The Retreat of the State

The Retreat of the State

Deregulation and Privatization in the UK and US

Dennis Swann

The University of Michigan Press

Ann Arbor

First published in the United States of America by
The University of Michigan Press 1988

First published 1988 by
Harvester • Wheatsheaf
Hemel Hempstead, Hertfordshire, England

1991   1990   1989   1988   4   3   2   1

Library of Congress Cataloging-in-Publication Data

Swann, Dennis.
     The retreat of the state: deregulation and privatization in the
  UK and US/Dennis Swann.
           p.   cm.
     Bibliography: p.
     Includes index.
     ISBN 0-472-10108-0
     1. Privatization—Great Britain.   2. Privatization—United States.
     3. Deregulation—Great Britain.   4. Deregulation—United States.
I. Title.
HD4145.S93 1988   88–26034
338.941—dc19   CIP

To Beryl

Contents

Part IV Conclusion

List of Figures

List of Tables

Preface

The idea of writing a book about privatisation and deregulation in the UK and US was first put to me by an editor at Wheatsheaf Books. My first reaction was to say no. I was less than convinced that the two topics were linked. Further persuasion and more thought led to a change of mind on my part. There was indeed a case for considering the two within one book. Various linkages suggested themselves. The most obvious is contained in the title. Both privatisation and deregulation represent a retreat from state involvement in industry—a retreat which has been taking place in varying degrees in many parts of the world. But the idea that, in both cases, the frontiers of the state are being pushed back is not the whole of the story. There are other aspects which to a degree run counter to the idea of retreat. Thus where newly privatised firms have faced competition, the UK government has been able to affect a virtual total withdrawal. But where competitive pressures have not been deemed sufficient to discipline the newly privatised firms, the government has chosen to institute a system of regulation. In other words the UK government has been adopting a mechanism of surveillance and control which has given rise to considerable disenchantment in the US during recent years. The causes of that disenchantment are clearly worthy of some consideration. Then again, whilst one form of regulation may be abandoned, the market may not be left to free competition. Instead some other form of regulation, perhaps designed to maintain stability and protect consumers, may be instituted. Therefore in some instances the state may not totally retreat but may substitute one form of involvement for another.

It should be added that the comparative approach has much to offer the study of regulation. Thus the US has already carried out a substantial programme of deregulation in sectors where competition is a possibility and there are of course areas of regulated activity in the UK and the EEC which are also potentially competitive. The experience of the US is therefore a useful guide to future action on this side of the Atlantic.

A thorough discussion of both privatisation and deregulation in the US and UK is a major undertaking, and the sheer size of the issues involved has exercised a powerful influence on the way the book is organised. Chaper 1 provides a very broad survey of the field. The rest of the book narrows down the focus to more manageable proportions.

Central to Chapter 1 is the point that privatisation is preceeded by public enterprise whilst deregulation is preceeded by regulation. The primary purpose of Chapter 1 is to paint a broad brush picture of the nature, scope and timing of the public enterprise/privatisation and regulation/deregulation processes in the UK and US. In addition, we also provide a thumbnail sketch of the extent to which the processes of privatisation and deregulation have been at work outside the UK and US.

The introductory discussion of public enterprise and privatisation contained in Chapter 1 gives rise to few difficulties in terms of the organisation of the study. The only point of importance which needs to be mentioned at this stage is that privatisation is capable of being defined in a variety of ways. Following our initial analysis of the concept, our focus will be on the idea of selling off public corporations, government stakes in Company Act companies and Trading Fund activities (i.e. commercially organised sections of government departments) and on the related issue of whether the privatised firm is to be subjected to competition, regulation, or some mixture of the two.

By contrast, regulation and deregulation pose a major problem in terms of the organisation of the book. The problem is quite a simple one—regulation and deregulation cover a wide range of activities. Antitrust policy is a form of regulation. It is obviously possible to reform such a system of regulation. It is also possible to water it down—which is a form of deregulation. Then there is economic regulation. This refers to the imposition of controls over prices, entry, exit, etc., in a particular industry. Economic deregulation includes reforming the system as well as easing or removing such controls. Finally there is social regulation which takes in matters such as the protection of the consumer, the protection of the environment, the imposition of occupational safety and health standards and affirmative action (i.e. equal rights in employment, etc., as between sexes and racial groups). The rules and regulations to which such policies give rise can be modified or abolished—in other words it is possible to envisage a process of social deregulation. Clearly a detailed discussion of all these topics would be overwhelming. In order to keep the discussion within manageable proportions the following plan of campaign has been adopted. In Chapter 1 we provide a broad brush picture of the extent of antitrust, economic and social regulation and deregulation in the US and UK. Since one of the ultimate goals of the book is to discuss the deregulation process, and since that process has been most dramatically at work in those parts of the economy which have been subjected to economic regulation, the rest of the book will concentrate on that aspect.

From all this the reader will gather that Chapter 1 presents a broad canvas. Thereafter the discussion will concentrate on (a) public enterprise, and the subsequent sale of certain publicly owned assets and (b) economic regulation, and the subsequent movement towards economic deregulation. That, to a large extent, is what the great privatisation and deregulation debate is all about.

In Chapter 2 we seek to explain why firms and industries were subjected to economic regulation or were publicly owned. Why, in other words, was free competition and/or private ownership deemed to be inappropriate? In Chapters 3, 4 and 5 we consider US experience. The US has steered away from public ownership (although not totally). Instead it has in the main preferred to leave industries in private ownership and to regulate their activities. In Chapter 3 we discuss the nature of that economic regulation together with the

xiv *The Retreat of the State*

limited amount of public enterprise. In Chapter 4 we discuss the forces which have led the US increasingly to abandon such regulation and enterprise. In Chapter 5 we examine the actual process of economic deregulation and privatisation. In Chapters 6, 7 and 8 the spotlight switches to the UK. In policy terms there has in the past been a clear contrast between the UK and the US, in that the UK indulged in public ownership on a significant scale, although this was coupled with economic regulation in a few sectors. In Chapter 7 we discuss the approach to public enterprise and economic regulation adopted in the UK. In Chapter 8 we seek to explain why public enterprise was replaced by a policy of privatisation and why economic regulation gave place to economic deregulation. In Chapter 9 we survey actual UK privatisation and economic deregulation policy. In Chapter 10 we stand back and appraise these British and American policies of disengagement. To what extent were the intellectual foundations of the policies open to criticism? What have they in fact achieved?

The book is intended to appeal to undergraduate and postgraduate students in a wide range of disciplines including economics, politics, public administration and business studies. In order to make the book as accessible as possible I have sought to present the argument in non-mathematical terms.

Writing about countries is always a hazardous business. I hope that I have not done too much violence to the facts of American experience. In truth any violence is inexcusable given the enormous outpouring of scholarship in the field of regulation. Not only is it vast, it is also impressive in its depth and penetration. My first debt of gratitude is to the army of American scholars who have already worked over the field. My second debt is to Kenneth Button. Hardly a day has passed during the last two years when we have not discussed some aspect of regulation policy. I have in particular been able to draw upon his impressive knowledge of transport economics. I was also extremely fortunate in that my colleague David Llewellyn was invited to give the Gilbart Lectures and chose as one topic the subject of the role of regulation in financial services. I have therefore been able to take full advantage of his stimulating appraisal. My acquaintance with financial regulation was further assisted by ideas and material supplied by two other colleagues, Brian Tew and Max Hall. Richard Collins at the Centre for Communication and Information Studies at the Polytechnic of Central London kindly gave me the benefit of his ideas on UK and US broadcasting. Needless to say any errors are mine. Thanks are also due to the French Embassy, the US Embassy and the Canadian High Commission for putting material at my disposal. Eric Davies at the Loughborough University of Technology library has been a tower of strength in helping to locate material on the US and UK. I am also grateful to my secretary Brenda Moore who with her customary dedication and skill has helped to get my thoughts into print.

Dennis Swann

Part I
Introduction

1 Overview

1 INTRODUCTION

This book is concerned with two policies—privatisation and deregulation—in two countries—the UK and the US. Both policies involve a wide range of possible actions and in the main body of the book—Chapters 3 to 9—it will be necessary in the interests of reducing the discussion to manageable proportions, to narrow the focus somewhat. Within that narrower focus the treatment of privatisation will concentrate selectively on the transfer of public assets to private ownership whilst the discussion of deregulation will concern itself with the economic variety. Typically economic regulation is concerned with the imposition of controls on entry, exit, prices, outputs, services supplied, markets served, consolidations and profitability in particular industries. Not all of these items may be subject to control in any particular instance. Deregulation is therefore concerned with the total abolition, the reduction in scope and intensity and the modification of such systems of control.

There is of course a broad connection between these two policies. They both involve a retreat from state involvement in industry. Sometimes however, a retreat from one form of involvement may be accompanied by the advance of another. Thus, following the abolition or reduction of economic regulation and the introduction of competition, it may be felt that some other form of regulation is necessary in order to protect consumers, deposit owners, etc., from potentially adverse effects of competition. Equally, the state may decide to privatise an enterprise or industry even though there may not be enough competition to exercise an effective control over its pricing and other behaviour. In such cases some form of regulation may be instituted. In truth the processes we are observing may not always take the form of a rolling back of the frontiers of state, but may on occasions involve to some degree the replacement of one form of state involvement by another.

More technically there are other connections between them. For example, the process of economic deregulation is designed to give scope for greater competition. But the process of competition may be frustrated by the absence of privatisation. Thus whereas we may expect competition to drive inefficient suppliers out of particular markets, public ownership may enable them to hang on because they can continue to draw on operating subsidies provided by the state. If deregulation was accompanied by privatisation a more responsive system might arise—i.e. firms would be less able to frustrate desirable readjustments.

Whilst, as we indicated above, the focus will in due course be narrowed, in this chapter we will adopt a broader canvas—notably in the case of regulation and deregulation. This will enable us to gain a broader insight into the process of deregulation of the US, the tentacles of which have reached beyond the areas traditionally subject to economic regulation.

2   PRIVATISATION IDENTIFIED

As David Heald has pointed out, privatisation is an ugly word, scarcely heard of in the UK before 1979, which thereafter gained quickly in popular currency.[1] What does it mean? Some UK commentators have preferred to define it narrowly to mean the sale of government corporate assets, other government industrial assets, local authority houses and government owned land to the general public. However this is a relatively narrow definition.

As an umbrella term, privatisation can best be defined as the introduction into the public sector, or what has previously been the public sector, of conditions which typify the private sector.

It is therefore possible to envisage privatisation taking place even though no change in the ownership of public assets takes place. Thus public enterprise may remain in existence but may be required to adopt a more commercial approach—i.e. to behave more like a privately owned enterprise. Instead of aiming merely to balance the books, making available a universal service at uniform prices, providing employment for certain groups, purchasing the outputs of certain prescribed suppliers and so forth, the enterprise may be enjoined to maximise profits, to provide goods and services only if the price covers the cost involved and to adopt cost minimising procedures in employment and procurement.

Private ownership is clearly a key feature of the private sector. Therefore in the context of the UK the sale of (a) the assets of public corporations, (b) government shareholdings in Company Act companies (i.e. private companies) and (c) the assets of Trading Fund bodies such as the Royal Ordnance Factories are three examples of a change in that direction and therefore of privatisation. Some commentators have tended to restrict this definition. Thus Peacock sees privatisation as a process whereby a *predominant* share of assets is transferred to private shareholders.[2] Beesley and Littlechild refer to it as a situation where a Companies Act company is formed and *at least fifty per cent* of the shares of the Company are sold to private shareholders.[3] Presumably what these writers have in mind is that for privatisation to have its maximum effect it is necessary that the balance of power between government, as owner, and private individuals and institutions, as owners, should change so as to give the latter at least an equal and hopefully a predominant influence over the use of the underlying assets. Whilst this point has undoubted validity, it is nevertheless reasonable to argue that even the sale of one per cent of assets to the general public is an act of privatisation, and in this context it should be pointed out that whilst privatisation has been motivated by a desire to improve the management of assets it has also been inspired by a desire to achieve a wider spread of property ownership. The latter is accomplished whatever the percentage of assets transferred. It should be added that privatisation in the ownership sense refers not merely to the sale of the whole or part of the assets of an enterprise but also to the sale of the whole or part of a division of an enterprise—e.g. the sale of the Jaguar division of BL (later Rover Group). This is sometimes referred to as hiving off.

Privatisation may take other forms which are not concerned with changes in the ownership of existing assets. Thus the public sector may continue to finance the provision of a good or service by means of taxes or local rates, but the actual production may be contracted out to the private sector. Contemporary Japanese city government is largely a matter of handling services contracted out. A survey in 1982 indicated that in the US forty-four per cent of cities and counties paid private contractors to collect commercial refuse; twenty-eight per cent contracted out their street repairs, forty-one per cent their street lighting.[4] Education vouchers, provided by a local authority, which could be redeemed by private schools in competition with the state system are another example of this form of privatisation. It is possible to distinguish a somewhat different kind of contracting out. In the above instances we have implicitly assumed that some or all of the government's productive capacity is closed down and is replaced by expanded private capacity. But it is possible that the capacity could remain in existence and continue to be owned by the government but be *managed* by private contractors. Such an approach has, as we will see later, been adopted in the UK in the case of the Royal Dockyards.

Then again privatisation may refer to changes on the financing side. Thus the public sector may continue to produce a good or service but may seek to charge a price for it. Here again the introduction of private enterprise conditions has nothing to do with changes of ownership. Rather what we are drawing attention to is the introduction of a key feature of the private enterprise system, namely price.

Privatisation may also take the form of load shedding. Thus the government might decide totally to divest itself of responsibility on both the production and financing side. In other words it might leave private expenditure and private production to fill the gap. For example, the UK government might totally abandon the business of running a health service. At the same time it might compel all citizens to take out private insurance in order that they should have the means to purchase health care. This would then pave the way for the emergence, on a larger scale than already exists, of privately provided health care facilities which would be priced. In principle no change of ownership arises. There is however a change in the locus of production and in the method of financing.

Then again a form of privatisation arises when a public enterprise joins with some private concern to develop some particular venture. Heald also includes within his definition the idea of liberalisation—i.e. the relaxation of state monopolies or licensing arrangements which keep private firms out of markets previously served exclusively by the public sector.[5]

From all that has gone before it is evident that privatisation can be taken to encompass a wide variety of possible changes—some of which are concerned with alternative approaches to the supply and indeed financing of local and central government services generally, and services such as health and education in particular. However we will not attempt to discuss such possibilities in detail. Instead we will focus on the transfer of public assets into private ownership. In the UK context this has taken the form of the public or privately negotiated sale of the assets of public corporations and of government shareholdings in public limited companies. These have constituted the bulk of the public enterprise to which we refer in the next section. In addition our later discussion will take account of the sale of the productive assets of government departments. Some of these had previously been put on a more commercial basis under the title of Trading Funds. We shall not concern ourselves with the very considerable sales of council houses and government owned land which have occurred in the UK. We shall as far as possible observe a similar line of demarcation in discussing privatisation in the US.

3   PUBLIC ENTERPRISE—A PRIVATISABLE INHERITANCE

At this stage we will merely provide a brief overview of the scope and size of public enterprise in the UK and the US. Detailed surveys are reserved for Chapters 3 and 6. It is necessary to point out that on this side of the Atlantic there is a tendency to think that whilst public enterprise has played a significant role in the economy of the UK, the US is essentially free enterprise in character and has afforded no role for such a form of organisation. That perception of the position in the UK is undoubtedly correct but the contrast with the US tends to be overplayed.

i The United Kingdom

In the UK, as in France, some public enterprise existed prior to the spate of public ownership which occurred in the immediate post-war period. Some of it was associated with the municipalities and goes back to the era of 'gas and water socialism' at the end of the nineteenth century. The rest was a product of a relatively new organisation known as the public corporation. The nature of that form of organisation will be discussed later in Chapter 6. It was however under the Labour governments of 1945 to 1951 that the public corporation came to exercise a really significant role in the economy. Basic industries including electricity, gas, coal, steel and transport were brought into public ownership—i.e. they were nationalised. The emergence of a Conservative government in 1951 did not lead to a wholesale reversal. Whilst doctrinally opposed to nationalisation, the Conservatives confined their activities to limited denationalisation (steel and some road haulage) and in fact a number of new public corporations arrived on the scene. When Labour was returned to office in 1964 it was to be expected that the frontiers of the state would advance and indeed they did to a limited extent as a result of the renationalisation of steel and the taking into public ownership of some road haulage and road passenger enterprises. Ostensibly the Heath Conservative administration of 1970–74 was doctrinally opposed to industrial involvements, but despite that actually added to public ownership by virtue of

'lame duck' rescues which occurred *force majeure*. The return
of Labour between 1974 and 1979 extended the frontiers still
further as a result of major acts of nationalisation in the
manufacturing base, affecting aerospace and shipbuilding.

In 1976 the National Economic Development Office
(NEDO) produced a study of UK nationalised industries. It
listed the public corporations and estimated that they contributed 11.0 per cent of the Gross Domestic Product (GDP)
and were responsible for 8.0 per cent of employment.[6] It
should be added that whilst NEDO was aware of the decisions
to nationalise shipbuilding and aerospace, the above data do
not include their contribution. Nor do the data above take
account of the fact that the government, directly or indirectly,
had equity stakes in a number of limited companies. By virtue
of taking account of items not included by NEDO, Richard
Pryke estimated the GDP contribution of public enterprise in
1977 as being 12.7 per cent and the employment share as 9.4
per cent.[7]

These two dates provide a useful point at which to terminate our brief account of the emergence of public enterprise in
the UK. By that point in time the impressive size and scope of
the state enterprise which was to be inherited by the Thatcher
government, when it came to power in 1979, was already
apparent. Moreover it was in the years after 1974, when it was
out of power, that the Conservative Party was to contemplate
in radical fashion its performance and implications from both
an economic and political standpoint. It should however be
said that subsequent first hand experience in office had an
equally profound effect on Conservative philosophy. What
happened after 1974 was that the bi-partisan element in the
approach to public enterprise (i.e. the Conservatives had
tolerated it and Labour had been enthusiastically in favour of
it) began to disappear. The detailed reasons for this will be
reserved for Chapter 7. At this point all we need to note is that
the Conservative Party began to move to the right. A broad-
based economic philosophy began to emerge which emphasised reliance on the free market mechanism and disengagement from industrial involvements. This radical change of
emphasis was to have profound implications for public enterprise, since the view was increasingly taken that the state

should not merely seek better performance from its public enterprises but should divest itself of such involvements—in short it should privatise. More will be said on the actual privatisation programme in Chapters 7 and 8.

ii The United States

Whilst the size and scope of public enterprise in the US did not match that of the UK in the seventies, it is nevertheless important to recognise that the US has not been a land devoted to unshackled free enterprise production. Firstly, there was a significant amount of public enterprise. Secondly, even when enterprises were investor-owned (i.e. private) some form of regulation was usually applied. In the US public opinion has not been especially favourable to concepts such as nationalisation. Thus where there have been conditions of natural monopoly—where, for example, economies of scale have indicated that for efficient production only one producer was required—rather than take the enterprise into public ownership the frequent though not universal reaction has been to leave it in private hands and to subject it to some form of regulatory surveillance and control. More will be said about this regulatory approach later—at this point we are concerned with the admittedly comparatively small public enterprise sector.

Before we turn to that discussion, it is important to recognise that the alternatives to investor operation are conditioned by the nature of the US governmental system. Apart from the federal government, there are state governments and beneath them local governments. The latter can be divided further into municipalities, counties and public utility districts. It follows from this that the alternatives to investor-owned activity include public enterprise at federal, state or local government level.

Data which can be directly compared with that provided by NEDO and Richard Pryke are not available. The best we can do is to cite the figure provided by the US government in respect of 1979. It indicates that in that year public enterprises (primarily publicly-owned utilities and the post office) produced 1.5 per cent of the national income.[8] In recent years at federal level there has with one exception (the US Postal

Service) been a notable absence of country-wide public corporations similar to those in the UK in utility sectors such as transport, electricity, gas and telecommunications. Equally at federal level there was nothing to compare with the dominating public enterprise stakes in key UK manufacturing and mining industries—e.g. coal, steel, shipbuilding and aerospace. Federal involvements have been sporadic—e.g. the Tennessee Valley Authority, a few airports and (a more recent feature) 'lame duck' rescues in rail transport. The bulk of consistent public enterprise involvements are to be found lower down at state and local government level in traditional utility sectors where conditions of natural monopoly often exist. Public enterprise dominates in activities such as municipal mass transit, ports, airports and water, and plays a significant but smaller role in electricity.

In contrast to the UK, privatisation in the US in the form of the sale of public enterprise assets is of relatively recent vintage. Indeed at the time of writing it is still largely a matter of promise rather than fulfilment. A substantial programme of asset sales was proposed in 1982 but little emerged. The most recent programme of possible privatisations appeared in 1986 and was a product of the need to reduce the US budget deficit. Since President Reagan did not want to raise taxes but did want to raise defence spending, the only alternative was to cut other programmes, such as welfare, and to exploit other devices, such as asset sales, to the full. Privatisation in the US thus appeared to have been largely grounded in expediency whereas in the UK it was a product of a deeply held philosophy which began to emerge in the mid 1970s. More will be said about US privatisation proposals in Chapters 4 and 5.

4   PRIVATISATION—A UBIQUITOUS BUSINESS

Privatisation is not a new phenomenon and not one confined to the UK and US. As we have indicated, some public enterprise was returned to the private sector by British Conservative administrations prior to those presided over by Mrs Margaret Thatcher. It is also possible to point to other countries where the state has during the post-war period divested itself of public enterprise involvements—e.g. Austria,[9] Canada[10] and Italy.[11] Indeed in the latter connection Giorgio Stafani has indicated that by the mid-seventies the political mood in Italy had begun to swing towards privatisation in reaction to the financial burden which followed in the wake of lame duck rescues and debatable industrialisation policies in the 1960s. It is however apparent that in the 1980s the pace of privatisation around the world greatly speeded up. Whilst it would be unduly presumptious to suggest that the UK programme was a precipitating influence, it is nevertheless true to say that it attracted widespread attention. Press reports indicate that the staff of foreign government departments from various parts of the globe descended on the British Treasury to study the reasons for and mechanics of privatisation.[12]

In recent years substantial privatisation plans have been announced and significant public asset sales have been undertaken in various parts of the world. Japan indicated that it proposed to privatise its telephone system (Nippon Telegraph and Telephone—NTT), its railways (Japan National Railways—JNR), its largest airline (Japan Air Lines—JAL) and its national tobacco firm (Japan Tobacco). NTT was to be turned into a private company and up to thirty per cent of its stock sold to the general public—this latter process has already taken place on the Japanese stock exchange. JNR has been broken up into seven private companies which it is hoped will be sold off to the general public. The tobacco monopoly has been disposed of and the Japanese government has sold off its minority holding in JAL. Canada, whose public sector is large relative to that of the US, has also chosen to indulge in privatisations. This decision followed in the wake of the election of a Conservative government in 1984. The Minister of Finance declared that 'Crown corporations with a commercial value but no ongoing public policy purpose will be sold off.' The federal government subsequently sold off crown corporations such as the Northern Transportation Company Ltd and Canadian Arsenals Ltd (a munitions producer) and holdings for which another crown body, Canada Development Investment Corporation (CDIC), had a responsibility. These latter disposals included De Haviland

and Canadair (aerospace manufacturers), Canada Development Corporation (a conglomerate with involvements from
pharmaceuticals to mining) and Teleglobe Canada (an international telecommunications carrier). At the time of writing
several further privatisations are planned including another
CDIC holding, Eldorado Nuclear Ltd (a uranium producer
and processor), Air Canada and Petro Canada.[13] In Italy
public enterprise takes two forms. There are those enterprises
owned by the state, local authorities and other agencies in
traditional public utility sectors such as railways, urban transport, electricity and water supply. In addition the central
government has created state holding companies which have
injected capital into existing and new enterprises of all kinds
on a participating (but controlling) basis with private equity
owners. The most important of these holding companies have
been *Istituto per la Riconstruzione Industriale* and the *Ente
Nazionale Idrocarburi*. Whilst the position of enterprises in
the traditional public utility sectors has not been in question,
and policy has focussed on seeking better performance, the
state holding companies have in recent years in a significant
number of instances either totally sold off enterprises or disposed of part of the states' shareholding. The latter process
has applied in the case of banks, manufacturing enterprises
and the airline *Alitalia*. In Spain the *Instituto Nacional di
Industria* has been the spearhead of government involvement
in industry. The state until recently had a stake in some 750
companies with controlling interests in close to 380. *INI* has
now initiated a policy of disengagement via the sale of assets.
These are just four examples, which illustrate a general trend
in developed economies. In developing countries too privatisation has been proceeding apace in recent years. Here the
ultimate stimulus has been external rather than internal. In
many such countries public enterprise has been a drain on the
central exchequer. In 1983 the World Bank found that in a
sample of twenty-seven developing countries net budgetary
payments to state-owned enterprises averaged three per cent
of GDP.[14] Whilst the flow of aid and bank lending was
expanding this burden was tolerable, but in the more recent
tightened circumstances it has ceased to be so. The response
has been to privatise—a move which has been encouraged by

bodies such as the World Bank, the IMF and right-wing aid donors such as the Reagan administration.

It should be noted that there are three limiting factors which quite frequently obtrude:

(1) Unlike the UK where the hybrid (a company in which the government retains a stake alongside the new private owners) seems to be a stage on the road to a total disposal, many foreign governments prefer to sell off only a minority stake in the assets they own.

(2) Nor does it follow that foreign governments are always set on a course which will lead to total disengagement from industry. Thus the Japanese government has not set its sights beyond the four privatisations mentioned earlier. Here we encounter something of a contrast with the UK since it is apparent that the Thatcher administrations have increasingly set their sights on a more or less total disposal of public enterprise. It should also be emphasised that UK government policy has been based on an ideological antipathy to public enterprise whereas the impression emerges that in some of the countries cited above the policy has been more pragmatic. The issue has been one of finding remedies for the problem of inefficient and loss-making enterprises and has not been primarily inspired by an ideological desire to roll back the frontiers of the state. Stefani has emphasised this point in relation to the Italian privatisations.[15]

(3) Even if states were disposed to go the whole way, they would in many cases run up against the problem that state enterprises making losses (a not unknown phenomenon) are not attractive to the private investor. This gives rise to a related point, namely that governments are strongly tempted to render their enterprises more saleable by allowing them to retain various forms of monopoly privilege. This has given rise to concern in both the developing and developed contexts.[16]

There was of course until recently one notable exception to the general trend, namely France. During the early 1980s the central government was engaged in vigorously advancing the frontiers of the state through a policy of further nationalisations. These substantially increased the share of public enterprise in economic activity—the figure for production rose from 13 to 17.2 per cent and for employment from 11.8 to 16.6 per cent.[17] However in 1986 right wing parties led by Jacques Chirac, which were pledged to introduce a substantial programme of privatisations, succeeded in gaining power. An interesting 'cohabitation situation' then emerged in which the government was pledged to pursue a policy which was vigorously opposed by President Francois Mitterand. Despite Presidential opposition, a bill was passed through the French Parliamentary Assembly in 1986 which provided for the privatisation of sixty-five concerns (38 banks, 13 insurance companies, 9 industrial groups, 4 finance companies and a firm engaged in communications).

At the time of writing the partial sale of the oil company *Elf Aquitaine* and the privatisations of the industrial group *Saint Gobain* and the investment banking group *Parisbas*, together with the banks *Société Générale Alsacienne de Banque*, *Banque du Bâtiment et des Travaux Publics* and *Crédit Commercial de France* together with *Compagnie Générale d'Electricité* have already been accomplished and there are more to come. It should be added that even the Mitterand government showed some flexibility. Nationalised industries were permitted to sell off minority stakes in some branches of their activities. In addition they were allowed to raise private capital through the issue of the *certificat d'investissement* (a form of non-voting preference share) and the *titre participatif* (a non-voting loan stock).[18]

It should also be noted that privatisation had been proceeded with at the municipal level whilst the Mitterand government was in office. This was notably the case in Paris where in 1984, under a right-wing city government presided over by Mayor Jacques Chirac, water supply was transferred to private hands—the *Compagnie Général des Eaux* now supplies the left bank and the *Société Lyonnaise des Eaux* the right.

5   REGULATION IDENTIFIED

Dictionary definitions of regulation emphasise the idea of the imposition of controls and restraints and the application of rules. In other words freedom of action is curtailed.

Regulation may take a self-regulatory form. Alternatively it may be imposed by departments of state or by bodies specially created by government which are external to the industry or enterprise which is being regulated. Then again the system of regulation may lie between these two limiting cases.

Self-regulation is indeed a phenomenon with many facets. There are self-imposed group codes of conduct which are sometimes a form of consumer protection. At the extreme such codes may be devised by private firms without any involvement on the part of official regulatory bodies or for that matter the consumer. An example is the *Jury d'Ethique Publicitaire* in Belgium which collectively regulates advertising.[19] In other cases producer groups may involve consumers in decision making but again exclude official involvement. Again Belgium affords an example in the form of standard contract terms, negotiated by producer bodies and consumer representatives, covering trades such as dry cleaning and travel agency. Somewhat less extreme, and really lying between pure self-regulation and pure external regulation, are the codes of practice drawn up under the UK Fair Trading Act 1973. Section 124(3) of that act imposes a duty on the Director General of Fair Trading to encourage trade associations to prepare such codes. These largely voluntary efforts are an alternative to the issuing of statutory orders which would of course constitute external regulation.[20] The mixture of the self- and external varieties is also apparent in the professions where standards of competence and conduct are often governed by institutions which may owe their existence to government but are then very much left to themselves to devise and implement the standards.

Self regulation also arises when competition laws exempt some area of activity from control and as a result the firms may be left free to fix prices, etc. This has frequently been the case in liner shipping and international airline operation, where respectively shipping conferences and the International Air Transport Association (IATA) have been allowed to fix rates. It is only fair to point out that governments or their regulatory bodies have sometimes hovered in the background. However, in the case of IATA they seem in the past to have been happy to rubber stamp what has come out of its deliberations. In the case of shipping conferences, external regulatory bodies have sometimes existed. But if the US case is typical we should not overestimate the degree of control exerted. It is generally agreed that the Federal Maritime Commission (FMC) has lacked teeth and that in reality the conferences were really regulating themselves.[21]

All these are examples of group activity, but self-regulation may be an individual reaction as when a company recognises that an active safety policy is good management and in effect regulates itself as opposed to being instructed by government safety officials. Much the same happens when producers or retailers are sensitive to the preferences of consumers in matters such as food additives, and adapt their goods appropriately in the absence of an official standard.

We turn now to the other main form of regulation—the externally imposed variety. In practice such control is exerted by a wide variety of bodies—government departments, but more often agencies which enjoy a degree of independence from government such as commissions, boards, corporations and executives and of course courts. In federal systems a particular industry may be regulated at both federal and state (province, land) level. There is no guarantee that the state system of regulation will be the same as that adopted at the federal level or that every state within a union will adopt the same regulatory approach.

Externally imposed regulation can, for expositional purposes, be divided into three categories—antitrust, economic regulation and so-called social regulation. The nature of these three forms can best be appreciated by considering, as an alternative to regulation, a policy of *laissez-faire*. Under such a policy, government would step back from the economic arena and (with few exceptions) would leave the course of events to be determined by market forces. Why may this be deemed inappropriate?

The reader will first notice that we have avoided describing *laissez-faire* as a matter of leaving matters to be determined by *competitive* market forces. The significance of that difference was well summed up by that canny economic observer Adam Smith when he declared:

> People of the same trade seldom meet together, even for merriment and diversion, but the conversation ends in a conspiracy against the public, or in some contrivance to raise prices.[22]

Most economists would probably agree that, if left to themselves, businessmen would prefer not to compete. Whilst we cannot say that in a purely *laissez-faire* context competition would totally disappear, experience suggests that it would be severely attenuated. This is where antitrust comes into the picture. It is a form of regulation since it seeks to force businessmen to compete. Typically it is a policy which addresses itself to phenomena such as dominant firms, oligopolies, mergers and restrictive business practices. In practice national systems differ in at least four ways. Firstly, the range of antitrust phenomena covered by the legislation varies from country to country. Secondly, the stances vary. Thus the US takes a *per se* view of many restrictive business practices. That is to say they are in and of themselves illegal and no mitigating arguments will be admitted in defence. In the UK and West Germany, on the other hand, the approach tends to be that agreements are contrary to the public interest or prohibited but exemptions are provided for. In other countries yet a different approach is adopted. The law is neither against nor for such practices but judges them on their merits. Thirdly, even if the formal stances of national policies were all the same, they can differ in practice because such policies often grant to those who operate them a significant degree of discretion (e.g. guidelines for the reference of mergers). Fourthly, the impact of antitrust policy partly depends on the severity of its sanctions and these vary. Thus in the US fines, treble damages and incarcerations have been possible penalties for those who transgressed the law, whereas the UK, for example, has taken a more lenient line.

We turn now to economic regulation. Antitrust is a form of regulation which is appropriate where competition is feasible. But there are some industries where it is alleged that competition is not feasible. This is generally agreed to be the case where natural monopoly conditions exist—where therefore it is most efficient if only one firm serves the market. It is generally accepted that water, gas, electricity and telecommunications are industries where, certainly in the past, elements of natural monopoly have existed. However, if the force of competition has to be suspended, supply being left in the hands of a private monopolist, then it is essential that the consumer be protected against exploitation. This is where regulation comes in. In the US such regulation typically takes the form of a control over the level and structure of prices which guarantees the utility a fair rate of return on the capital embodied in its 'rate base'.

There are other industries where some competition is possible but where the number of competitors has been limited by natural features. The most obvious has been broadcasting, where the electromagnetic spectrum has set limits to the number of broadcasting stations which could operate without interference. In such circumstances it has been necessary to introduce some form of regulation which allocates the available space on the spectrum (on the basis of prescribed criteria) to broadcasters, and this has often been coupled with some control over the nature of the broadcast material—i.e. balance of subject matter, quality, frequency and volume of advertising, matters affecting public taste, etc.

Then there are industries where factors such as economies of scale and nature do not appear to restrict the number of competitors and where, on the face of it, competition is feasible. Nevertheless it is decided that a completely free market is not acceptable because it will lead to excessive competition which will in turn give rise to instability and damage to consumers and other producers. Whether such a conclusion is sound is open to doubt. It is also quite possible that such reasoning, which may take on a public interest guise, is largely bogus and conceals motives which are really grounded in the self-interest of particular groups of producers or consumers. The latter could also be extended to include governments which in the past have, for example, sought to defend their (sometimes publicly owned) railways from the competitive depredations of private road hauliers. Whatever the reasons, the response has been to suspend the operation of a free market.

The regulators may control prices. The latter may be fixed, may be subject to a floor or a ceiling, or may only be allowed to fluctuate within prescribed upper and lower limits. Regulatory authorities may merely recommend prices. Then again firms may be required to file prices with the regulatory authority which has the power to refuse approval. Prices may be left to collusion under the supposedly watchful eye of the regulator. Typically controls are imposed on entry—often through the agency of licensing. Even if a firm is allowed to enter, it may nevertheless be restricted as to the markets in which it may operate. Thus the number of airlines allowed to fly on a particular route may be limited and financial institutions may be limited as to the markets in which they can borrow and lend and the kind of operations which they can engage in simultaneously. The entry of foreign firms may be absolutely precluded. Control may also be placed on exit as when a railway wishes to close a line. Output may also be controlled—e.g. the number of flights on a particular route may be limited. It is not untypical for firms subject to regulation to be exempted in some degree from normal antitrust rules. In respect of some antitrust phenomena, such as mergers, control may be assumed by the regulatory authority.

The instability argument has also been used to justify regulation in the financial sphere and bank regulation in particular. Governments have been reluctant to leave banks to conduct their affairs freely because of the fear that they might behave imprudently, might therefore fail and drag the rest of the economy down with them. Because of this, banks have tended to be subject to external control. Some of the controls are similar to the ones discussed above but sometimes the regulation of banks has involved fairly detailed supervision of their day-to-day activities. Typically entry has been controlled—a bank would have to obtain a licence or its equivalent before it could operate. Typically it would have to satisfy rules regarding the adequacy of its capital. The conduct of its affairs would have to be open to inspection and if necessary to interference. Changes which affected capital or gave rise to amalgamations and expansions have sometimes been subjected to regulatory approval. Typically banks would have to satisfy certain basic liquidity rules. However control might be more detailed—the composition of assets and liabilities, the level of interest rates and the amount which could be lent to any one individual might be subject to regulation. In addition financial institutions have been subject to systems of insurance—e.g. insurance of deposits. Whilst such activity could be regarded as consumer protection and thus a form of social regulation (see below), we shall treat it as an aspect of economic regulation on the grounds that, like some other controls mentioned above, it is designed to maintain the stability of the system.

In other sectors of the economy even more specialised motivations have been at work. Take for example the case of agriculture. If we seek to account for the emergence of the EEC's Common Agricultural Policy then the following points seem to be germane. Firstly, the member states were merely continuing at Community level a policy approach which had been previously implemented at national level. Secondly, political forces were at work. Those who advocated European unity sought to attract political support for the cause by appealing to the powerful farm lobby. They did so by promising to redress the income imbalance between the industrial and agricultural sectors. Since the price levels necessary to redress the balance were well above world levels, a system of external protection was essential. Thirdly, it could also be argued that agriculture was by its very nature unstable. It was at the mercy of the elements and that, combined with short run price elasticities of demand and supply, was likely to produce marked instability of prices and incomes. Fourthly, and of crucial importance, was the tendency for supply to outstrip demand, thanks to the remorseless onward march of technology in conjunction with the low income elasticity of demand for food. This gave rise to a need for a system of support buying whereby surpluses were bought up and stored or disposed of on the world market. By the latter device Community producers solved their problems at the expense of outside suppliers.

Regulation may also be a means of dealing with structural problems. The European Community policy in respect of steel is a case in point. The immediate reaction to the depressed conditions which followed the first oil price hike was to assume that the problem was cyclical. Only later was it realised that it was structural—that there was excess capacity, that much steel capacity was inefficient and uncompetitive and that the industry would have to shift up market to products where competition was less intense. That point having been realised, the European Community then decided to install a system of minimum prices, voluntary (and ultimately mandatory) sales quotas, together with devices designed to reduce import competition (i.e. fast-track anti-dumping duties and voluntary export restraints). The theory was that severe social shocks had to be avoided at a time when alternative employment was increasingly difficult to provide. The regulatory system was designed to provide a breathing space during which structural adjustments could take place. Subsidies would be allowed but would have to be directed to restructuring and would eventually have to be phased out. The target date was the end of 1985. Regulation in these circumstances is usually conceived of as being temporary, although it is a well known fact that once installed such systems sometimes prove difficult to terminate.

We now come to the third of our categories of regulation. Industries which are subject to competition and also industries which operate under a system of economic regulation may nevertheless fail in some degree. Such failures may be concerned with externalities (e.g. pollution), the difficulties faced by consumers in respect of information and safety, the possibility of injury or death at the workplace and the problem of discrimination in access to jobs. This gives rise to regulation concerned with environmental protection, consumer protection, occupational health and safety and affirmative action. Unlike economic regulation, such social regulation, or what some economists call 'new style' regulation, often applies across the economy. Typically it takes the form of the provision of information (e.g. unit pricing, product content labelling), prescription of standards (e.g. work safety, permitted levels of pollution, permitted contents, product testing) and rights of redress (e.g. consumer rights in relation to deception, defective goods and product-related injury).

6   REGULATION IN THE US AND UK

i The United States

The evidence indicates that for many years regulation has been a growth industry in the US. One of the oft-cited methods of judging the growth of federal (as opposed to state) regulatory activity in the US is to point to the increase in the number of federal regulatory pages in the Federal Register. In 1936 it was 2599, by 1970 it had grown to 424,000 but by 1977 it was 742,000 and was expected to grow rapidly.[23] Clearly something of a regulatory explosion occurred in the 1970s. Various estimates have also been made of the contribution of regulated industries to the national product. MacAvoy calculated that in 1965 they represented 8.2 per cent of GNP and that by 1975 the figure had grown to 23.7 per cent.[24] Thompson and Jones calculated that the regulated sector accounted for 25.7 per cent of GDP in 1978.[25]

Quite apart from the fact that these figures relate to different measures of national income, they are not directly comparable. MacAvoy included not just those areas subject to economic regulation (specifically these were sectors involved in price regulation together with regulated financial markets), but also activities significantly burdened by health and safety regulation. Thompson and Jones excluded this latter factor but included in their list of sectors subject to price and supply controls community services such as health, education and welfare. These latter were excluded by MacAvoy. In summary, the Thompson and Jones figure is based on a fairly generous definition of economic regulation since it covers areas which were fairly lightly regulated. The MacAvoy figures were based on a conservative view of economic regulation to which were added sectors considerably affected by one form of social regulation.

Whilst it is apparent that there was an explosion of regulatory activity in the 1970s, it is also important to recognise that regulation in the US is a very long-standing phenomenon. The earliest and basic antitrust enactments go back to 1890 and 1914. The former date witnessed the introduction of the Sherman Act which provided the key powers to deal with conspiracies such as price fixing, market sharing, etc., and with monopolisation. The Antitrust Division of the Department of Justice was specially created to enforce the Act. In 1914 the Clayton Act provided powers to control mergers and to attack specific practices such as exclusive dealing, tying contracts and price discrimination. In the same year the Federal Trade Commission Act created an independent regulatory commission of the same name which, in alliance with the Antitrust Division, was empowered to apply the Clayton Act provisions.

It is broadly speaking correct to say that by 1914 the foundations of the US antitrust system were in place, though it is true that there were subsequent enactments which modified or reinforced these basic provisions. For example, the Robinson-Patman Act 1936 modified the section 2 provisions of the Clayton Act concerning price discrimination, the Celler-Kefauver Act 1950 stiffened section 7 of the Clayton Act in respect of mergers and the Hart-Scott-Rodino Act 1976 in particular required advance notice of large mergers.[26]

The origins of economic regulation go even further back in time. Indeed it is sometimes referred to as 'old style' regulation. State regulatory commissions[27] designed to supervise banking, insurance and railways go back in some cases to the 1830s. In the early days, some of the independent regulatory commissions were 'sunshine' bodies.[28] That is to say they relied primarily for the effectiveness upon powers of investigation and the bringing of publicity to bear.[29]

Subsequently four main developments occurred. Firstly, because the activities of the regulated enterprises began to transcend state boundaries, and since only the federal government was vested with power over trade between the states of the union, supposedly regulated activities were in danger of eluding the grasp of the regulators. In order to get to grips with these inter-state (as opposed to intra-state) activities, the federal government had to step in and discharge a regulatory role. In practice the government chose not to do the job itself but usually assigned it to bodies of commissioners. The earliest of these developments came in 1887 with the Act to Regulate Commerce, which gave rise to the railway regulating Interstate Commerce Commission (ICC). With few exceptions regulation came to exist on two levels, federal and state, and this became a permanent feature of the US regulatory scene. (Incidentally the latter is also true in the field of anti-trust and social regulation). Secondly, regulation ceased to be sunshine and developed economic teeth (e.g. rate making and entry controlling powers) of the kind discussed earlier. Thirdly, regulation tended to spawn more regulation. Thus, as we have seen, the ICC started out by regulating the railways but since other forms of transport competed with the railways it was deemed necessary in the interests of effectiveness and equity that its regulatory remit should be widened to include inland waterways, oil pipelines, road haulage and buses—to mention only a few instances. Fourthly, federal regulation spread to other parts of the economy—that progressive expansion is detailed in Table 1.1.

The object of Table 1.1 is to leave the reader with some impression of the range of activities which were subject to federal economic regulation prior to the onset of deregulation. It is worth noting that in the 1930s economic regulation intensified noticeably and that point is not fully brought out in the table. The financial sector was one area in particular where that intensification took place—it was a response to the financial collapse of 1929 and after. The Securities and Exchange Commission was an attempt to eradicate the kinds of abuses surrounding the stock market crash. In addition the banking sector was subjected to reform in response to weaknesses in the system which manifested themselves in widespread bank failures. This latter regulatory response took the form of the Glass-Steagall Act of 1933 and the Banking Act of 1935. They strengthened the position of the Federal Reserve Board in relation to the banks. They also provided for a closely regulated system which was not paralleled in any other developed country. In addition the Federal Deposit Insurance Corporation was set up. All national and all federal reserve banks were required to insure their customers'

*Table 1.1: Scope of federal economic regulation prior to
deregulation movement**

Enactment date of first named body	Regulatory body(ies)	Regulatory role
1863	Comptroller of the Currency, Federal Reserve Board (1913), Federal Deposit Insurance Corporation (1933), Federal Home Loan Board (1933), and Federal Savings and Loan Insurance Corporation (1934)	Supervision of banking and other deposit-taking institutions and provision of insurance for depositors, etc.
1887	Interstate Commerce Commission	Control over rates, entry and exit in railways, road haulage, buses, inland waterways and other related activities
1913	Federal Reserve Board and Securities and Exchange Commission (1934)#	Control of margin requirements in security dealing, supervision of security dealing on stock exchanges and supervision of public utility holding companies
1916	United States Shipping Board (ultimately† replaced in 1961 by the independent Federal Maritime Commission)	Control of rates and service frequency of trans–ocean freight shipments
1920	Federal Power Commission (replaced in 1977 by the Federal Energy Regulatory Commission in the Department of Energy)	Regulation of wellhead price of natural gas and wholesale price of natural gas and electricity sold for resale in interstate commerce
1927	Federal Radio Commission (replaced in 1934 by Federal Communications Commission)	Regulation of price of telephone and telegraph service. Control of entry into the above telecommunications activities and into television and radio broadcasting. Remit also extends to international telecommunications

1938	Civil Aeronautics Authority (replaced in 1940 by Civil Aeronautics Board)	Control over entry, exit, rates and mergers in air transport, both passenger and freight. Remit also extended to international operations although fares, particularly in earlier years, were agreed in IATA. Provision of subsidies for local services
1970	National Credit Union Share Insurance Fund	Provision of insurance facilities in respect of credit unions
1970	Securities Investor Protection Corporation	Provision of insurance to protect investors dealing with brokers on stock exchanges

Notes

*The reader is once more reminded that the above are federal regulatory bodies. For example the Federal Energy Regulatory Commission would regulate the wholesale price of electricity sold by a generating utility in state A to a distribution utility in state B. But the price charged to consumers by an investor-owned utility in state B would be governed by the state B regulatory commission—municipally-owned utilities are not regulated.

†Maritime regulation has led a chequered existence. The independent US Shipping Board was replaced in 1933 by the US Shipping Board Bureau of the Department of Commerce. In 1936 the regulatory task was taken up by the independent US Maritime Commission which in turn was replaced in 1950 by the Federal Maritime Board in the Department of Commerce. In 1961 the independent Federal Maritime Commission was established.

The Securities and Exchange Commission regulatory role was not wholly economic—its Truth in Lending activities were essentially a form of consumer protection. However it did in practice choose to preside over the self-regulatory activities of the stock exchanges and these were economic in character. The control of margin requirements exercised by the Federal Reserve Board after the great crash was really designed to achieve stability and therefore seems to fit into our economic regulation category.

deposits. Whilst this was a form of consumer protection, it was also a device for producing greater banking and monetary stability since runs on banks were less likely to occur if customers were assured of protection.[30]

One interesting feature of bank regulation in the US is that, apart from the state banking commissions, the four agencies

named in the table all share in the overall scheme of regulation. Moreover the agencies' activities tend to overlap. This
being so, a bank can often choose which agency to be regulated by. Putting it another way, there is competition between
agencies for the custom of those whom they regulate.[31]

We turn now to social regulation in the US—this of course
is not a new phenomenon. Thus in the consumer protection
field we can point to the Pure Food and Drug Act 1906 which
created the Food and Drug Administration (the Act was
strengthened in 1938) and to the Federal Trade Commission
Act 1914, to which we referred earlier, which empowered the
FTC to attack deceptive practices. The FTC was originally
only allowed to attack deceptive practices if they restricted
competition but that restriction was withdrawn in 1938 by the
Wheeler Lea Act. Nevertheless, despite these and other
parallel developments, there is absolutely no doubt that the
really major advances in social regulation were a product of
the 1960s and 1970s. Regulatory developments in that period
reflected the growth of societal values which gave rise to calls
for major advances in matters such as consumer and environmental protection, health and safety in the workplace and
affirmative action. Much of the vast growth in regulatory
activity reflected in our proxy measures discussed earlier was a
product of these developments. Much of the expansion
revealed by the MacAvoy data was due to the introduction of
health and safety legislation. Some of this growth in social
regulation was also to prove highly controversial.

We will not attempt to describe in detail all the more recent
developments, but merely highlight those legislative steps
which led to the creation of new social regulatory agencies.
These agencies are show in Table 1.2. The reader will note
that a number of them were located in the executive branch
and were not based on the hitherto traditional independent
regulatory commission model. The reader should also bear in
mind that, in parallel with these institutional developments, a
considerable number of laws were introduced which provided
powers for the establishment of protective standards. For
example, in the field of consumer protection alone, the 1960s
and 1970s witnessed the introduction of laws which tightened
up the long-standing food and drug legislation, provided for

standards in relation to labelling and disclosure and the development of standards in relation to certain more dangerous products.

Table 1.2: New social regulatory agencies in the US

Year established	Agency	Location	Regulatory Role
1964	Equal Employment and Opportunity Commission	Independent	Investigation of charges of job discrimination. Equal Pay and Civil Rights Acts were passed in 1963 and 1964 respectively
1970	Environmental Protection Agency	Executive branch	The enforcement of environmental protection. A series of acts was passed between 1965 and 1972 dealing with air, water and noise pollution and automobile emissions
1970	National Highway Administration	Executive branch	Setting of motor vehicle safety and fuel economy standards
1972	Consumer Product Safety Commission	Independent	Setting of consumer product safety standards
1973	Occupational Safety and Health Administration	Executive branch	Setting and enforcing of workers' health and safety regulations

ii The United Kingdom

In the UK antitrust as a form of regulation is of relatively recent vintage when compared with the Sherman and Clayton Acts. Whilst it is true to say that long-standing common law doctrines existed which in principle could have been applied to monopoly, conspiracy and restraint of trade, in practice they proved of little utility.[32] It was not until 1948, with the Monopolies and Restrictive Practices (Inquiry and Control) Act that the UK introduced a specific piece of legislation. The broad lines of monopoly control as presently practised date from that enactment. Currently the referring for investigation of monopoly situations is in the hands of the Office of Fair Trading (OFT)—a body created by the Fair Trading Act 1973. The actual investigation is carried out by the Monopolies and Mergers Commission (MMC). The 1948 Act had no great impact on the antitrust problem, but the investigations to which it gave rise did serve to highlight the widespread and damaging nature of restrictive business practices. This paved the way for the more effective Restrictive Trade Practices Act 1956 which embodied broad principles of control which are still applied. Currently cases are referred to the Restrictive Practices Court by the OFT. In 1964 a similar pro-competition approach and method of adjudication was adopted in respect of individual resale price maintenance under the Resale Prices Act 1964. Then in 1965, by virtue of the Monopolies and Mergers Act, a power was provided over mergers and in 1980 anti-competitive practices were singled out for attack under the Competition Act. In both cases the final investigatory body is the MMC. Thus by 1980 the UK disposed of a broad range of antitrust controls, although its less than full-hearted posture and weakness in its enforcement powers have been strongly criticised.[33]

The economic regulation which existed when the Thatcher government began to shift away from involvement in industry was altogether much less extensive than that of the US. Indeed there was a clear contrast between the two countries. The US had opted for a small amount of public ownership and a large amount of economic regulation. By contrast the UK had a lot of public ownership and that undoubtedly reduced the need to indulge in economic regulation. Economic regulation in the UK tended to concentrate mainly in four areas. One was transport—specifically road freight (lightly regulated), express coaching and buses and domestic and international air transport. The second was financial institutions—the latter being broadly defined so as to include banks and other deposit-taking institutions, building societies, insurance companies and the Stock Exchange. The third was broadcasting. The fourth was the professions.

Whilst economic regulation in transport was a clear cut system, built on conventional lines, the economic regulation of financial institutions was more complex and amorphous.

Considering the area as a whole, the system was a mixture of self-regulation and the externally imposed variety. The main ingredients apart from monetary policy controls were licensing; the restriction of ownership stakes; restrictions on the range of business which institutions might engage in; the prescription of margins of solvency, liquidity and capital asset ratios; systems of depositor and policy-holder protection; agreements on interest rates and minimum brokerage commissions together with less formal, but important, regulatory influences emanating from the Bank of England. Regulatory systems were also imposed by virtue of UK membership of the European Community. More will be said about this topic in Chapters 6 to 8.

Social regulation in the UK was extensively established by the 1970s. Whilst the origins of the system of consumer protection can be traced back to the nineteenth century, the great bulk of the protection which was in place in the late 1970s was a product of the post-war period, and much of it stemmed from the second half of the sixties onwards as Table 1.3 indicates. Much the same could be said about environmental and safety and health at work legislation. Environmental protection was not solely a post-war phenomenon, but it received a great boost notably from the Clean Air Acts 1956 and 1968, the Noise Abatement Act 1960, the Civil Aviation Act 1971 (aircraft noise) and the Control of Pollution Act 1974 (water pollution). Equally health and safety at work legislation goes back to the Factory Acts of the nineteenth century and after. However, by the post-war period some 12 million people were engaged in non-manufacturing activities which were outside the scope of the Factory Acts system. Hence the importance of the much more embracing Health and Safety at Work Act 1974, presided over by the Health and Safety Commission and the Health and Safety Executive. By contrast, equal opportunity legislation is essentially a post-war phenomenon—a product indeed of the 1970s. The important pieces of legislation were three in number. The Equal Pay Act 1970 was designed to ensure that employers paid men and women equally for the same or broadly similar work. This was followed by the Sex Discrimination Act 1975. Discrimination against both men and women became unlawful in areas such as education, training, advertising and employment. This legislation was presided over by the Equal Opportunities Commission. The following year the Race Relations Act, with its Race Relations Commission, was introduced in order to eliminate racial discrimination and thereby promote equal opportunities between racial groups.

Table 1.3: Main consumer protection statutes in operation in the UK in the late 1970s

Date of enactment	Act	Main regulatory purpose
1893	Sale of Goods Act	Basic rights of consumers in connection with sale of goods
1955	Food and Drugs Act	Control of food hygiene, composition, additives, contaminants and labelling
1960, 1972	Road Traffic Acts	Motor and other vehicle safety
1963, 1976, 1979	Weights and Measures Acts	Regulation of sales in respect of quantities
1968	Medicines Act	Screening of drugs in respect of efficacy, quality and safety
1968	Trade Descriptions Act	Protection against false statements in respect of goods, services and prices
1973	Sale of Goods (Implied Terms) Act	Protections additional to those in Sale of Goods Act 1893
1973	Fair Trading Act	Regulation of trading practices which adversely affect consumers' economic interests. Encouragement of voluntary trading codes
1974	Consumer Credit Act	Comprehensive protection against unfair credit practices
1977	Unfair Contract Terms Act	Restriction on ability of sellers to exclude liability in sale of goods
1978	Consumer Safety Act	Provision of safety standards in respect of consumer durables

Source: P. Smith and D. Swann, *Protecting the Consumer* (Martin Robertson, Oxford, 1979)

7 DEREGULATION IDENTIFIED

Just as in recent years public ownership has been followed by privatisation, so regulation has been followed by deregulation. But what exactly is deregulation?

Useful though the word is, it is also extremely imprecise. Strictly interpreted it can be taken to refer to the removal of all regulation. But that is an improbable development. Thus even when we contemplate the decision of the US congress in 1978 to deregulate American internal airline passenger operations, it was not intended that all forms of regulation which impinged upon the airlines should be abandoned. Congress was in fact formally disposing of the *economic* regulation which had been operated by the Civil Aeronautics Board (CAB). The matter of aircraft safety standards was still to be regulated by the Federal Aviation Administration (FAA) and every traveller in American built aircraft is glad to be assured of that fact. In practice, when we use the word deregulation we are employing a term which encompasses (a) differing degrees of deregulation and (b) a variety of possible changes in the way in which regulation operates. All this can best be described as regulatory reform.

Regulatory reform may take the form of total economic deregulation—i.e. the whole panoply of controls over price, entry, exit, the range of business which firms may engage in, etc., may be removed and the industry left to be disciplined by competition and the forces of the marketplace. But economic deregulation may also take the form of a partial removal of restrictions. Thus fixed prices may be replaced not by free prices but by prices which can fluctuate within limits. Quantitative licences, which may rigidly restrict the number of entrants, may be replaced by qualitative licences which stipulate that anyone may enter provided they meet certain, perhaps quite low, standards of professional competence and financial strength. The latter is partial deregulation in the sense that the overall scheme of control is rendered somewhat more flexible. But deregulation may be partial in the sense that only a segment of an industry is deregulated. Thus in electricity, one or more stages in the generation, transmission, distribution process may be natural monopolies which must go on being regulated, but the remaining stage or stages may be deemed to be workably competitive and therefore not in need of regulation. Technological change sometimes renders part of a system competitive whereas previously the whole of the system may have been naturally monopolistic—this seems to have happened in telecommunications.

The reform of economic regulation is not always concerned with the elimination of restrictions which prevent competition. It may also be directed towards creating conditions of greater competitive equity. That is to say the previous system of regulation may have discriminated against and borne more heavily on some enterprises than others, thus placing the former at a disadvantage. Recent regulatory changes in the financial sector have at least in part reflected a desire to put enterprises on a plane of competitive equality.

The reform of economic regulation also covers situations where there is no intention to cease to regulate, but where there is a desire of modify the system in order to render it fairer or more economic. Two examples may suffice to illustrate this point. Thus the structure of regulated electricity prices may be modified in order to provide for life-line tariffs (designed to help small consumers by lowering the price of a limited initial amount of electricity consumed) or time-of-day tariffs (designed to induce consumers to adopt a more economic (off-peak) pattern of electricity consumption). Reform has also been much in evidence in the area of social regulation as we shall see later.

12   DEREGULATION IN THE US AND UK

The purpose of this section is not to discuss the rationale and process in detail—those matters will be dealt with in subsequent chapters—but to leave the reader with some impression of the scope and timing of the deregulation movement.

i The United States
Economic deregulation in the US was essentially a product of the second half of the 1970s and after. It has to be admitted

that it is possible to point to certain deregulatory decisions in the late 1950s—these occurred in telecommunications and broadcasting, and had their origins in the fact that technological change was beginning to undermine the existing regulatory system. Nevertheless, if we look for the turning point in recent US regulatory history, *when the action began to quicken*, then 1975 seems a not unreasonable date to choose. In that year the SEC indicated to the New York Stock Exchange that the latter could no longer set and enforce minimum brokerage commissions in common stock (i.e. equity) trading, and Congress accompanied this with an act which guaranteed that competitive forces would play a bigger role nationally. In subsequent years deregulation occurred in other areas of the economy and these developments are detailed in Table 1.4. The reader should note that deregulation began as *economic* deregulation. It is also apparent that whilst some deregulation waited upon Congressional action, some was carried out by the regulatory body itself. That process was most clearly at work in telecommunications where no deregulatory statute was passed but where nevertheless the Federal Communications Commission (FCC) took a series of decisions, the earliest going back to 1959, which began to introduce competition into the field—indeed to usher in a phase which can be described as managed competition.[34] The process was also at work in transport, notably the airlines, where the CAB began to loosen the regulatory shackles before Congress delivered the *coup de grace* in the shape of the Airline Deregulation Act 1978.

Whilst economic deregulation gathered pace from 1975, its practical and intellectual origins are to be found much further back in time. Criticism of regulation is not new. A long line of official reports, reaching back to the 1930s, expressed concern about the effectiveness of regulatory commissions. But the impression emerges that whether or not industries should be regulated was not a central issue. Instead the reports tended to focus on the efficiency with which the regulatory role was discharged, and suggestions for reform tended to point to the need for better personnel, more effective management structures and procedures and so forth. However it is apparent that, notably from the 1940s onwards, evidence and theories

Table 1.4: Economic deregulation in the US from 1975
(key deregulatory initiatives and statutes)

1975	Securities Exchange Commission: abolition of minimum brokerage commissions on New York Stock Exchange. Securities Amendments Acts: development nationally of interlinked competitive securities markets.
1976	Railroad Revitalisation and Reform Act: increased rate setting freedom for railways.
1977	Air Cargo Deregulation Act: progressive entry and rate deregulation.
1977	Court judgement striking down anti-siphoning restrictions in cable TV and subscription TV.
1978	Air Passenger Deregulation Act: progressive and ultimately total deregulation of rates and entry. Sunset for CAB. In the case of antitrust issues, CAB control was to be passed to Department of Justice.
1978	National Gas Policy Act: gradual decontrol of gas prices focussing mainly on newly discovered gas.
1978	Department of Justice 'show cause' move regarding price fixing exemption of IATA.
1978	Public Utility Regulatory Policies Act: electricity wheeling (see Chapter 4) and inter-connection powers granted to FERC. Requirement to consider rate structure reform—e.g. electricity.
1978	Presidential statement on need for increased competition in bi-lateral air services agreements with other countries.
1979	International Air Transport Competition Act: maximum reliance on competitive market forces in international airline agreements.
1979	Supreme Court: upholds termination of own programming and public interest rules imposed on cable TV.
1979	FCC: radio programme content rules dropped.
1980	Staggers Rail Act: emphasis on more flexibility for rail carrier management.
1980	Motor Carrier Act: increased entry and rate freedom and reduced role for rate fixing bureaux.
1980	Household Goods Transportation Act: deregulation of household goods transport.
1980	Depository Institutions Deregulation and Monetary Control Act: equalisation of reserve requirements among all financial institutions offering similar types of deposits; phasing out of limitations on deposit interest rates; easing of restrictions on the permitted range of lending activities.
1981	FCC: approval of direct broadcasting satellite programme.

1981	Decontrol of Crude Oil and Refined Petroleum Products (Executive Order): complete lifting of crude oil price controls. Under President Carter's National Energy Plan of 1977 controls had in any case been scheduled to be lifted by October 1981.
1982	AT&T divestiture consent decree.
1981	Bus Regulatory Reform Act: entry and exit conditions eased, zones of rate freedom established and role of rate bureaux reduced.
1982	Garn-St Germain Depository Institutions Act: removal of restrictions on thrift institutions both in the acceptance of deposits and in their lending and acquisition of securities.
1982	US–European discussions leading to introduction of zones of rate freedom on North Atlantic air routes.
1983	FCC: TV programme content rules dropped.
1984	FCC: complete deregulation of rate and service regulation of satellites.
1984	Cable Telecommunications Act—virtual completion of deregulation of cable TV.
1985	Supreme court ruling on inter-state banking pacts. Agreements between states, whereby a bank in one state may be controlled via the shareholding of a bank in another state, were upheld even if New York banks were specifically excluded from benefiting from such an arrangement.
1986 and 1987	FRB and court rulings eroding restrictions contained in Glass Steagall Act. Proxmire-Garn bill to repeal Act introduced in Congress in 1987.

began to accumulate which increasingly questioned the wisdom of the existing modes of regulation. Economists, political scientists and historians all contributed to that end.

In particular, studies of the transport sector, some under government aegis, and others which were products of independent academic activity, provided a growing body of contrary evidence. As early as 1942 J. C. Nelson was recommending the virtual repeal of the Motor Carrier Act of 1935 by which ICC control was extended to trucking.[35] From the late 1950s onwards a series of economic studies pointed to the costs of road, rail and airline regulation and prompted economists to ask the question—do we really need to regulate? Thereafter this shift of opinion began to manifest itself on the political plane in the shape of Presidential proposals for transportation reform. The first of these occurred in 1955 under

President Eisenhower. In 1962 President Kennedy, in his special transportation message, called for more reliance on the forces of competition and less on the restraints of regulation.[36]

Significant also as straws in the wind were the studies on antitrust policy commissioned by both President Johnson and President Nixon. The respective Neal and Stigler Task Force Reports both recommended policies leading to increased competition in regulated industries.

Nevertheless, looking at the regulation field as a whole, it was not until the 1970s onwards that there occured a critical amalgam of factors which finally led to action. That combination consisted of:

(a) The accumulated economic evidence about the harm done by regulation and the favourable evidence provided by the performance of unregulated markets.

(b) The theorising and evidence of economists, political scientists and historians which cast doubts on the public interest basis of existing legislation and upon the effectiveness and independence of independent regulatory commissions.

(c) New theoretical developments and the rediscovery of old ones which stressed the potentiality of competition as a regulator.

(d) The need to combat inflation and the undermining effect which inflation had upon the existing regulatory system.

(e) The effect which technological change had in undermining existing modes of regulation notably in the higher technology sectors and transport.

(f) The fact that deregulation in one transport mode tends to undermine the regulation of others.

(g) Consumer pressures for change.

(h) Presidents (notably President Carter), politicians (notably Edward Kennedy), and indeed regulators (notably Alfred Kahn at the CAB) who saw that the time to act had come.

One of the interesting features of US regulatory developments is that whilst the evidential tide was flowing against economic regulation, the US was engaged in a veritable spate of social regulation—according to Table 1.2 1964 to 1973 was the key period for agency creation. It should be added that the flow of protective legislation did not end in 1973—further acts and amendments were passed in the second half of the seventies. In due course these agencies and powers produced a rising tide of regulation. This in turn provoked a reaction which centred on the burden which it imposed upon the economy. Commentators also pointed out that however heavy the burden had become by the late 1970s, it was by no means certain that it would not increase yet further. Thus Murray Weidenbaum observed:

> Unfortunately, the rapid growth of regulation has not ended, and it is not about to end soon. If you look at the pipeline of regulation, you will see that a host of statutes passed in the 1970s are still generating regulations whose costs will not hit us until the 1980s.[37]

The result was a form of deregulation in the social sector—particularly in the fields of health and safety, environmental protection and consumer protection. Deregulation partly manifested itself as reform of the way in which the system operated but at a later state it gave rise to numerous cancellations of regulatory rules, i.e. actual deregulation. The process got under way during the Ford and Carter administration and was considerably intensified under President Reagan. The latter's antipathy to regulation matched Mrs Thatcher's dislike of public enterprise.

Two developments stand out in what is a complex field of activity. Firstly, it was recognised that agencies had a strong incentive to obtain regulatory benefits since they thereby justified their existence, but to a large extent they ignored the attendant costs—these were borne by other parts of the economy, notably industry and ultimately no doubt the consumer. There was no system for setting the costs against the benefits prior to the making of a decision as to whether or not to introduce a regulation. From the Ford administration onwards it was therefore decided that social regulatory agencies should assess both the costs and the benefits of major proposed regulations. Apparently such procedural reform was largely ineffective, notably under President Ford but also under President Carter. It is true that under President Carter the social regulatory agencies did produce estimates of costs as well as benefits but a net benefit was not required as a condition for approving a regulation, and net benefits and net costs were not in any formal way employed as the primary factors in making decisions. When President Reagan came on the scene he altered all this by, amongst other things, requiring that the condition for approving a regulation was that a net benefit should be demonstrated. He set on foot a vigorous counter-attack against unjustified social regulation. For example, he set up a Presidential Task Force on Regulatory Relief. This group was given the power to identify particularly burdensome regulations for investigation by the regulatory agency and by the Office of Management and Budget. This led in a significant number of cases to the cancellation of regulatory rules. The rolling back of regulation was further promoted by cuts in agency appropriations. Secondly, it was recognised that more flexible market-type methods of control were needed. Thus specification standards should be replaced by performance standards. For example, in the case of pollution, particular details of the way that it should be reduced should cease to be prescribed. Instead an acceptable degree of pollution should be identified and the regulatory system should give the polluter an incentive to achieve the required reduction by the least-cost method i.e. a cost-effectiveness approach.

More recently under the Reagan administration regulatory reform has begun to creep into the field of antitrust. There are some who claim that members of the administration have seen antitrust in the same light as social regulation—i.e. a burden that needs to be lifted from the back of hard pressed industry. Whilst we cannot rule out that such a relatively crude calculation has inspired policy changes and policy proposals, it seems likely that other more subtle influences have been at work.

Before we seek to identify those influences it is important to emphasise that in the field of antitrust, as indeed in any kind of regulation, reform can proceed along two lines. The substantive law may change. Alternatively the law may not change but the guidelines used in implementing it may change. Thus merger guidelines (which indicate which mergers will be challenged) may be altered—depending on how they are changed more or fewer or different kinds of mergers may be attacked. It is equally important to recognise that historically American antitrust has tended to emphasise the prime importance of maintaining competition. Thus under section 1 of the Sherman Act various forms of collusion came to be regarded as illegal *per se*. That is to say, if the courts found evidence of collusion, adverse judgement followed automatically. There was no scope for giving consideration to counterbalancing advantages—e.g. greater efficiency. Equally section 7 of the Clayton Act attacked mergers which might significantly lessen competition or tended to create a monopoly. It made no explicit reference to the possibility that gains such as scale economies should be taken into account.

What seems to have been happening in recent years is that, by virtue of new statutory powers and through changes in administrative guidelines, the balance has swung towards giving more weight to efficiency gains. Two straws in the wind are the National Cooperative Research Act 1984, which limited the damages that can be collected from participants in collective R & D ventures which turn out to restrict competition, and the 1982 and 1984 merger guidelines, which have allowed the Department of Justice to consider efficiency gains as grounds for not attacking mergers. The attack on mergers slowed down under President Reagan as compared with President Carter, and yet merger activity in recent years has been running at a high level.

The reform process entered a potentially more intensive phase in 1986 when the administration put before Congress five bills which if carried into law would represent the most sweeping antitrust reform for many decades. The proposals consist of an interlocking directorates bill, a foreign trade antitrust improvement bill, an antitrust remedies bill, a merger modification bill and a distressed industries bill. The first two are not really controversial and may succeed. The third touches upon the ability of those adversely affected by a competitive violation to claim treble damages from the perpetrator. This is a hallowed feature of US antitrust and may therefore meet some resistance. It is however the last two bills which are the really important ones.

The merger modification bill seeks to change the wording of section 7 of the Clayton Act so that a merger is attacked not when it *may* substantially lessen competition or *tends* to create a monopoly but when there is a *significant probability* that it will increase the ability to exercise market power. What effect this change of wording would have is not clear. Indeed some who are not favourable to the proposal have argued that it may amount to very little since the courts have regularly ruled that there must be a probability and not just a possibility that a merger will be anti-competitive.[38] Altogether more important is the point that the new act would put into statutory form what are presently merely administrative guidelines. Here a particularly important point is that efficiency gains would become a statutory defence.

The shift in emphasis during the Reagan period picks up a new trend in thinking, sometimes called the new learning, which stems very much from work done at the University of Chicago. In the past economists have established a positive correlation between concentration and profitability. In traditional theory the enhancement of profits arising from concentration (possibly arising from horizontal mergers) has pointed to adverse consequences in distributional and efficiency terms. But the new learning provides an alternative interpretation. For example, it is argued that higher profitability in concentrated industries is a reflection of the superior efficiency of bigger firms. Put crudely it suggests that big is best. Mergers are therefore viewed in a more favourable light. There is no doubt that administrative practice and the merger modification proposal have been influenced by this school of thought. A reading of the academic defence of the proposal by Douglas Ginsberg (then Assistant Attorney General, head of the antitrust division of the Department of Justice) leaves that point in no doubt.[39] It should be mentioned that Commerce Secretary the late Malcolm Baldrige would have happily scrapped section 7 but that line of attack was not adopted (see end note 46).

The other proposal on distressed industries is highly controversial and could well fail. Briefly it proposes that industries that are suffering from an increase in imports should enjoy a three year exemption for any merger or acquisition. Critics point out that the only remedy for import penetration is a leaner and fitter industry, and that to make life somewhat easier and in such a blanket fashion is not likely to be beneficial. The possibility that this proposal is really an attempt to take steam out of the pressure for trade protection measures cannot be ruled out.

ii The United Kingdom

By contrast, economic deregulation in the UK has been a relatively modest affair. Prior to 1979 the main instance was the substitution of qualitative for quantitative licensing in road freight transport as a result of the Transport Act 1968. Under the post-1979 Thatcher governments, the policy of economic deregulation has been pressed forward with enthusiasm. Nationalised industries have been stripped of their statutory monopolies. The process of deregulation and the introduction of competition has been noticeably at work in the financial markets (a development which can be traced back to 1971), although the actual contribution of the Thatcher government should not be exaggerated—a significant part of the change can be ascribed to domestic and international competitive pressures—on the latter see below. As a result of the Transport Act 1980 the economic regulation of express coaching (road passage transport over 30 miles) and buses has been largely dismantled. In domestic airline operation the CAA has been pursuing a policy of route liberalisation together with a relaxation of control over fares. Internationally the new policy approach manifested itself most vividly in 1984 in the agreement between the UK and the Netherlands which significantly deregulated air services between the two countries. In the field of broadcasting, notably TV, technological developments (cable, satellites) have been a major factor in creating the possibility of greater competition, and policy has been based on the proposition that these changes should be accepted (rather than resisted) within a lighter regulatory framework. Changes on the EEC front will be discussed in Chapter 8.

Whereas in the US social deregulation has been at work on a significant scale in recent years, that tendency has not made much headway in the UK. It is of course true that public expenditure cuts have affected agency appropriations. As a result the Health and Safety Executive has had to cut down on its force of inspectors and policy seems to be swinging towards self-regulation and the privatisation of inspection. Currently there is no commitment to deregulate in the field of antitrust. Opinion among informed commentators tends to the view that British antitrust is somewhat lacking in credibility and needs to be stiffened up. Time alone will tell whether UK antitrust policy is to be strengthened, weakened or left where it currently stands. Clearly, as the state retreats from regulation and privatises enterprises which have dominant positions, the importance of competition policy as a means of checking market power and anti-competitive practices increases (recent signs suggest a strengthening).

13   DEREGULATION FOR EXPORT

Just as the British privatisation programme has attracted the attention of governments in other parts of the world and may at least have acted as an encouragement to right-wing administrations, notably in Canada and France, so the US programme of deregulation has disposed governments in other parts of the globe not merely to subject their regulatory controls to closer scrutiny but to reform and indeed abolish them.

Having said that, it has to be admitted that just as the UK was not first in the privatisation field, so the US was not the first to deregulate. Notably in surface transport other countries had already trodden that path. Australia led the field in 1954 when all state licensing and taxation restrictions on interstate motor carriage were declared unconstitutional.[40] Sweden adopted legislation in 1963 which led to a significant easing of quantitative licensing although the final stage, which could have led to total abolition, is reported not to have occurred.[41] As we noted earlier, the UK substituted quali-tative for quantitative licensing as a result of the Transport Act 1968. In 1977 South Africa removed some of the restric-tions which prevented road hauliers from competing with the railways.[42] There was also some deregulation in rail transport, the most frequently cited example being the federal deregu-lation of Canadian railways under the National Transpor-tation Act 1967. This was actually a case of partial deregu-lation which consisted of the granting of wide commercial freedom over rates.[43] Mention should also be made of the EEC Common Transport Policy—the basic features of which were spelled out as far back as 1961 and 1962. This was really a proposal for the deregulation of surface modes in the sense that fair and undistorted inter-modal and inter-enterprise competition was to be progressively substituted for quite rigid controls over entry and rates, and for distorting government interventions. The proposal was quite far-sighted since it was at that time still widely accepted that free competition in transport was undesirable because it would be excessive, destructive, etc.[44]

A particular feature of US deregulation which rendered it highly influential was the scope of the policy; across the board the system of regulation was subjected to intense inquiry and in some cases to radical treatment (e.g. internal air passenger transport). The impact of US deregulation was not however purely based on the fact that the Americans were doing it on an impressive scale. Its influence was also due to three other factors.

Firstly, attention focussed on its alleged beneficial effects. Thus in the case of airline operation commentators and indeed regulators in, for example, the UK and the EEC drew attention to the lower fares, distance for distance, in the US as compared with Europe where tight controls existed in the case of scheduled services. Secondly, the American conversion to deregulation had a direct impact when the US and other countries had joint jurisdiction over regulatory systems. This was the case where traffic between the US and other countries was governed by bilateral air services agreements. Oppor-tunities to exert a deregulatory influence also arose when US enterprises joined with those from other countries in fixing rates—e.g. IATA. Thirdly, American deregulation had a direct impact on geographically contiguous economies and on economies which, whilst not geographically continuous, were nevertheless in competition. The contiguity factor is well illustrated by Canadian airline experience. From the mid-seventies regulation began to give place to competition in US airline operation. This had two effects in Canada. Firstly, US carriers diverted considerable trans-Canadian traffic to US services running parallel with Canadian trans-continental routes. Secondly, the Canadian public became increasingly aware of low US fares and began to press for deregulation. The result was a move towards greater competition, notably in Southern Canada.[45] The effect of competition even in the absence of geographic contiguity is illustrated by events in the world of security dealing. Thanks to technological developments all the main financial centres are now linked—this is often referred to as the globalisation of the financial system. Once one centre deregulates and prices fall other centres are forced to follow suit—otherwise trade is deflected to the lower cost centre. Thus competition from the New York Stock Exchange after the events of 1975 helped to bring about deregulation in London, and this kind of knock-on effect was felt throughout the world.

The international commerce of ideas has not however been a one way flow from the US to the rest of the world. There are some instances where the old world has influenced the new. Thus the reform of electricity regulation in the US has involved the application of peak load pricing principles which were pioneered in Western Europe and notably France.

NOTES

1. D. Heald, *Public Expenditure; Its Defence and Reform* (Martin Robertson, Oxford, 1983), p.298.
2. A. Peacock, 'Privatisation in Perspective', *Three Banks Review*, 144 (1984), p.3.
3. M. Beesley and S. Littlechild, 'Privatisation: Principles, Problems and Priorities', *Lloyds Bank Review*, 149 (1983), p.1.

4. *The Economist*, 11 February 1986, p.43. For an interesting study of contracting out by cities in the US, which is a practice of long standing, see E. S. Savas, *Privatizing the Public Sector* (Chatham House, Chatham, New Jersey, 1982). For a recent study of contracting out public services in the UK see K. Ascher, *The Politics of Privatisation* (Macmillan, London, 1987).
5. D. Heald, *op. cit.*, p.299.
6. National Economic Development Office, *A Study of UK Nationalised Industries*, Appendix Volume (London, 1976), p.8.
7. R. Pryke, *The Nationalised Industries* (Martin Robertson, Oxford, 1981), p.2.
8. US Bureau of Census, *Statistical Abstract of the United States* (Government Printing Office, Washington, 1981), p.425 cited in P. R. Gregory and R. C. Stuart, *Comparative Economic Systems* (Houghton Miflin, Boston, 1985), pp.199–200.
9. R. Platzer, 'The Privatisation Debate in Austria', *Annals of Public and Cooperative Economy*, 57 (1986), pp. 277–8.
10. T. M. Ohashi *et al.*, *Privatization Theory and Practice: Distributing Shares in Private and Public Enterprises* (Fraser Institute, Vancouver, 1980).
11. G. Stefani, 'Privatizing Public Enterprises of Italy', *Annals of Public and Cooperative Economy*, 57 (1986), p.234.
12. For an excellent worldwide survey of privatisation see *The Economist*, 21 December 1985, pp. 69–84.
13. *Globe and Mail* (Canada), 28 February 1987, p.8.
14. M. M. Shirley, *Managing State-Owned Enterprises, World Bank Staff Working Papers*, No. 577, (Washington, 1983), p.13 and A. Kaletsky, 'Everywhere the State is in Retreat', *Financial Times*, 2 August 1985, p.8.
15. G. Stefani, *op. cit.*, pp. 234–5.
16. See, in the developing country context, the reported views of Eliot Berg in *Financial Times, op. cit., loc. cit.*, and, in the UK context, the views of John Kay in *The Economist*, 21 December 1985, p.84.
17. P. Bance and L. Monnier, 'The Privatization of Public Enterprises in France', *Annals of Public and Cooperative Economy*, 57 (1986), p.182.
18. *The Economist*, 11 May 1985, pp.70–1.
19. J. Stuyck, 'Consumer Soft Law in Belgium', *Journal of Consumer Policy* 7 (1984), pp. 125–35.
20. R. Cranston, *Consumers and the Law* (Weidenfeld, London, 1978), pp.29–64.
21. E. Mansfield, 'Federal Maritime Commission', in J. Q. Wilson (ed.), *The Politics of Regulation*, (Basic Books, New York, 1980), pp.42–74. We should not of course ignore the countervailing power which shippers exert through the collective agency of Shipping Councils.
22. A. Smith, *The Wealth of Nations*, Vol. 1 (Dent, London, 1947), p.117.
23. Quoted in S. G. Breyer, *Regulation and Its Reform* (Harvard, Cambridge, Massachusetts, 1982), p.1.

24. P. W. MacAvoy, *The Regulated Industries and the Economy* (Norton, New York, 1979), pp.17–25.
25. F. Thompson and L. R. Jones, *Regulatory Policies and Practices* (Praeger, New York, 1982), pp.33–5.
26. D. Swann, *Competition and Consumer Protection* (Penguin, Harmondsworth, 1979), Chapters 5 and 6.
27. There are alternative devices such as the insertion of regulatory clauses in charters of incorporation. But these do not seem to have been effective—see H. H. Liebhafsky, *American Government and Business*, (Wiley, New York, 1971), pp.438–9.
28. For an entirely fascinating account of the activities of a sunshine commissioner, see T. McCraw, *The Prophets of Regulation* (Belknap, New York, 1984), Chapter 2.
29. Not all commissions were sunshine affairs. The Granger movement, which attacked the high and discriminatory rates of the railways, led some states to create commissions with powers to control extortionate rates and discriminations. These were later watered down but undoubtedly the Granger commissions anticipated the nature of subsequent federal regulation—see S. J. Buck, *The Granger Movement* (Harvard, Cambridge, Massachusetts, 1913), p.205.
30. J. R. Barth, R. D. Brumbaugh, D. Sauerhaft and G. H. K. Wang, 'Insolvency and Risk-Taking in the Thrift Industry: Implications for the Future', *Contemporary Issues*, 3 (1985), pp.2–3.
31. T. G. Herrick, *Bank Analysts' Handbook* (Wiley, New York, 1978), pp.264–5.
32. D. Swann, D. P. O'Brien, W. P. J. Maunder and W. S. Howe, *Competition in British Industry* (Allen and Unwin, London, 1974), pp.49–51.
33. D. Swann, *Competition and Consumer Protection op. cit.*, Chapter 9.
34. S. M. Besen and J. R. Woodbury, 'Regulation, Deregulation and Antitrust in the Telecommunications Industry', *The Antitrust Bulletin*, 28 (1983).
35. J. C. Nelson, 'Regulatory Performance in Surface Freight Transportation in Australia, Canada, Great Britain and the USA', *International Journal of Transport Economics*, 7 (1980), p.134.
36. M. T. Farris, 'Evolution of the Transport Regulatory Structure of the US', *International Journal of Transport Economics*, 10 (1983), pp.185–6.
37. M. L. Weidenbaum, 'An Overview of Government Regulation' in J. F. Gatti (ed.), *The Limits of Government Regulation*, (Academic Press, New York, 1981), p.94.
38. *Congressional Quarterly* 5 (44), 1986, p.191.
39. D. H. Ginsburg, 'The Reagan Administration's Legislative Initiative in Antitrust', *The Antitrust Bulletin*, Winter (1986), pp.851–69. For a critical view see P. G. Harris and L. A. Sullivan; 'Horizontal Merger Policy: Promoting Competition and American Competitiveness', *ibid.*, pp.871–933.

40. G. Chow, 'Economic Regulation of Motor Freight in Foreign Countries', *ICC Practitioners Journal*, November–December 1979), p.48.
41. Chow *op. cit.*, pp.49–50.
42. T. R. Jacobson and T. L. Kennedy, 'A Study in Contrast U.S. Versus South African Transportation Policies', *Transport Research Forum*, 24 (1983), p.411.
43. J. C. Nelson, *op. cit.*, p.155.
44. D. Swann, *The Economics of the Common Market* (Penguin, Harmondsworth, 1988), Chapter 8 and K. J. Button, *Road Haulage Licensing and EC Transport Policy* (Gower, Aldershot, 1984), Chapters 2 and 3.
45. T. H. Oum and M. W. Trethaway, 'Reforming Canadian Airline Regulation', *Logistics and Transportation Review*, 20 (1985), pp.261–84.
46. All five bills ultimately failed but the regulatory reform influence of Chicago thinking is apparently exercising a strong influence on those who are responsible for the implementation of US antitrust policy.

2 The Rationale of Regulation and Public Enterprise

Various theories have been advanced which seek to explain why regulation came into existence. It may of course be necessary to distinguish between the original legislative enactment and the subsequent regime imposed by the regulatory body. In the first part of this chapter we will survey theories of regulatory origin. In the second part we shall attempt to explain why it has been deemed desirable that some enterprises and industries should be in public ownership.

1 REGULATION—COMPETING THEORIES

It is tempting to argue that regulation, other than that concerned with the maintenance of competition, is irrelevant. The argument might run as follows. A free market, which in this context means perfect competition, will lead to the most efficient allocation of resources. That is to say, for a given distribution of income, the maximum social welfare will be produced when conditions of perfect competition obtain. Such efficiency implies that the correct combination of goods will be produced and that each good will be produced with the minimum input of resources. The former is referred to as allocative efficiency. The latter may be termed productive efficiency.

In Figure 2.1 (a) we present the long run equilibrium position of the perfectly competitive firm. In Figure 2.1 (b) we show the total demand for and total supply of the product in the market in which each perfect competitor operates. The equilibrium price will be OP1 and the equilibrium quantity will be OQ1. In Figure 2.1 (a) we can see that at price OP1 each perfectly competitive firm just breaks even (normal profit—i.e. a return on the entrepreneurial capital which is just sufficient to retain it in its existing use—is included in average cost) by producing output OQ1. Because of the ability of the individual form to expand or contract (both its capital stock and its output), and for firms to enter and exit, this is the position to which firms will gravitate in the long run. If the price was above OP1, existing firms would enjoy abnormal profits, new firms would enter, supply would increase and price would fall—thus eliminating the abnormal return. If price fell below OP1, existing firms would make losses, sooner or later some would exit, supply would diminish and price would rise—thus wiping out the losses.

In what sense is the equilibrium position in Figure 2.1 (a) optimal? Firstly, it is assumed that productive efficiency would be maximised since in order to survive in conditions of free competition the firm will have to seek to be as efficient as possible. Cost will therefore be minimised—i.e. the long run average cost curve will be as low as current technology, current managerial best practice, etc., will allow and output will take place at the minimum point along it. Secondly, the accompanying property of allocative efficiency refers to the fact that price is equal to marginal cost. That is to say, the price which consumers are willing to pay for the last unit they are willing to consume (which we take to be a measure of the welfare or utility they derive) is equal to the resource cost of producing it. If all industries are producing under conditions of perfect competition then in all cases at the margin, price will be equal to marginal cost. No gain can therefore be made by reallocating resources—i.e. increasing the output of one industry and decreasing the output of another. The reader who is less familiar with economic analysis should appreciate that if at the margin price does not equal marginal cost then a reallocation of resources would be beneficial. Thus if good A costs 80 pence (cents) to produce but sells for £1 ($1), whilst good B costs £1 ($1) to produce but sells for 80 pence (cents), then we ought to shift resources from industry B, where they produce relatively little utility or welfare, to industry A,

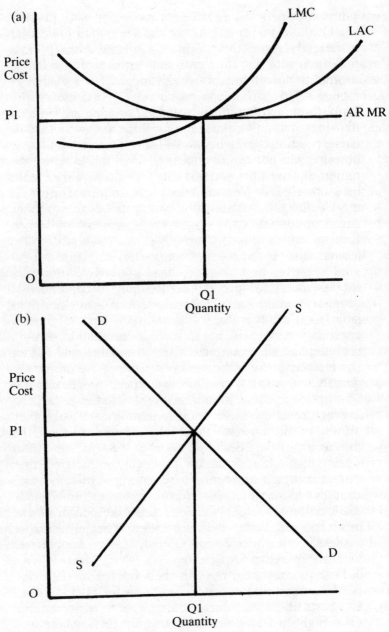

Figure 2.1: Perfect Competition Equilibrium

where they produce relatively more utility or welfare. Only when the ratio of price to cost is the same in both industries will the process of transfer cease to be advantageous.

We can compare the supposedly optimal nature of perfect competition with what would happen if the industry was monopolised. For this purpose we will focus on the total supply and demand for the good in question and will assume that marginal cost is constant and that therefore the supply curve is perfectly elastic. In Figure 2.2 we assume the equilibrium condition under perfect competition to be the combination of price OP1 and quantity OQ1. Now let the industry be monopolised. We will assume that the monopolist is no more efficient in production than the collection of perfectly competitive firms which existed previously. There are therefore no economies of large scale production. We will also assume that the monopolist, like the perfect competitors, will seek to maximise profits. Profits will be maximised when the increase in total cost as a result of producing one more unit of output (i.e. marginal cost) equals the increase in total revenue as a result of selling it (i.e. marginal revenue). The supply curve of the perfectly competitive industry and the marginal cost curve of the monopolist are one and the same. Likewise the demand curve of the perfectly competitive industry is the demand curve (or average revenue curve) of the monopolist. The monopolist's marginal revenue curve lies below his average revenue curve. In the light of what we have said above, profit will be maximised when the monopolist produces output OQ2 and charges price OP2—i.e. the quantity where maginal cost equals marginal revenue. The (non-discriminating[1]) monopolist produces a smaller output and charges a higher price than the previous competitive industry. Total cost is OP1BQ2. Total revenue is OP2AQ2. Abnormal profit (normal profit, it will be recalled, is treated as a cost and is therefore included in area OP1BQ2) or monopoly revenue will be P1P2AB.

How is social welfare affected by the change? Under perfect competition the total welfare derived from quantity OQ1 was the area under the demand curve up to Q1—i.e. ODCQ1. We derive this conclusion from the assumption that the price consumers are willing to pay reflects the welfare or utility they expect to derive from consuming it. Clearly the utility expected from the first unit is high (i.e. approximately OD) but it diminishes as consumers enjoy more of the good until at quantity OQ1 it is only Q1C. The reader will observe that on all units up to Q1 the price the consumer is willing to pay exceeds the cost of producing a unit of the good. Therefore there is an excess of welfare or utility over cost, which in total is equal to P1DC. On the last unit (Q1) the price (welfare) just equals the resource cost of producing it—there is no excess on that good.

The area P1DC also represents consumer surplus. The latter may be defined as the excess of what consumers would be willing to pay over what they actually do pay. In this case consumer surplus and the excess of welfare over cost exactly coincide.

When the monopolist restricts output, what happens to this surplus area? Part of it is transferred to the monopolist in the form of monopoly revenue P1P2AB. *If* we are prepared to accept, as is typical in this sort of analysis, that a pound in the pocket of the monopolist has the same welfare significance as a pound in the pocket of the consumer, then the transfer has no welfare significance on balance. Consumer surplus is of course reduced to P2DA and previous consumer surplus P1P2AB is pocketed by the monopolist. Therefore we must look elsewhere for a monopoly loss. One possible measure of the latter could be the area Q2ACQ1 because less output is now produced and consumers would lose the welfare deriving from it. However we cannot assume that to be automatically so, since resources Q2BCQ1, which are no longer used by the monopolist, can presumably be transferred to other uses. If when transferred to other uses they produce welfare equal to Q2ACQ1 then there is no loss at all—i.e. resources OP1BQ2 in the monopolised industry produce welfare ODAQ2 and transferred resources Q2BCQ1 produce welfare Q2ACQ1 elsewhere. In terms of total welfare nothing has changed! Why therefore bleat about monopoly!

The answer at this stage is twofold. Firstly, the above conclusion is not valid. If we assume that the other industries to which the resources are transferred are operating under conditions of perfect competition then at the margin their

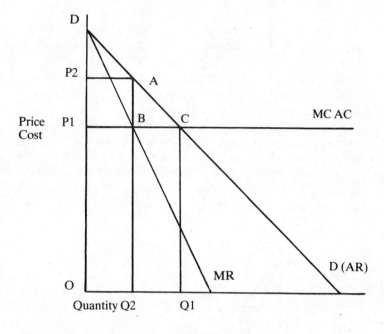

Figure 2.2: Deadweight Welfare Loss

prices will be equal to their marginal costs. It follows that at best when we transfer resources Q2BCQ1 the welfare they produce will be equal to what they produced *at the margin* in the previous perfectly competitive state. We recollect that the last unit cost Q1C and gave rise to a good whose utility was also Q1C. Therefore transferred resources Q2BCQ1 will at best produce welfare equal to Q2BCQ1. There is therefore a net loss of welfare equal to BAC. This is referred to as the deadweight welfare loss due to monopoly.

Secondly, it can be argued that if competitive pressures are removed then the incentive to be productively efficient will be reduced. The carrot remains but the stick is absent—i.e. the monopolist gains by keeping his costs low but his continued existence does not depend on being maximally efficient. This possibility is enhanced when a division between ownership and control permits managers to pursue their own goals as opposed to those which best suit the equity owners. We may therefore expect the average and marginal cost curves to drift up—this will eat into monopoly profits. It is indeed possible to imagine that the monopoly profits are totally eroded so that the monopoly industry is no more profitable than the perfectly competitive one. This tendency for productive efficiency to decline, which Leibenstein has termed X-inefficiency[2], is an additional source of loss. The process is illustrated in Figure 2.3 where the effect of monopolistic security is to allow the average and marginal cost curves to drift up from AC and MC to AC^1 and MC^1. As a result in order to profit maximise the monopolist produces a smaller output and the deadweight loss is therefore EFC. Also the cost of producing the smaller output OQ3 is increased by the amount P1GHE. The idea

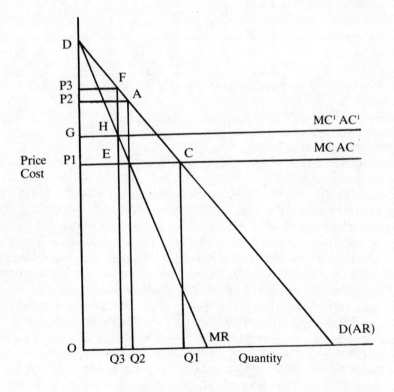

Figure 2.3: X Inefficiency

that monopoly conduces to X-inefficiency, with a consequential loss of welfare, is highly relevant in a regulatory context since the object and/or effect of regulation may be to lessen or indeed eliminate the pressure of competition by controlling entry, etc.

Four points must be mentioned at this stage. Firstly, whilst second–best considerations may complicate the above allocative efficiency argument, it is generally agreed that the productive efficiency (i.e. X-efficiency) which springs from competition and enables additional goods to be created is preferable in terms of Paretian optimality.[3]

Secondly, the argument so far has focussed on *static* welfare effects. But it could equally be argued that monopoly has dynamic disadvantages in that it reduces the incentive to innovate whilst competition has a beneficial effect on technical progressiveness.[4]

Thirdly, the previous argument appears to imply that in the absence of market rivals (actual or potential) there will be a tendency for X-inefficiency to creep in and for firms to rest on their technological oars. Whilst such rivalry may be an important source of pressure, we have to acknowledge another source associated with the concept of the market for corporate control. If firms are insulated from competition, inefficiency will be encouraged, costs will drift up, profits will thereby decline and the share price will tend to be depressed. This will make the firm an attractive takeover target for an entrepreneur who believes that he can make better use of the assets. It is also argued that the threat of takeover as well as actual takeover will act as a check on X-inefficiency. This point relates to the likelihood that a takeover will be followed by a managerial shake-out and that managers will therefore seek to avoid takeovers by being efficient.[5] This point is of considerable relevance in the context of our subsequent discussion of privatisation, since those who advocate such a policy argue that even if the privatised firm has no effective rivals it will nevertheless be subject to a new form of discipline—i.e. that inherent in the concept of the market for corporate control.

Fourthly, it should be said that not all economists accept the idea of X-inefficiency. Richard Posner, for example, in his

analysis of the effects of monopoly rejects it.[6] He does however draw our attention to another way in which restrictions of
competition may lead to costs drifting up at the expense of
profits. Let us assume that a group of firms engage in collusion. They collectively restrict output, raise price and as a
result are able to earn monopoly profits. Posner suggests that
they may seek to increase their share of the monopolised
output by engaging in non-price competition. This has the
effect of raising the cost of production. Posner suggests that
firms will compete by progressively escalating the non-price
competition until all the monopoly profits are competed away
and the incentive to yet further non-price competition is
therefore eliminated. We can describe this as the process of
transforming monopoly profit into a social cost. We cannot
conclude that welfare will decline by the full amount of the
cost escalation, since the consumer may to some extent
benefit from the product differentiation. However it seems
likely that there will be some welfare loss in that the consumer
might have preferred a lower price and less frills to a higher
price and more frills. Posner's suggestion has considerable
relevance in a regulatory context since it seems to be reflected
in the behaviour of regulated airlines in the US. With prices
fixed, they tended to compete by offering more in-flight entertainment, lusher meals and more frequent departures (i.e.
less efficient load-factors).

The above argument suggests that rivalry within the
market, supported by the influence of the market for corporate control, will maximise welfare and that regulatory
activity ought to be confined to rooting out anti-competitive
elements and minimising the factors which inhibit the
influence of the corporate control market.[7] But is it as simple
as that? Unfortunately the answer is no. Economists point to
the fact that the sort of free market we have been considering
would not necessarily produce the kind of optimal results we
have suggested. The market may fail. The sources of that
failure are numerous and we shall not attempt to discuss them
all.[8]

One with which we are already familiar is connected with
economies of scale. We mentioned this in Chapter 1 in connection with the influence of the new learning on US antitrust

policy. There the emphasis was on merger situations where efficiency gains might have to be traded off against some loss of competition. Here however we will focus upon the much more extreme situation where economies of scale are so pronounced that it would be grossly uneconomic to insist upon any competition at all. In other words we are pointing to the existence of natural monopoly. But the private monopolist cannot be left to himself. Somebody has to prevent the monopolist from exploiting the consumer—not least because, whilst we have not placed any welfare significance on the ability of the monopolist to raise price and thus line his pocket at the expense of the consumer, the consumer is likely to take a different view! Not only that, but if competition is not available to produce the appropriate welfare maximising prices and to keep the monopolist on his toes in terms of productive efficiency and technical progressiveness, then some surrogate mechanism has to be devised which will hopefully achieve these ends. There are of course other issues, such as those concerning price structures (e.g. the life-line tariff discussed in Chapter 1), about which the consuming public may have decided views but which the monopolist, not having to contend with more obliging rivals, may safely choose to ignore.

Another cause of market failure is associated with externalities. An externality is an effect which arises incidentally in the production or consumption of a good and thereby affects other people's welfare. Such external effects may be beneficial or disbeneficial. Where a beneficial effect arises, too little of a good will be produced. Where a disbeneficial effect arises too much will be supplied. Let us consider the disbeneficial case. Suppose a firm is producing a good under competitive conditions. As we have noted, one of the virtues of competition is that it forces producers to be as productively efficient as possible—e.g. to use the lowest cost technology available. Not to do so would be to invite market failure but in another sense—i.e. bankruptcy! However this minimisation of *private* costs may also be accompanied by other costs—e.g. pollution. The cost to society as a whole—social cost—is the private cost plus the pollution cost, the latter being an external cost or cost spillover. This might suggest that an alternative technology, involving no pollution but higher private cost, would be best. But this is by no means inevitable since we have to set the gain from the elimination of the pollution loss against the increased resource cost of using a non-polluting technology. Whilst the former may outweigh the latter, the latter may outweigh the former—where the balance lies is clearly an empirical matter. What is clear is that the social benefits derived from producing goods have to be set against the social costs of producing them—the latter involves internalising the externality. It also follows that the optimum may not be zero pollution but *an optimum degree of pollution*.

One way of achieving the optimum is to apply a tax—a pollution tax. Thus in Figure 2.4 DD is the marginal social benefit curve derived from consuming a good. SS is the marginal private cost of producing the good, but social cost is not the same as private cost because the technology used gives rise to pollution. S^1S^1 is the marginal social cost curve, which is made up of private cost plus the external cost arising from pollution. Prior to the application of the tax the equilibrium point is E1, equilibrium output is OC and the equilibrium price is OP1. However this is not optimal since the OCth unit costs society CB and not CE1, but produces welfare or utility equal to only CE1. However if we impose a tax equal to the marginal external cost, the tax internalises the externality and this is shown in the shift of the supply curve to S^1S^1. Equilibrium is now at E2, output falls to OA and the consumer has to pay the higher price OP2. The efficiency gain is the area E2BE1, which is equal to the inefficiency loss which arose prior to the tax.

Taxes and subsidies are not the only ways of dealing with externalities. Property rights[9] offer another approach. If it is possible to invest individuals or institutions with property rights in things such as clean air then, rather than rely on official regulation, we could envisage the property right owners bribing the polluters to reduce or eliminate their emissions. However in practice there are difficulties in applying the property rights approach to problems such as smoky chimneys. These are connected with the cost of collecting the bribe, securing agreement on appropriate contri-

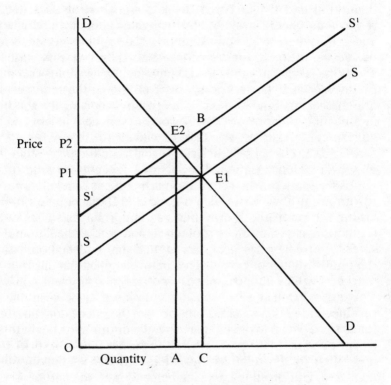

Figure 2.4: Internalising the Externality

butions from affected individuals and coping with the fact that some (free riders) may hope to benefit without paying. In practice, when pollution arises, governments often have recourse to detailed emission specification standards. However, as we pointed out in Chapter 1, this is not always the most cost-effective way of securing a given reduction in pollution.

Then there is the phenomenon of the public good—which should not be equated with the output of government. In other words, not all goods supplied by governments are technically public goods. Public goods are those goods whose consumption has the quality of non-excludability and non-depletability. That is to say, if a good is supplied to one group, it is not possible to exclude those outside the group from benefiting and the fact that the latter do benefit does not reduce the benefit available to the group. Defence and law and order, are oft-quoted examples. The problem in essence derives from the existence of free riders. In the worst case everyone relies on someone else paying. The upshot is that a private supplier has no prospect of obtaining the remuneration necessary if he is to cover the cost of supplying the good in question. Therefore it will not be supplied unless the government takes on the task of calling forth supply and forcibly bills citizen beneficiaries, usually via the tax system. However defence, law and order etc., are not the kind of goods we think of when considering the origins of regulation. Information however is such a good and the adequate provision of it (in truthful form) plays an important role in social regulation–e.g. consumer protection and worker health and safety. Moreover it is generally argued that information has the quality of a public good. That in turn implies that in a free market it will be undersupplied or possibly not supplied at all. This arises from the fact that information may be costly to produce in the first instance but, once in the public domain, it tends to be cheap to disseminate. Ideally information ought to be supplied up to the point where the marginal benefit (price) has fallen to the relatively low marginal cost of making it available. But profit maximising behaviour on the part of the originator will dictate a smaller supply where marginal cost equals marginal revenue. However the situation may be worse than this. The producer may not be able to tap the benefits derived by consumers by virtue of free riding or processes which approximate thereto—i.e. borrowing, taping, photocopying, word-of-mouth, etc. This will cause demand to fall (the demand curve shifts to the left) and could lead to a situation where the producer does not have the prospect of raising enough revenue to cover the total cost of supplying the information. In this case he will not generate it and consequently there will be nothing to disseminate.

Of course, this is a fairly general argument and it does not by any means cover all aspects of information failure in a free market context. For example, the problem may not be one of an inadequate supply of information but of an inability on the part of the consumer to evaluate it (as in the case of drugs, food additives, etc.) or even a reluctance to take the trouble. It may therefore be deemed appropriate that those who are supposed to be in a position to make accurate judgements should impose standards. This would be regarded as preferable to relying on free but uninformed, and possibly harmful, choice. Then again the problem may be one of the way information is presented. If consumer search costs are to be minimised and consumer purchasing errors are to be avoided, it may be deemed desirable that goods be sold in standard quantities, at stated prices per unit and so forth. The reduction in cost to consumers may outweigh the extra costs incurred by the supplier.

The above are all arguments, based on the concept of market failure, which can be adduced in favour of economic and social regulation. They involve interventions in the free market which are intended in some way to compensate for market failure and as such are designed to serve *the public interest*. It should be added that whilst it is relatively easy *a priori* to identify the possibility of market failure, it is much less certain that we can come up with interventions which will remedy that defect in an optimal way. For example, our pollution tax will lead to an optimum degree of pollution only if we can set the tax at an appropriate level, which in turn implies that we can measure the cost of pollution to those polluted. In practice this is no easy task.

We are now in a position to identify the source of the controversy which surrounds the issue of regulatory origin. The source may be stated in terms of an economic syllogism which runs as follows:

- Market failure provides a rationale for a system of regulation in the public interest.
- Governments do in fact regulate.
- Therefore such regulation has its origins in a desire to protect the public interest.

The first two are not likely to be disputed. The last is. A variety of theories have been put forward which suggest alternative explanations. Some of those who support alternative explanations point out that *economic* regulation usually moderates or even eliminates the force of competition. This is a very valuable concession to those already in the industry to be regulated, since restrictions of competition are normally frowned upon by the state and private collusion is often unstable. How attractive then is the prospect of restrictions blessed by the state and underpinned by law. More generally regulation may not be the product of benign legislators and regulatory bodies seeking the public good but of the political market place in which particular interest groups and coalitions seek and/or are granted favours by legislators and regulators who may receive some sort of benefit in return. We shall consider the public interest theory in more detail and then move on to consider these interesting alternatives. As indicated earlier in the book, we shall now focus exclusively on economic regulation.

2   ECONOMIC REGULATION

i The Public Interest Theory

A key element is the concept of natural monopoly. The traditional explanation of natural monopoly emphasises the role of scale economies. If, as inputs are increased by some proportion, output increases more than proportionately, then we have increasing returns to scale. Other things being equal, unit cost falls as output increases. Introductory textbooks cite a number of reasons for this but we shall not review them here. In more recent years emphasis has been placed on the idea that some organisations may enjoy a cost advantage which derives from economies of scope.[10] This applies in the case of multiproduct firms. Such economies are based on the idea that certain costs may be joint—thus a particular production facility may be shared by a range of different products. A multiproduct firm will be able to utilise more fully the cost arising from that shared facility, whereas a firm producing perhaps only one product will not enjoy that advantage. In short economies of scale derive from producing long runs of one product. Economies of scope arise from producing a wide range of different products. Whilst the latter are important, we will concentrate on the traditional economies of scale aspect of natural monopoly.

The explanation of the existence of the natural monopoly condition does not derive from the absolute size of the output of a firm. It is a product of the combination of, on the one hand, what happens in the long run to average cost as output increases and, on the other, the size of the market. Thus in Figure 2.5, if the market demand is D^1D^1 then it is possible to have two equal optimally sized firms each with demand curve D^2D^2. But if market demand is only D^3D^3 then the existence of two producers would be either economically undesirable, or unstable and potentially monopolistic. Let us assume that they continue to share the market equally—i.e. each has the demand curve D^4D^4. If they collude then unit cost and price

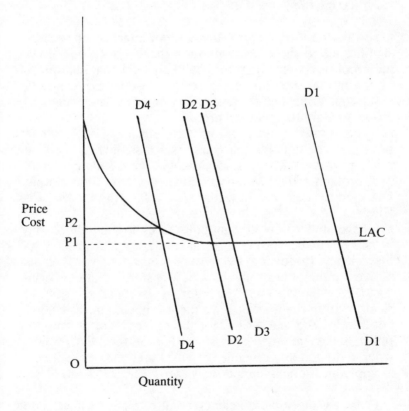

Figure 2.5: Scale Economies and Market Size

would be higher (OP2) than in the case of monopoly (OP1). If they compete there will be a temptation to cut price, increase sales, lower unit costs, etc. Ultimately it is likely that one firm will drive out the other and that monopoly will be the end product.

The need to regulate where natural monopoly exists is illustrated in Figure 2.6. Clearly in such a situation it is essential that only one firm should be allowed to produce and the regulatory body may so decide. But if the firm was otherwise unregulated, and sought to maximise profit, it would choose to produce output OA where marginal cost equals marginal revenue. It would also charge monopoly price OP3 and make monopoly profits LP3FK. There are three reasons for rejecting this outcome:

(1) Whilst in our previous analysis we attached no welfare significance to the redistribution of income in favour of the monopolist, consumers would be likely to object on grounds of *equity* that the monopolist (who, as we have just noted, enjoys an exclusive privilege sanctioned by law) ought to enjoy no more than normal profits.
(2) The optimal output for allocative efficiency is OC where price (OP1) is equal to marginal cost—assuming competitive pricing exists elsewhere, since otherwise we encounter second best-problems. If the monopolist is allowed to produce output OA then the deadweight welfare loss will be the shaded area EFH.
(3) Since the incumbent monopolist faces no competition and in this particular instance is making abnormal profits, X-inefficiency (following Leibenstein) may creep in. Alternatively monopoly profits may be transformed into a social cost (following Posner). The latter possibility arises not from rivalry within the market since there is none, but from competition for the market i.e. for the role of being the monopolist and retaining it. In short Posner sees the process whereby monopoly revenue is transformed into a social cost as applying as much to monopoly as to cartel collusion.[11]

From an allocative efficiency point of view we have seen that the regulatory ideal is output OC. However under condi-

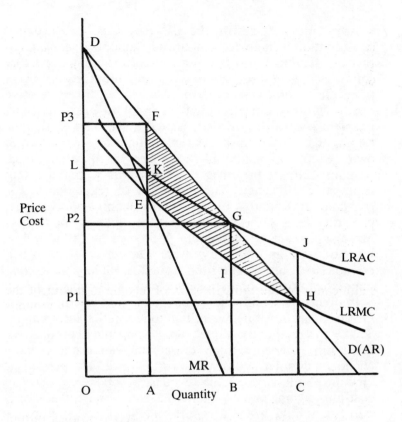

Figure 2.6: Regulatory Approaches to Natural Monopoly

tions of declining marginal cost, average cost will be greater than marginal cost. Therefore, if the regulated firm was required to charge marginal cost it would also be condemned to make losses HJ per unit. One simplistic solution would be to pay it a subsidy of HJ per unit—there are other alternatives which are discussed later. The firm would also just cover its total cost of production and that would satisfy the equity requirement of normal profit (assuming that was all that was permitted by the regulator). In the absence of abnormal profit it might be argued that losses of the kind envisaged by Libenstein and Posner would not arise. However that might be too optimistic an expectation—see below.

In practice, at least in the US, it is usually argued that subsidisation is likely to be politically unpopular. Because of this the tendency has been to opt for different regulatory solutions. One approach is to produce output OB and charge price OP2—which is equal to *average cost*. There is some deadweight loss but it is only IGH and not EFH. The equity problem is satisfied provided, as we observed earlier, that the regulator is successful in restricting the return embodied in average cost to a normal level. The big question which remains relates to the other components which are relevant to productive efficiency. The defenders of regulation would presumably argue that the regulator will only approve prices provided he or she is satisfied that the other components of average cost are at a minimum. Moreover he or she will be invested with appropriate powers. On the other hand it is possible to doubt whether the regulator will be able to command the information necessary to make such judgements.

In practice it is difficult to know just how low costs can be. Generally we rely on competition to reveal that information. That is to say, if entry is free, and it is possible to produce the good more cheaply, then those who can produce more cheaply will enter and drive down the price. The pessimistic view of regulation sees the regulator as operating a sort of cost-plus arrangement. Unless he can dispute the monopolists' costs, he has to accept them and add the appropriate profit component. If that is so, can we be sure that, even though profits are normal, the lack of a competitive stimulus will not lead to X-inefficiency creeping in? Equally can we be sure that the regulator will be able to prevent the monopolist from passing on expenses which are designed to maintain the monopoly privilege? If on the other hand the regulator is vigilant and effective, we may wonder whether there is any advantage to the monopolist in seeking to reduce costs if the regulator immediately calls for a compensating cut in price. Clearly a regulatory lag could be beneficial—the parallel with Schumpeter's theory of innovation is close.[12] But under conditions of inflation regulatory lags can be crippling.

The above discussion does suggest an alternative, advocated by Demsetz and originally suggested by Chadwick.[13] Rather than install a monopolist and then hope to keep his costs down to something like a competitive level (whatever that might be), why not establish a franchise system? Those who wish to occupy the monopoly position could tender competitively for the privilege. Provided that the tendering is competitive, those who have the potential to produce the good more cheaply than anyone else will presumably tender the lowest supply price and should be given the franchise. In short, and adopting Chadwick's language, when competition within the field is not possible (because of natural monopoly), competition for the field could be substituted. To put it another way, natural monopoly and competition are not mutually exclusive. Regulation in this case would consist of letting the original tender and then supervising the holder of the franchise in order to guarantee that he or she subsequently delivers the goods. In practice it could prove to be more complicated than that. What happens if the tenderer has underestimated the cost? What happens if, over time and due to unforeseen circumstances, costs rise more or less rapidly than expected? Renegotiations may be needed and the system in practice begins to sound more like the continuous rate surveillance of traditional utility regulation.[14]

The unregulated natural monopolist has hitherto been assumed to charge one price—i.e. monopoly price OP3 in Diagram 2.6. But a monopolist may choose to charge more than one price—i.e. to indulge in price discrimination. A second strand of the public interest theory of natural monopoly regulation relates to the need to exercise surveillance over such activity. It does not however suggest that price discrimination should be abolished *per se*. Some commentators suggest that the objective is to prevent undue price discrimination.[15]

Firstly, we need to ascertain what is meant by price discrimination. It is defined as the charging of different prices for a good to different customers when the cost of supplying them does not vary or, where the cost of supplying them does vary, charging prices which differ by more than the difference in cost. Perfect price discrimination would involve the monopolist in charging each customer what he or she would be prepared to pay for each unit purchased. The latter is an interesting theoretical notion rather than a phenomenon which is likely to be encountered in practice. The form which is encountered is usually imperfect—as when a monopolist divides his customers into groups and charges each group a different price. In the US context the examples often cited are business telephone users being charged more than private subscribers and industrial users of electricity paying less than domestic consumers.

Price discrimination is feasible when (a) it is possible to divide the market into such different categories; (b) the monopolist controls each such category; (c) as between categories price elasticities differ; (d) there is no possibility of arbitrage whereby price differentials are undermined by supplies being shipped from low price to high price markets.

On the face of it a monopolist who practices price discrimination is even more in need of regulation than one who does not. The argument runs as follows. If a monopolist discriminates, he does so because he makes bigger profits by discriminating than by not discriminating. Therefore from an equity point of view the case for regulation to control profits is even stronger. It could also be argued that if monopoly profits encourage X-inefficiency or social costs, then all the more so will the profits of discrimination. What about allocative efficiency—how will it be affected? In the case of perfect discrimination the output of the monopolist will be the same as that under competition—there will be no deadweight welfare loss. However if we focus on the imperfect variety then, Posner argues, on average the output is not expected to be greater or less than it would be under single price monopoly—a deadweight loss does occur.[16]

Does this mean that, for one reason or another, price discrimination ought to be disallowed? Apparently not. Firstly, although discrimination has perjorative overtones, there are cases where it can be justified. For example, the textbooks habitually cite the case of the community which requires the services of a doctor. Unfortunately there is no point on the community's demand curve where, by charging one price, the doctor's revenue will cover total cost—i.e. the demand curve (average revenue curve) lies to the left of the falling branch of his average cost curve. However if he charges his wealthier clients a higher fee, he may be able to raise his total revenue sufficiently to cover his total cost—the service can then be supplied. This of course has applications outside the field of medicine. Secondly, price discrimination may offer a way out of our marginal cost pricing dilemma— assuming subsidies to be ruled out. The approach here is to adopt some form of Ramsey pricing. The point is that price cannot be set at marginal cost for all customers if the natural monopolist is to avoid losses. If the monopolist's customers can be broken down into separate categories it will be possible to treat them differently. The fundamental question is—how far can price be pitched above marginal cost in each case? In the simplest version of the Ramsey pricing rule it is postulated that welfare will be maximised if the deviation from marginal cost is inversely related to a consumer's price elasticity of demand. In non-technical terms that means that in the case of a group of consumers with relatively high elasticity of demand, price must not rise much above marginal cost, but in the case of a group with a relatively inelastic demand, the deviation above marginal cost can be relatively greater. The effect of this is to minimise the impact on consumption.

We now move away from conditions where one supplier seems inevitable to situations where conventional scale economies do not preclude the possibility of having more than one supplier. Why has regulation been deemed appropriate in such situations? There is of course the case of over-the-air broadcasting which we mentioned in Chapter 1. This is a special case—it is the electromagnetic spectrum which limits the number who may supply. Let us consider those other cases which are more interesting and indeed more controversial.

Firstly, there is banking where, according to Barth *et. al.*,[17] the object of economic regulation is to protect the community against the potential externalities, or larger social costs, generated by widespread bank runs. In other words, if the banking system collapsed, the whole economic system would go down with it. In the US the regulatory regime seems to have had a belt and braces character since apart from the Federal Reserve Board, which acted as lender of last resort, two other safeguards were put in place. An attempt was made to protect individual banks from failures stemming from excessive risk taking and competition. The general nature of the measures adopted in various countries was discussed in Chapter 1 and the specifically US measures will be explained in more detail in Chapter 3. If, despite all this, a bank failed, there was a further safeguard, namely deposit insurance. The latter was designed to reduce the likelihood of widespread bank failure by virtue of bank runs rippling through the system.

Secondly, it has been suggested that intervention may be necessary to protect particular industries against what is variously called destructive competition or excessive competition. This was commonly advanced as an argument in favour of the regulation of airlines, trucking and shipping. It was in fact a general justification which encompassed a number of different rationales—the most important of which are singled out below. Breyer argues that some of these rationales are no longer acceptable as justifications for regulation and indeed he describes the whole matter as being an empty box.[18]

One version of the argument applies in the case of industries with heavy and specialised fixed investment and relatively low operating costs. Petersen cites railways as a case in point.[19] Such industries are said to be prone to price cutting when business conditions deteriorate as a result of a recession or the overbuilding of capacity. Prices will be cut in order to attract business, spread heavy fixed costs over a larger output, lower unit costs and thus reduce losses or even move into a state of profitability. This is likely to provoke retaliatory cuts and may lead to situations where price falls to marginal cost. Either in order to preclude such a development, or to bring the rate war to an end, firms may conclude price fixing or market sharing agreements.[20] Another version of the argument envisages that in the rate war only the firms with the greatest financial strength will survive whilst the weaker ones will be forced into bankruptcy or will be absorbed by the stronger. Ultimately there emerges a monopoly which will be able to determine price without fear of being undermined by inconvenient competitors. In both these cases the consumer may enjoy a short term benefit but will pay for it in the long run. A third version of the argument sees excessive competition as forcing firms, notably in transport, to economise on expenditures concerned with the safety of equipment. This gives rise to the possibility of a disbeneficial externality affecting transport operatives, pedestrians and passengers. A fourth version argues that competition in a slump will eliminate productive capacity which will be needed when demand recovers.[21]

Arguments of this kind are involved in defence of the proposition that regulation should be instituted to avoid the dangers of excessive competition. Entry restrictions are presumably designed to prevent the build up of excessive productive capacity which would otherwise lead to rate wars. But the emergence of excess capacity cannot be totally precluded since it may result from recessions and regulators cannot stop recessions. Therefore price controls are also introduced as an additional safeguard. The public interest element in all this is presumably based on the proposition that prices under regulation will in the long run be lower than they would be under collusion or monopoly and that if prices are profitable safety standards will not be jeopardised.

Other more specialised justifications for economic regulation exist—as in the case of European agriculture and steel discussed in Chapter 1. We will not pursue these points further.

ii Private Interest Group Theories
The public interest theory holds that regulation is supplied by politicians and regulators who seek the public good in response to a demand by the public for the correction of inefficient and inequitable outcomes in the market place. Clearly it does not follow that because economic regulation exists, and there are public interest justifications for it, then economic regulation must be a product of a desire to protect the public interest. Posner argues that one of the reasons which have led some economists to reject the public interest explanation is the substantial body of evidence which demonstrates that regulation is not positively correlated with the presence of such things as externalities and monopoly elements.[22]

Alternative explanations have been advanced including the idea that regulation is supplied in response to the demands of particular pressure groups who have an interest in the outcome of the regulatory legislation and the decisions of regulatory bodies. These are often described as capture theories in that the legislators and regulators are portrayed as being in the pockets of particular interest groups—usually producers. Kolko, for example, has argued that early railway regulation in the US was designed to serve the interests of the railroad owners—the latter successfully sought to use the coercive power of the state for their own benefit.[23] In the words of Mitnick

> only a minimum of regulation was desirable—enough to eliminate instability, but not to interfere with the collusive practices that guaranteed over-built, unnecessary railroads their incomes.[24]

Bernstein produced a study of the independent regulatory commissions in the US in which he envisaged, rather like Shakespeare's seven ages of man, that the commissions went through a series of stages—gestation, youth, maturity and finally debility and decline. In the latter the commission sees its prime mission as maintaining the *status quo* and protecting the interests of the industry it is is supposed to be regulating on behalf of the community.[25]

One of the most interesting of these capture theories was advanced by Stigler.[26] It has been described as an economic theory of regulation. Stigler recognises that regulation may be sought by an industry or it may be thrust upon it. In practice regulation is usually acquired by an industry and is designed and operated primarily for its benefit. The benefit which industries seek proceeds from the power of the state to coerce its citizens. The four main ways in which a state may coerce are as follows. It may extract money from some of its citizens in order to pay subsidies to others. It may restrict entry. It can benefit particular producers by affecting the goods which are substitutes for or complements to the ones they are producing. It can fix prices. All such interventions give rise to wealth transfers. Stigler views regulation as a commodity upon which the forces of demand and supply play. Interest groups, wishing to benefit from wealth transfers, demand it. Politicians, anxious to be elected or re-elected, supply it. The price consists of political votes, campaign contributions and the like.

Stigler's theory was subsequently further developed by Peltzman[27] with the politician more towards the centre of the stage. In the Peltzman model, contending interest groups seek wealth redistribution through the regulatory process. Each group is seeking the privilege of taxing the remainder of the community. The politician chooses between them with the intention of maximising his majority—i.e. the chance that he will be elected or re-elected. One of the weaknesses of both the Stigler and Peltzman models is that strictly speaking they are not models of the regulatory process but of the passage of regulatory legislation. This criticism derives from the fact that the suppliers in each case are politicians looking for electoral advantage.

Regulators on the other hand are not directly involved in the electoral game—indeed the whole idea behind US regulatory commissions was that the actual process should be taken out of politics and placed in the hands of professionals who had the expertise. If regulatory statutes closely prescribed actual regulatory practice, then those who supplied the legislation would also supply the detailed practice. But in fact regulatory statutes tend to be broad and because of this a good deal of discretion is available to commissioners. Not surprisingly therefore theories have been evolved to explain why commissions do what they do within their discretion. In some models regulators are assumed to maximise their utility and the latter is a product of a variety of factors. It may include their survival (i.e. protection against those who have been harmed by commission decisions) which they endeavour to assure by building up coalitions. They may also seek (a) to assure their futures after they leave the commission; (b) to uphold their reputation among their peers and associates and (c) to maintain their integrity by not supporting propositions which offend their notion of the public interest.[28] Of course if we believe Bernstein, ultimately they will simply become tools of those they are supposed to control.

iii Taxation by Regulation

Posner has proposed an alternative explanation of regulation. He sees it as performing a function normally discharged by the budgetary branch of government.[29] That is to say when regulation is observed it is seen to give rise to cross-subsidisation arrangements. Some groups of citizens pay more than the economic price for a good or service (i.e. they are taxed) in order that other groups may enjoy that good or service which is supplied to them at a loss (i.e. they receive a subsidy). This he calls internal subsidisation since the subsidy is generated within the industry as opposed to being financed by the government. Posner argues that such subsidisation is not accidental—it is part of the objective of regulation to produce such a result. Governments who wish to appease certain groups but who do not wish to foot the bill are likely to find this an appealing idea.

He also argues that neither the public interest nor the private interest group theory is consistent with internal subsidisation. The public interest view looks to competitive markets as its model of desirable resource allocation, and internal subsidisation involves allocative results which are unthinkable in a competitive market context. To put it another way, a regulator imbued with a desire to serve the public interest, *as conceived in the public interest theory*, would order firms to end the subsidisation. The private interest group view assumes that regulators are captured and clearly it is not in the interests of the captors to supply goods at a loss—terminating such sales would add to profits.

Posner therefore goes on to observe:

> The internal subsidy, it seems to me, is an aspect of public finance in what is at once a more exact and a more natural sense. Taxation in common parlance refers to the powers of the state to extract money from its citizens in order (1) to defray the costs of services that the politically dominant elements in the state wish to provide and that the market would not produce in the desired quantity and at the desired price, or (2) to transfer money from one group to another, or (3) often, to do both. By this test regulation is part of a system of taxation or public finance. The basic mechanism is the internal subsidy.[30]

He concedes that this view does not mean that the other views are to be totally rejected. Either could be tenable explanations *provided they were broadened*. For example, the public interest could be viewed as including the desirability of subsidies. The private interest might include certain customer classes within the overall pressure group.

Whether internal subsidation is an economically efficient way of achieving the state's objectives is a separate question. Generally economists take the view that if society wishes to be more egalitarian it is best to proceed via lump sum transfers, leaving it to the consumer to allocate to best advantage his or her income, rather than to induce him or her to consume more of certain goods. Posner retorts that such criticisms of internal subsidisation tend to measure it against an ideal standard. But the proper comparison is with other forms of taxation. He argues that all forms of taxation tend to distort the allocation of resources. Internal subsidisation is *a priori* no better and no worse than those methods.

The Posner theory is particularly valuable because it, unlike some others, recognises that the emergence of regulation may not be capable of explanation by one theory alone. Indeed it is possible to imagine that, however untidy and inconvenient it may be, the emergence of regulation may be based on a variable mixture of all the causes we have mentioned—and possibly others as well.

2 PUBLIC OWNERSHIP

In this section we endeavour to identify the reasons why public ownership has come into existence. For the most part they are public interest in character—capture explanations of the kind discussed earlier have little or no role to play.[31] Whilst the reasons we shall consider are for the most part grounded in the public interest, in political terms they encompass widely differing perceptions of what constitutes the public interest. It should also be noted that whilst public ownership may be a way of serving the public interest, it is not always a unique way. Quite often *private* ownership combined with regulation and/or subsidies constitutes an alternative means of achieving some of the ends which are regarded as being in the public interest.

Natural monopoly is a frequently cited reason for public ownership. The rationale is much the same as that which is used to explain the emergence of economic regulation. In other words, there are economies of scale which dictate the need to have only one supplier. But a private monopolist would be in a position to exploit the consumer and of course there are other welfare losses. In order to enjoy the fruits of natural monopoly but to eliminate the possibility of excess profits, etc., existing enterprises are taken into public ownership and newly created ones have to be publicly owned.

Marginal cost pricing is an approach which such publicly owned natural monopolies might be expected to follow—although second-best considerations might dictate some adjustments. Early advocates of marginal cost pricing, notably Lerner and Hotelling,[32] recognising the accompanying problem of the deficit (see the above discussion on regulation), suggested that the latter should be financed by government subsidies. This has been criticised on the grounds that the taxes required to finance the subsidies may themselves give rise to a distortion in the allocation of resources. Moreover income distribution is affected since those who pay the taxes may not be consuming the good produced by the natural monopolist.

A number of alternative approaches have been suggested. One is that the natural monopolist should operate a system of perfect price discrimination—it would produce an optimum amount but would scoop out all consumer surplus. Another consists of the two-part tariff. The running part of the tariff would be related to marginal cost whilst the fixed part would be designed to appropriate consumer surplus. Both these are interesting but not very practical ideas since the determination and extraction of consumer surplus on an individual basis would be an extremely tedious process. A more practical proposal would be for a two-part tariff in which the running part is related to marginal cost but the fixed part is designed so that the other accounting costs are recouped without attempting to allocate that recoupment on the basis of each individual's consumer surplus.[33]

The natural monopoly argument illustrates the point we

made at the beginning of this section. Although it is advanced as a justification for public ownership, it would be equally possible to envisage a privately-owned natural monopoly being required to charge maginal cost and being subsidised by the government (following Lerner and Hotelling) or being allowed to practice some form of two-part tariff, etc. Why, if such a private ownership arrangement is available, has public ownership nevertheless been adopted?

A variety of reasons can be found. Let us take the case of electricity in the UK. As we shall see in Chapter 6, by the time the post war Labour government came to nationalise electricity, fifty-seven per cent of production and sixty-six per cent of sales were already in the hands of the municipalities. The decision to nationalise the whole industry was a product of Labour Party ideology—we will discuss that later. The question still remains—why had about three fifths already found its way into the hands of the municipalities? The answer is revealed by a most unexpected source. In 1905 the National Civic Federation, a US body, decided to carry out a scientific and impartial survey of the relative merits of the public and private ownership of utilities. The investigation produced evidence relating to British experience. It ascribed British municipal ownership to a variety of factors. Two are of particular interest. One was the fact that earlier attempts to regulate gas, water and transport utilities had been unsatisfactory. Private utilities had exploited consumers as to price and had provided poor levels of service. Regulation, or at least that form which had been sanctioned by Parliament, had not worked. A second reason which led to municipal operation was concerned with the profits enjoyed by private companies. Municipalities, lacking funds for their own development, saw utilities as a useful source of income.[34]

Publicly owned utilities may also arise not because they are inherently more efficient or more socially responsible than the private regulated variety but because they enjoy certain artificial advantages. Two Canadian commentators, Trebilcock and Prichard, point to the fact that Canadian crown corporations are immune from federal income tax. The decision of the provinces of British Columbia and Quebec to nationalise their electricity utilities was motivated by such tax avoidance and the prospect of consequentially lower electricity prices.[35] Petersen indicates that in the US certain federal projects can sell low cost hydroelectric power to municipally-owned utilities but not to the investor-owned variety. Thus by shifting to public ownership a municipality can be eligible for lower cost power.[36] A distortion in favour of public ownership also arises when governments are prepared to guarantee the debt of publicly owned utilities but not that of private ones. The former are able to attract capital at lower rates of interest, etc., and therefore supply cheaper electricity. Such financial assistance has been standard practice on the part of provincial governments in Canada.[37]

Trebilcock and Prichard also suggest another reason for the preference of public over private ownership:

The superior ability to co-ordinate multiple objectives by internalising them and certain of the functional limitations of the substitute instruments can also be seen as powerful influences on the choice of instrument in the electric industry. The provision of electric power is central to the industrial and economic structure of the province. As such, the provision of electricity as an incentive for development must be co-ordinated with the full range of government programmes and plans for the economic industrial development of the province. The availability of electric power at differential rates can be used as an incentive or disincentive for industrial location, private investment decisions, population distribution and almost any other aspect of the development of a province. Given the centrality of these objectives to provincial planning schemes, it is understandable that considerable stress would be put on the need to integrate the structure of electric prices and system expansion with these other policies. To the extent this can be achieved more readily through the internalisation of decision-making in the public sector, crown corporations become relatively more attractive.[38]

It has also been pointed out that a preference for public ownership in natural monopoly situations may be due to the novelty of, and uncertainty as to, the regulatory issues which may arise in certain cases. Trebilcock and Prichard cite the case of the Canadian communications satellite Telesat Canada where the government was unwilling to commit itself in advance and preferred to allow decisions on matters such as access by different potential users to evolve over time. Because of the resulting uncertainty, private enterprise was not willing to take entire financial responsibility and a joint venture between the federal government and the private sector was therefore chosen.[39]

Public ownership may be a product of a desire to benefit from yardstick competition. In other words public operations can be used as a yardstick to evaluate the performance of private firms. Petersen points out that in the inter-war years there was some disillusionment with US private electricity utilities and it was hoped that the performance of publicly owned utilities would help in evaluating the costs, rates and rate structures in investor-owned firms. He also points out that there are problems in practice. It is essential that the public and private utilities should be operating under comparable conditions—as we have already seen that may not be so. On the one hand public utilities may be subsidised but on the other they may fail to act as a benchmark because they may be regarded as sources of funds for municipal treasuries. Petersen further points out that electricity derived from multi-use projects may be under- or overpriced depending on how fixed costs are allocated among the various project uses.[40]

Public ownership may also be espoused because it provides competition, or the threat of it, which may act as a control over the behaviour of privately owned utilities. Whilst it may not have been conceived with this end in mind, in practice the Tennessee Valley Authority has had that effect on electricity pricing in and around its area of operation.[41]

Public ownership may also be advocated not because it creates competition but because competition has been absent as between existing private firms. Part of Herbert Morrison's case for amalgamating all the different modes of transport in London under one organisation (the London Passenger Transport Board) was that the various modes had preferred cartels and consolidations to free competition. Morrison's answer was coordination—a public corporation would allocate traffics to those most suited to deal with them.[42] The sprawling British Transport Commission of later years was another example of that philosophy. Failure to compete was also an ingredient in the decision to nationalise the British steel industry. In the inter-war years it had been cartelised. After it was denationalised by the Conservative government in 1953 it was accused of competitive malpractice. Specifically the steel companies treated the Iron and Steel Board's maximum prices as minimum prices. By so doing they helped to seal their own fate.[43] Trebilcock and Prichard cite the example of the public ownership of electricity utilities in Saskatchewan as being a response to a cartelised private electricity industry.[44]

Public ownership may also be conceived as a means of dealing with externalities both disbeneficial and beneficial. The provision of mass transit in urban areas is an obvious way of dealing with the disbenefits of traffic congestion and pollution. It may be economic to provide such facilities at a loss in order to avoid such disbenefits. A private operator, on the other hand, would not be prepared to provide the service unless his revenue was expected to cover his own costs, and would ignore the benefits to society derived from an abatement of congestion and pollution. Of course this is not an argument which uniquely recommends public ownership—it would be possible to subsidise a private operator (but see below). A report of the US Senate Committee on Governmental Affairs cites the case of the beneficial externalities proceeding from public enterprise:

> River basin development by the Department of the Interior's Bureau of Reclamations and the Army Corps of Engineers provides another example in which public enterprise may be justified by the importance of external costs and benefits. Dams on the Columbia River provide not only electricity but also flood control and irrigation. These benefits are widely diffused; it would be very difficult for a private enterprise to fully collect the value of the service. Thus, full private enterprise might underprovide such services. In addition, upstream dams assure a more stable flow and, therefore, more power out of the river downstream.

There is a case for developing a river basin as a whole. Private enterprise may be unable or unwilling to organise such projects. Therefore, some form of Government intervention is justified.[45]

The Committee goes on to say:

That, however, need not mean public enterprise is the best option. One alternative would be subsidies to private firms, perhaps administered under competitive bidding arrangements. Yet especially for projects of vast scale, such as the initial TVA, the Federal co-ordination and regulatory role would necessarily be so large as to render the effort essentially a public enterprise.[46]

Government may also wish to supply uniform levels of service even though some users are high-cost. This may be the product of a desire to foster political cohesion. Railways may be required to provide passenger and goods services to some localities when the rates do not even cover marginal cost. The provision of low-price mail services to rural areas is another example which is frequently cited. As we saw earlier, regulation is one way of achieving this process of cross-subsidisation. It is also attractive to governments since they do not have to find the revenues to pay the subsidies. On the face of it a regulated monopoly should be able to perform this function. However this may not be possible for at least two reasons. Firstly, whilst the regulated monopolist may enjoy the sole right to supply some particular service—e.g. rail freight—it may not be in a position to exploit the market because it does not control substitutes. It may, for example, be faced by competition from other transport modes—e.g. trucking. It will not therefore be able to generate the profits necessary to finance the losses elsewhere. Secondly, the government may envisage a uniform level of price for a good or service which is so low that even if the monopolist is able to extract profits from some markets, those profits may be too low to finance the losses in other markets. Internal subsidisation will therefore prove inadequate. Government subsidies will therefore be necessary. Trebilcock and Prichard argue that such subsidies will be least visible if the service is provided by a public body. But there is another problem apart from visibility. Governments may be reluctant to provide subsidies to private firms for the simple reason that they may lack access to data which enables them to check on the validity of the level of subsidy claimed by such firms. If the firms are internalised within the public sector more effective scrutiny may be possible.

A major reason for public ownership is connected with what may be called the sick industry problem. It should be added that before enterprises are taken into public ownership or government shareholdings are acquired, other measures are often introduced. In other words public enterprise is often a last resort after all else has failed. For example, prior to the nationalisation of the British coal industry the UK government had introduced a system of statutorily backed cartelisation in the hope of restoring profitability. In the case of the British shipbuilding industry, between 1966 and 1977 when the industry was nationalised, close to £300 million was granted or committed by the taxpayer in order to promote reorganisation and new investment. This was in addition to substantial non-selective assistance.[47]

The sick industry problem can be broken down into a number of categories although actual cases may in practice overlap. In some cases private enterprise seems to have failed miserably. The classic example is the British coal industry which had a history of poor management, low investment and backward technology. As a result wages were low and industrial relations were abysmal. Shifting the industry into public hands was felt to be the only way to end the bitter industrial relations. W. G. Shepherd in his analysis of motivations refers to 'improvement of content and "social relationships" within the enterprise' as a possible gain from public enterprise and probably he had the British coal industry in mind.[48]

Industrial sickness may take the form of a decline which is either the result of superior competition from other industries or from the same industry located abroad. The decline of railways in various parts of the world in the face of competition from other transport modes is an example of the former.

The progressive shrinkage of the UK shipbuilding industry in the face of foreign competition is an example of the latter. The British industry, riddled with restrictive labour practices and afflicted with bad industrial relations, was undercut on price and out-delivered by foreign shipbuilders. To all this was added, as we noted in Chapter 1, intensive competition in the wake of the post 1973 oil shock recession. The sick industry argument for public ownership is sometimes referred to as the industry restructuring and revitalisation justification. Whilst it is possible that public ownership may be motivated by such aspirations, it is also possible that it is inspired, at least in part, by a desire to slow down the inevitable decline. Particularly if there is a shortage of alternative employment, wholesale bankruptcies may create severe social shocks. This does not however explain or justify the decision not to proceed via subsidies. The answer is probably the fear that subsidies will merely be used to prop up inefficient structures. Governments may feel that if they are going to have to continue to grant assistance they need to be in a position to 'call the shots'. This is more likely if the industry is in public ownership.

Industrial sickness may take yet other forms. One is structural maladjustment. The size of firms may be too small to take full advantage of economies of scale. This justification was advanced in favour of the renationalisation of the UK steel industry in 1967 and the nationalisation of the British aerospace industry in 1977. The latter was regarded as having good prospects but being too fragmented. The sickness of enterprises may be a product of cost overruns on dominating contracts. Rolls Royce in the UK when producing engines for the Lockheed Tristar, and Canadian railway companies engaged in constructing trans-continental routes are examples of firms taken into public ownership because they miscalculated costs and were in danger of going bankrupt. Public enterprises have also emerged on the scene in order to assist industries in difficulties because of general depressions of demand. *Istituto per la Riconstruzione Industriale* in Italy and the Reconstruction Finance Corporation in the US are examples of such responses in the period of the Great Depression.

Public ownership may also arise for a variety of other reasons. One is national security. A good example of the latter is provided by the half stake which the UK government held in British Petroleum. That involvement goes back to 1914 when, at the instigation of Winston Churchill, the British government acquired a shareholding in the then Anglo-Persian Oil Company in order to safeguard supplies of oil for the navy in the light of the imminent hostilities.[49] Public ownership may also be regarded as an appropriate device in the case of industries where the need to maintain secrecy is of paramount importance. Petersen also argues that government involvement may be inevitable where projects call for large amounts of capital which are beyond the means of private industry and where the pay-off may only occur over a long period.[50] Where a large part of the output of an industry or firm is purchased by the government, the latter may decide that supply will be most efficiently organised if it is internalised within the public sector. Pryor subjected this hypothesis to a statistical test but did not find much support for it.[51] However it has undoubtedly been an important ingredient in some instances—e.g. the nationalisation of the British aerospace industry. Petersen also points out that nationalisation may also be a form of punishment—he cites as an example Renault which was taken over by the French government because the owners had collaborated with the Nazi regime.[52]

Finally public ownership may be a product of political ideology. The immediate post-war nationalisation programme in the UK was a product of British Socialist doctrine. One of its central tenets was that basic industries should be owned by and operated for the benefit of the whole community. They were to be run by public corporations and this involved a rejection of earlier syndicalist ideas about the desirability of worker control. Public ownership was also a product of a dislike of the profit motive on moral grounds. Nationalisation would also facilitate effective economic planning—the course of economic events would be determined by government on behalf of the people and not by the capitalist system of demand and supply. Public ownership of the Bank of England was necessary if monetary policy was to be in the grasp of government and was to be effectively mobilised to avoid a recurrence of depression. The Bank of England in its more independent days was regarded as having pursued policies which engendered mass unemployment and had served financial interests. Very similar motivations seem to have lain behind the parallel nationalisation programme in France.[53]

NOTES

1. The property of producing a smaller output than that of perfect competition is not an inevitable outcome of monopoly. Where a monopolist discriminates as to price, and where that discrimination is perfect, the monopoly output will be the same as the competitive output—see below.
2. H. Leibenstein, 'Allocative Efficiency vs X-efficiency', *American Economic Review*, 56 (1966), pp.392–415.
3. See T. Gale Moore, 'Deregulating Surface Freight Transport' in A. Phillips (ed.), *Promoting Competition in Regulated Markets* (Brookings Institution, Washington, 1975), p.57.
4. *Ibid., loc. cit.*
5. H. G. Manne, 'Mergers and the Market for Corporate Control', *Journal of Political Economy* 73 (1965), pp.110–20.
6. See R. Posner, 'Theories of Economic Regulation', *Bell Journal of Economics and Management Science*, (2) 1971, pp.335–58 and *Antitrust Law An Economic Perspective* (University of Chicago Press, Chicago, 1976), Chapter 2.
7. The reader should not conclude that the kind of arguments advanced above as to why competition is beneficial are also the kind of arguments which persuaded legislators to introduce antitrust laws. Arcane concepts such as deadweight welfare loss played little if indeed any role. Historically the proclivity of monopolists to line their pockets at the expense of the general public was a very persuasive factor. The deadening effect of monopoly upon productive efficiency and technological progressiveness has long been accepted although it was not described as X-inefficiency. Antitrust legislators were certainly concerned to maintain the freedom to compete, to eliminate unjustified discrimination and to prevent undue concentrations of economic power which were seen as being politically dangerous.
8. See F. M. Bator, 'The Anatomy of Market Failure', *Quarterly Journal of Economics*, 72 (1958), pp.351–79.
9. See R. H. Coase, 'The Problem of Social Cost', *Journal of Law and Economics*, 3 (1960), pp.1–44.
10. E. E. Bailey and A. F. Friedlaender, 'Market Structures and Multi-

product Industries', *Journal of Economic Literature*, 20 (1982), pp.1024–48.

11. See R. Posner, 'The Social Costs of Monopoly and Regulation', *Journal of Political Economy*, 83 (1975), pp.807–27.

12. J. A. Schumpeter argued that cost cutting, etc., innovations would be discouraged in a perfectly competitive environment because immediately the innovator introduced the new technology and gained a profit advantage he would be copied. There would be a general fall in cost and price which would wipe out the innovatory profit. Therefore he would not bother to innovate. However if there was a lag before his competitors copied him and reduced their costs and prices, he would enjoy a temporary advantage and would therefore have an incentive to devote resources to innovation.

13. H. Demsetz, 'Why Regulate Utilities?' *Journal of Law and Economics*, 11 (1968), pp.55–65; H. Chadwick, 'Results of Different Principles of Legislation and Administration in Europe: of Competition for the Field, as compared with the Competition within the Field of Service', *Journal of the Royal Statistical Society*, 22 (1859), pp.381–420.

14. For a survey of the issues see O. E. Williamson, 'Franchise Bidding for Natural Monopolies—in General and with Respect to CATV', *Bell Journal of Economics*, 7 (1976), pp.73–104. See also S. Domberger and J. Middleton, 'Franchising in Practice: The Case of Independent Television in the UK', *Fiscal Studies*, 6 (1985), pp.17–33.

15. H. C. Petersen, *Business and Government* (Harper and Row, New York, 1985), p.183.

16. R. Posner, *Antitrust Law op. cit.*, pp.64–5.

17. J. R. Barth, R. D. Brumbaugh, O. Sauerhaft and G. H. K. Wang *op. cit.*, *loc. cit.*

18. S. G. Breyer, *op. cit.*, p.29.

19. H. C. Petersen, *Business and Government op. cit.*, p.184.

20. See F. M. Scherer, *Industrial Market Structure and Economic Performance* (Rand McNally, Chicago, 1970), pp.192–8.

21. This account is closely based on the excellent summary by H. C. Petersen, *Business and Government op. cit.*, pp.184–5. Other accounts are to be found in S. G. Breyer, *op. cit.*, pp.29–32; D. L. McLachlan and D. Swann, *Competition Policy in the European Community*, (Oxford University Press, London, 1967), pp.316–20; the cyclical argument is to be found in A. Kahn, *Economics of Regulation*, Vol. 2, (Wiley, New York, 1970), p.198.

22. R. Posner, 'Theories of Economic Regulation', *op. cit.*, p.336.

23. G. Kolko, *Railroads and Regulation 1877–1916* (Princeton University Press, Princeton, 1965).

24. B. M. Mitnick, *The Political Economy of Regulation* (Columbia University Press, New York, 1980), p.179.

25. M. Bernstein, *Regulating Business by Independent Commission* (Princeton University Press, Princeton, New Jersey, 1955).

26. G. J. Stigler, 'The Theory of Economic Regulation', *Bell Journal of*

Economics, 2 (1971), pp.3–21.
27. S. Peltzman, 'Towards a More General Theory of Regulation', *Journal of Law and Economics* 19 (1976), pp.211–40.
28. M. Russell and R. B. Shelton, 'A Model of Regulatory Agency Behaviour', *Public Choice*, 20 (1974), pp.47–62.
29. R. Posner, 'Taxation by Regulation', *Bell Journal of Economics*, 2 (1971), pp.22–50.
30. *Ibid.*, p.28–9.
31. It is possible to imagine that private firms might seek to induce governments to take equity stakes in certain activities. The private equity owners might do so because they anticipate that the government, having committed itself financially, will be amenable to pressure to bend the rules in ways which safeguard the enterprise and *inter alia* the interests of private shareholders.
32. A. P. Lerner, *The Economics of Control* (Macmillan, New York, 1944) and H. Hotelling, 'The General Welfare in Relation to Problems of Taxation and of Utility Rates' *Econometrica*, 6 (1938), pp.242–69.
33. For a review of approaches see R. Millward, *Public Expenditure Economics* (McGraw-Hill, London, 1971), Chapter 7.
34. National Civic Federation, *Municipal and Private Operation of Public Utilities*, Vol. 1, (Martin B. Brown Press, New York, 1907), pp.186–9.
35. M. J. Trebilcock and J. R. S. Prichard, 'Crown Corporations: The Calculus of Instrument Choice' in J. R. S. Prichard (ed.), *Crown Corporations in Canada* (Butterworths, Toronto, 1983), p.48.
36. H. C. Petersen *op. cit.*, pp.396–7.
37. M. J. Trebilcock and J. R. S. Prichard *op. cit.*, p.49.
38. *Ibid., loc. cit.*
39. *Ibid.*, p.52.
40. H. C. Petersen, *op. cit.*, p.395.
41. *Ibid., loc. cit.*
42. H. Morrison, *Socialisation and Transport* (Constable, London, 1933), Chapters 4 and 5.
43. D. Swann and D. L. MacLachlan, 'Steel Pricing in a Recession: An Analysis of UK and E.S.C.S. Experience', *Scottish Journal of Political Economy*, 12 (1965), pp.81–104.
44. M. J. Trebilcock and J. R. S. Prichard, *op. cit.*, p.50.
45. United States Congress, Senate Committee on Governmental Affairs, *Study on Federal Regulation Prepared Pursuant Senate Resolution 71 to authorise a Study of the Purpose and Effectiveness of Certain Federal Agencies, Volume 6—Framework for Regulation*, (US Government Printing Office, Committee Print, 95th Congress, 2nd Session, 9 (1978), pp.116–17.
46. *Ibid., loc. cit.*
47. *Parliamentary Debates (Hansard)*, House of Commons, 5th Series, Vol. 901, Session 1975/76, Col. 1454.
48. W. G. Shepherd, *Public Enterprise op. cit.*, p.xii.
49. A. Sampson, *The Seven Sisters* (Hodder and Stoughton, London,

1975), pp.52–7.

50.   H. C. Petersen, *op. cit.*, p.398.
51.   F. L. Pryor, 'Public Ownership: Some Quantitative Dimensions' in W. G. Shepherd (ed.), *Public Enterprise op. cit.*, pp.3–22.
52.   H. C. Petersen *op. cit.*, p.398.
53.   J. B. Sheahan, 'Experience with Public Enterprise in France and Italy' in W. G. Shepherd (ed.), *Public Enterprise op. cit.*, p.125.

Part II
Evolution of Policy in the USA

3 Economic Regulation and Public Ownership in Practice

1 FEDERAL AND STATE COMPETENCES

Although it may sound like a statement of the monumentally obvious, no one who studies US regulatory policy can possibly escape the fact that it takes place within a context in which citizens place great store by the constitution and the rights it grants to them. Quite early in the history of US regulation the legitimacy of such state activity was put to the test.

This arose in *Munn* v. *Illinois* (1877)[1] where the state of Illinois sought to set maximum rates for the storage of grain in elevators. This was a Granger case. The Granger movement was a product of agrarian discontent, much of it focussed on the high and discriminatory rates charged by the railways, although this particular case fell outside that immediate area. Munn challenged the right of the state to pass legislation which infringed the rights of private property. Having lost, he appealed to the Supreme Court. It held that the state of Illinois had a right to fix prices since the business was 'clothed with a public interest'. In situations where business was of such a nature, public interest considerations took precedence over private property rights. Potentially this had implications for other areas such as railways. However the legitimacy of economic regulation did depend on the activity having a public interest character and from time to time the courts were saddled with the unenviable task of deciding whether some particular activity was or was not appropriately clothed. In the end the Supreme Court gave up.

This occurred in the case of *Nebbia* v. *New York* (1934).[2]

The case centred on a New York law which fixed a minimum price for milk. On appeal the Supreme Court decided that there was no clearly defined collection of activities which were clothed with a public interest. It was up to each state to decide what policies would promote the public welfare and in principle there was no limit to the range of industries which could be brought within the ambit of regulatory control. It was not the job of the courts to set limits.

However it was the job of the courts to prevent improper use of regulatory powers—e.g. powers used in an arbitrary or discriminatory way. The latter underlines the fact that amendments to the constitution forbid the federal and state governments to deprive a person of his property without 'due process of law'. A right of appeal against regulatory decisions is therefore an essential feature of the US system. It should be added that the law governing the decision-making processes of federal agencies is codified chiefly in the Administrative Procedure Act 1946. It allows affected parties to present evidence and requires agencies to present publicly reasons and evidence for their actions. This contrasts with UK economic regulatory agencies who tend not to provide detailed public explanations of why they decide in a particular way. American regulators are much more publicly accountable.

We have seen that in *Munn* v. *Illinois* the right of a state to regulate certain activities was clearly upheld. What that case did not do was to determine the relative competences of the federal government and the state governments. However in *Wabash, St. Louis and Pacific Railway* v. *Illinois*[3]—an action concerning the railway regulating activity of the state of Illinois—this matter was at issue. The Supreme Court in effect declared that states could regulate only intrastate railroad operations—interstate operations were deemed to lie within the province of the federal authorities. The Supreme Court was of course drawing attention to the commerce clause of the US constitution which declares that Congress has the power 'to Regulate Commerce . . . among the several States . . .'.[4]

2 ENERGY REGULATION

i Electricity

Today the regulation of electricity is both a state and a federal activity—more will be said about that dual aspect later. Regulation began at state level and emerged in the first decade of this century. Douglas Anderson points out that regulation was a product of a defensive coalition.[5] The coalition members consisted of the investor-owned utilities, progressive political forces and consumers. The utility owners would have preferred to have been given a free hand but recognised that unregulated monopoly would not be acceptable. Their main fear was municipal ownership. The reader will recollect that in 1905 the National Civic Federation initiated an investigation of the relative merits of public and private utility ownership (see Chapter 2). The utility owners decided that if they were willing to accept regulation they were likely to escape from public ownership. Progressive forces were opposed to municipal ownership for two reasons. They feared that it would lead to corruption—that possibility was admirably summed up by Ambrose Bierce who described a lighthouse as 'a tall building on the seashore in which the government maintains a lamp and a friend of a politician'.[6] They were also acutely aware of the dangers of monopolistic exploitation and neglect, were able to provide evidence of it and thus gathered additional consumer support for a regulatory approach.

The current dual system of regulation is a product of the constitutional limit on state activity combined with the fact that electricity supplies do enter into interstate trade. The price of electricity produced and sold within state A is regulated by the state A regulatory commission. However a utility in state A may be merely a distributor and may purchase its power wholesale from a utility located in state B. The regulatory commission in state B has no power to control the price of such interstate wholesale electricity sales. This is where the Federal Energy Regulatory Commission in the Department of Energy (FERC) exercises its role. In its absence the state A regulatory commission would be powerless to prevent the monopolistic exactions of the state B utility—its price approval activity would be largely reduced to the passing through of the unregulated energy costs incurred by the state A distribution utility.

The actual way in which regulatory commissions have operated in setting electricity rate levels can best be described as cost of service rate making. The process approximates to the average cost approach discussed in connection with Figure 2.6 in Chapter 2.

The object of rate making is to determine a Revenue Requirement which will *inter alia* produce the required return on the utility's capital. We will assume that a historical cost approach is adopted. The regulatory body will select a test year. Its processes in respect of the test year can be expressed in terms of the following equation:

$$RR = OC + D_1 + T + r(C - D_2)$$

where RR = Revenue Requirement
   OC = Operating Costs in test year
   D_1 = Depreciation in test year
   T = Taxes in test year
   r = Percentage rate of return
   C = Total historical investment
   D_2 = Prior Depreciation

Having determined the Revenue Requirement, the regulator can then set prices so that the volume of sales will cover the Revenue Requirement. Customers will not necessarily be treated alike or charged the same price for every unit of electricity they consume. These are matters which are reflected in the *rate structure*. In the past utilities tended to take a lead in this matter. More recently regulators have become embroiled in rate structure issues. We shall not discuss the matter here since it represents an element of regulatory reform which is more appropriately discussed in Chapter 5.

Returning to the equation, OC represents such costs as fuel and labour which have been incurred by the utility. D_1 is depreciation which the utility must recover in its sales if it is to maintain its capital stock intact. T represents the taxes it must pay. To these elements must be added a sum of money designed to remunerate the investors—i.e. r $(C - D_2)$—the latter being capital invested after allowing for previous depreciation.

The process of rate setting gives rise to a variety of problems— the most important of which are connected with the elements OC, $(C - D_2)$—this is called the rate base—and r. Taking OC first, it may appear to be relatively easy to determine operating costs. Petersen reports that typically commissions have tended to take the word of the utility when it comes to estimating operating costs.[7] Little time is spent in evaluating management's figures. Commissions do not have the staff or expertise to challenge anything other than the most obvious padding. This tends to cast doubts upon the ability of regulators to keep a check on X-inefficiency—a concern we expressed in Chapter 2.

Turning now to the other items namely $(C - D_2)$—the rate base and r—the rate to be paid upon it. Quite early on these matters were at issue in *Smith* v. *Ames* (1898)[8]—a railway case. The Supreme Court declared that regulated rates ought to allow a fair rate of return on a fair valuation of the assets employed. The Court did not explain what a fair rate was but it did trot out a whole series of bases upon which assets might be fairly valued. In practice only the historical cost and repro-duction cost bases were of practical significance—as we noted the above equation embodies the former. In a subsequent case *FPC* v. *Hope Natural Gas* (1944),[9] the Supreme Court departed from the stance it had previously adopted in review-ing rate determinations. In this particular case it was faced with a situation in which a regulatory body had called for a rate reduction because it had adopted a historical cost valuation whereas the company claimed that the regulator ought to have adopted a reproduction cost base. The Court did not endorse any particular method of determination. In its view rate making should be judged not according to whether it embodied some particular method but according to its impact. If the rates which emerged enabled the enterprise to operate successfully, preserved its financial integrity, allowed it to attract capital and compensated investors for the risks they bore, then such a rate was not invalid even if it produced a meagre return on some convenient (to the enterprise) basis of calculation.

In practice rate bases in electricity, gas and telephone regulation appear to be historical cost in character. The rate of return which has to be offered will vary according to the nature of the issued capital and as an average will depend upon the weighting of the different kinds of capital employed. Some will be loan stock. Some will be in the form of preference shares. The rest will be equity. Calculating the appropriate return for the latter gives rise to particular difficulties concerned with evaluating the degree of risk to be remunerated and allowing for the kind of growth which equity owners tend to expect. It should be added that regulation is not solely concerned with prices and profits—adequacy of service is also an issue in public utility supervision. Mention must also be made of the Public Utility Holding Company Act of 1935. It was introduced for a variety of reasons including the need to enable regulatory commissions to exercise control over rate making. Previous to that act the holding company systems were of such a complexity that they were beyond the reach of the regulators.

ii Natural Gas
Natural gas is a relatively new industry in the US. It arose from the discovery of large gas fields in the inter-war period. Its expansion was linked to the development of pipeline technology in World War II. This gave rise to seamless pipe which allowed gas to be transmitted over long distances from the producing states (Arkansas, Louisiana, Oklahoma and Texas) to the rest of the US. On an oil equivalent basis natural gas in 1980 supplied twenty-five per cent of the energy needs of the US.[10] The industry is divided into three sections: (a) production and collection from wells, (b) transmission and (c) distribution by utilities to users. In broad terms it is true to say that, whilst there are some company linkages between these activities, the industry is vertically disintegrated. Production has been characterised by relatively low concentration and relatively unimpeded entry.[11] In 1970 the fifth Circuit Court of Appeals described it as being structurally competitive.[12]

Pipeline activity is characterised by economies of scale.

Gujarati describes pipeline companies as being natural monopolies but that seems to be going too far.[13] Breyer and
MacAvoy portrayed the situation as having some of the
characteristics of natural oligopoly—economies of scale in
transmission would seem to have justified no more than two
or three pipeline sources of supply in any regional market with
a population of less than 10 million.[14] In attributing the quality
of natural oligopoly they were of course referring to the fact
that scale economies dictated fewness but fewness might
facilitate collusion. A case for regulation could therefore be
founded on the latter potentiality. Commentators generally
agree that distribution to final users is essentially naturally
monopolistic.

The price gas producers charge to pipelines is called the
wellhead or field price. The price charged by pipeline companies to distribution utilities is called the wholesale or city-
gate price. The price charged by utilities to consumers is of
course the retail price.

Originally regulation was confined to retail prices and was
subject to the kind of state commission rate making activity
discussed above in connection with electricity. However in
1938 the Natural Gas Act was passed which extended federal
regulation to the interstate activities of the pipeline companies. The role of regulating these wholesale or city-gate
prices was conferred upon the Federal Power Commission
(FPC)—predecessor of the FERC. The construction, alter-
ation and abandonment of interstate pipelines also came
under federal control. The decision to extend control was a
result of the fact that without it distribution utilities were
powerless to do anything but merely pass through the prices
imposed by the pipeline companies. Up to 1954 the wellhead
or field price was not regulated. In defence of that position it
could be argued that competition was itself a sufficient safeguard at the production stage. However as a result of the
Phillips Petroleum Co v. *Wisconsin* case (1954)[15] it became
part of the FPC's job to intervene in respect of wellhead prices
also. This was opposed by the industry—a point which incidentally does not support the capture hypothesis.

The FPC chose to approach the regulation of wellhead
prices on conventional rate making lines and this was to prove

its undoing since it was bound to give rise to difficulties. In the first place there were more than 4500 independent gas producers to regulate. Some were small and kept inadequate records. Regulation also gave rise to extremely difficult accountancy problems. In particular there was the problem of apportioning joint costs when oil and gas were produced together. In addition gas production is a very uncertain business—a given investment expenditure may produce a bonanza or little or nothing.

Because of the sheer size of the administrative task involved the FPC was forced to drop its company-by-company approach. Instead it divided the country into geographic areas and prescribed uniform ceiling prices for each region. This too seems to have proved to be too burdensome and it ended up by producing a ceiling price for the whole nation in which old gas (reserves already contracted for) was priced differently from new gas (newly discovered reserves). In order to cope with its task the FPC had to resort to a system in which prices were frozen for considerable periods. Whilst it is the task of the regulator to prevent prices from rising by an unjustifiable amount, the FPC seems to have been too successful. Its depression of prices had a disastrous affect on known reserves and supplies. More will be said about that in the next chapter.

3   TRANSPORTATION REGULATION

i Railways

Federal regulation began with the railways. The initiating legislation was that of 1887—the Act to Regulate Commerce which created the Interstate Commerce Commission (ICC). This act was apparently based on nineteenth century UK railway legislation. We have already referred to the abusive behaviour of the railways which helped to provoke the Granger movement and led to state (as opposed to federal) railway regulation. Apart from the ability of the railways to exploit local monopoly positions, there were a variety of specific practices which gave rise to vociferous compaints from consumers (i.e. shippers). Small shippers complained about the rebates given to large shippers. The other main bone of contention related to the differential treatment accorded to long and short hauls—the latter being discriminated against. A simple example will serve to indicate the nature of the problem. In the case of a long haul between terminal A and terminal B, a shipper at A might have an alternative means of reaching B by using a different route. Where such competition existed rates tended to be low. However shippers wishing to move goods between points along the A to B route (or wishing to shift goods from a point along the A to B route to terminal B) might have no practical alternative. The railways therefore tended to inflate the rates on such short hauls and thus compensated for low rates on competitive long hauls.

It was however the emasculating effect of the *Wabash* judgement which seems to have finally precipitated the legislation. As we have seen it prevented the state regulatory commissions from controlling rates on interstate journeys. Some thought was given to the possibility of publicly owned railways competing with private ones, but in the end Congress opted for private ownership and regulation.

The Act required rates to be reasonable and just. They had to be published. Rebates were not allowed. The pooling of traffic (market sharing) was prohibited. Charging more for a short haul than a long haul 'under substantially similar circumstances and conditions . . . in the same direction, the shorter being included within the longer distance' was prohibited.

The emergence of this regulation has been subjected to much investigation particularly in the light of the debate on regulatory origins discussed in Chapter 2. It has been regarded as an instance of regulatory capture although the background of Granger discontent suggests that it was likely to be a response to pressure for protection of consumers. Mitnick,[16] supported by Friedlaender,[17] sees it as being more complicated than that. There were undoubtedly consumer protection elements in the requirement that rates should be just and reasonable and in the ban on short haul/long haul discrimination. Mitnick also recognises a private interest element in that secret rebates, which were a source of competitive instability, were banned and price fixing as such was not proscribed. These elements would protect the over-built railways from destructive competition. In addition Mitnick and Friedlander also see evidence of a social goals factor at work. This they ascribe to the fact that value-of-service rate making was not precluded, and was indeed later commended by the ICC.

In value-of-service rate making, rates are not related to the cost of carrying particular consignments but reflect what the market will bear. Other things being equal, in the case of manufactured goods with a high value to weight or bulk, demand will tend to be relatively insensitive to the level of transport rates since they will have relatively little effect on the final delivered price. By contrast goods with a high weight or bulk in relation to value will be sensitive. Carriers will therefore price up on the first relative to the second. Mitnick argues that this pricing system supported the national social goal of western development. At first sight it might appear that, whilst the west thereby gained in respect of its export of bulk goods, it lost on its import of manufactures. But Mitnick argues that most manufactures were traded in the east and thus generated funds which gave rise to a transport subsidy on western bulk good exports. The practice therefore gave rise to a geographical income transfer.

In the early years the act was greatly weakened by Supreme Court judgements which undermined the ICC power to impose maximum rates and deal with rebates and the short/long haul issue. Further legislation was therefore necessary. The Elkins Act 1903 tightened up the power over rebates. The Hepburn Act 1906 empowered the ICC to specify maximum rates. The Mann-Elkins Act 1910 dealt with the short/long haul issue. In addition the power of the ICC was increased by extending its interstate jurisdictional scope. Oil pipelines as well as telephone, telegraph and cable companies were also brought under its control.

Up to 1920 the main thrust of federal legislation was concerned with railway monopoly power and associated practices. Thereafter, with road transport beginning to loom on the horizon and the railways in a weakened state, the emphasis of legislation began to change. Policy began to emphasise the importance of protecting the economic health of carriers. Under the Transportation Act 1920 a number of

provisions facilitated the new approach. Pooling was lega-
lised. Railways were to be provided with a fair return on their
investments.[18] In order to prevent competition from undermining the latter goal, the ICC was now allowed to set
minimum rates. It was also allowed to control entry and exit
and to approve or disapprove mergers and consolidations.
Gujarati characterises this as the regulated capturing the
regulators.[19] That may be somewhat too categorical a judgement, but undoubtedly the system was moving to the more
protective phase identified by Bernstein. Despite this more
supportive approach, and the ensuing legislation relating to
trucking (see below), which provided insulation from competition, the subsequent history of the railways was one of
progressive deterioration. Their later legislative history was
dominated by government attempts to ameliorate their position which culminated in the 1970s in lame duck rescues—
these are discussed in Section 6 below.

ii Trucking
The capture hypothesis seems to be well illustrated by the next
important episode—the Motor Carrier Act 1935. This related
to both trucking and buses. We will focus on the former.
States had by then begun to regulate trucking activities but, as
in the *Wabash* railway case, had been repulsed when
endeavouring to control interstate activities. The growing
competition from truckers and the effect of the depression led
the railways to clamour for protection from competition. This
particular episode is a good example of Stigler's point that the
state can confer valuable rights by restricting competition
from a substitute. The railways were indeed very vulnerable.
Rates were fixed by cartels (rate bureaux) with the approval of
the ICC. These rates tended to be relatively inflexible and
furthermore the railways refused to drop the value-of-service
approach to rate setting. The latter exposed the higher value
traffic to the competition of the truckers who were able to
capture much of this higher value business.[20]
  The trucking industry was divided about the merits of regulation although many firms did see it as a means of eliminating
undesirable competitive practices. Some shippers also envisaged benefits in the shape of stability and regularity of supply

(a point which supports Posner's broader version of the private interest theory) although many, including farmers who had benefited from rate cuts, were opposed to regulation. In passing it should be mentioned that the Transportation Act 1940 also brought waterway operations under ICC control.

Following the 1935 act the ICC divided truckers into three main classes. (a) Common carriers were available to the public for the carriage of goods. (b) Contract carriers did not hire themselves out to the general public but offered specialised services to particular shippers. (c) Exempt carriers hauled their owners' goods—they were the equivalent to UK own account operators. In practice regulation bore most heavily on the first category. Within that category it is important to distinguish between truckload and less-than-truckload cargoes. Regulation tended to bear most heavily on the latter. The reason for this was that shippers offering truckloads could if necessary turn to contract carriers or carry out their own haulage, whereas the less-than-truckload shippers did not necessarily have such alternatives open to them. For ease of exposition we will focus on the regulatory system as it affected less-than-truckloads carried by common carriers.

The ICC enjoyed various powers but two were crucial. Firstly, it could fix maximum or minimum rates and was required to see that they were just and reasonable and were neither discriminatory nor preferential. In practice it delegated its rate making role to rate bureaux which later, under the Reed-Bulwinkle Act 1948, were granted legal immunity from the antitrust laws. These bureaux filed rates with the ICC. There was some possibility of a competitive check in that individual firms could refuse to accept a bureau filing and file their own rate. Indeed such independent filings were quite common but they tended to deal with matters which had little competitive impact. Independent filings which had competitive implications were usually protested by other firms before the ICC and were not likely to be accepted by the Commission. It should be added that when the Motor Carrier Act was passed the ICC set trucking rates at levels comparable with those of the railways. In other words the ICC was using its powers to protect the older part of its constituency. Breyer emphasises the point that the rate structure continued to embody a significant element of value-of-service pricing. It should be noted that trucking rate regulation was based on setting limits on profits as a percentage of sales, as opposed to a return on a rate base.

Secondly, the ICC had a power over entry to routes. Under a grandfather clause in the 1935 act existing carriers were automatically allowed to continue to supply. New entrants were however subject to control. An applicant for a common carrier route had to show that he was fit, willing and able to perform the service and more importantly that the service he wished to supply was required by reference to existing or future convenience and necessity. The latter was difficult to prove and was likely to be protested by existing suppliers. In practice entry was severely restricted.

It is important to recognise that this system was imposed upon an industry which was structurally competitive. Economies of scale were not such that it would be reasonable to expect that competition would lead to concentration and therefore to an ultimate absence of competition.

iii Airlines

Federal regulation of *interstate* airline operation, both in respect of passengers and freight, began in 1938 under the provisions of the Civil Aeronautics Act. It created the Civil Aeronautics Authority which in 1940 was retitled the Civil Aeronautics Board (CAB). Under the Federal Aviation Act 1958 matters such as safety were vested in the Federal Aviation Administration. States continued to enjoy a power to issue certificates for *intrastate* airline operation and to regulate *intrastate* fares. In practice some states chose to apply a very light regulatory rein. The contrast between the results of heavy handed regulation at federal level and relatively free competition within some states was in due course to be of crucial significance.

The origins of federal regulation indicate that both public interest and private interest forces were at work—both pulling in the same direction but for ultimately different reasons. Some of the proponents of the need for the regulation of entry and pricing focussed on the threat posed by destructive competition which, it was argued, could lead to prices close to or below cost. In such circumstances safety standards, in what was still an infant industry, would be jeopardised and scheduling would be unreliable. Two points added credibility to this public interest argument. Firstly, although the industry was growing, in the period leading up to the act severe financial losses were sustained. Secondly, in the wake of the Great Depression the reputation of the free competition system was somewhat tarnished. It should also be added that equality of regulatory treatment as between modes was also a motivating factor. The railways had to operate under regulation and there was no prospect of retreating from that position. It was therefore argued that it was only fair that competing modes should be placed on an equal footing.

Not surprisingly the airlines found the destructive competition argument extremely convenient. They were of course primarily interested in maintaining their market shares and profitability, and were exceedingly active in seeking to persuade Congress totally to insulate them from competition. Bradley Behrman has observed:

> Few interest groups have ever been so overtly and uncontestably pre–eminent in legislative proceedings as the airline industry was during the congressional deliberations that led to the passage of the act.[21]

In the short term the airlines were concerned about the competitive bidding for airmail contracts. In the past these had proved to be an extremely valuable source of subsidy. However subsequently bidding arrangements were tightened up and the response of the airlines was to try to get rid of the bidding system. In the long run the existing airlines were worried that new airlines would begin to emerge which, even if they did not benefit from airmail subsidies, would be able to offer increasingly effective competition. As events transpired the existing airlines had things very much their own way. The only significant sources of opposition were the Post Office and the Department of Commerce. With great perception they felt that regulation would hinder technological change and undermine efficiency. Their arguments were however brushed aside. The economics profession it should be said were favourable to regulation. For the most part they are now against it.[22] Let us not dwell on that point!

Under the 1938 act the CAB had a power to control entry, exit, rates, mergers and collusive practices.[23] Entry to a route required the issue of a certificate of public convenience and necessity by the CAB. As in the case of motor carriers, a grandfather clause was inserted which protected the carriers who were already in operation. Route abandonment required CAB approval. Rates were to be just and reasonable and undue preference or prejudice was prohibited. They had to be published and filed with the CAB. If necessary the CAB could step in and prescribe the rate to be charged, or a maximum, or a minimum, or a combination of maximum and minimum. Consolidations, mergers and acquisitions had to be approved by the Board. Pooling and other agreements had to be filed with the CAB and approved by it—otherwise they were in violation of the antitrust law. The subsidy arrangements were very favourable to the existing airlines. The grandfather route certificates also carried with them permanent eligibility for mail pay for all airlines which had contracts in the four months prior to the act. Moreover the criteria for determining mail pay included 'the need of each . . . carrier for compensation'.

The system of federal regulation operated by the CAB proved to be highly protective. At the centre of that protection were the domestic trunklines. Originally 16 such airlines were granted grandfather route certificates. By the early 1970s mergers had reduced the number to 11—the four largest (the 'Big Four') were American Airlines, Eastern Airlines, Trans World Airlines and United Air Lines. They operated *scheduled* services and served primarily the larger communities and heavy density routes. On a revenue passenger mile basis they were responsible for ninety per cent of scheduled activity. Secondly, there were local and feeder service carriers. In the early 1970s there were 9 of these. They also operated *scheduled* services—in this case between smaller cities and between such cities and the larger traffic centres. Gujarati describes them as regional carriers, often providing service to lightly travelled areas in which the trunklines were not interested or which they had abandoned.[24]

They represented about eight per cent of scheduled passenger mile service. Thirdly, there was a group of *non-scheduled* operators. The CAB attitude towards them was initially, and in contrast to the two above, to exempt them from regulation. However after World War II men with wartime flying experience began to buy up planes at knock-down prices and set up in business. These free spirits began to operate in competition with the scheduled airlines and to provide services which in some instances were scarcely distinguishable from the scheduled variety.[25] The CAB therefore resorted to various devices to keep this competition within bounds. Eventually the larger of these carriers were designated as supplemental and were allowed to operate as long as they provided charter as opposed to scheduled service. Fourthly, there was a group of all-cargo carriers—by the early 1970s there were 3 of these. Freight handling was not however confined to these carriers—passenger operators were also involved in freight movement. Apart from certification, the CAB also prescribed minimum freight rates when competition got out of hand.

The scheduled services and notably the trunklines were highly protected. Quite simply, as Breyer points out, the CAB closed the industry to newcomers and stabilised the market shares of those already within it.[26] It totally blocked entry into the trunkline section of the industry. In particular it set its face against local carriers becoming trunkline operators.[27] The degree of protection accorded to the scheduled services is well illustrated by a Senate investigation which showed that between 1950 and 1974 the CAB received 79 applications from companies wishing to enter domestic trunkline service and it granted none.[28] In addition it also severely restricted applications for new routes from existing operators. Originally only one carrier served a particular route although this was modified later.

Exit was also controlled. Apparently in the case of the trunklines the policy was fairly lenient. When a route was unprofitable, provided another carrier was left to serve a city pair, exit was allowed. However in the case of local services, where only one carrier might be operating, exit was more difficult.[29]

The CAB also controlled fares. As in the case of railways

after 1920, cost of service rate making was not conducted on a company-by-company basis but related to the industry as a whole. Basically what the CAB did was to call for returns of costs and revenues. It eventually decided to calculate cost on the assumption that the trunklines operated on a fifty-five per cent load factor basis (local airlines were allowed a figure of 44.5 per cent). The Board adjusted both costs and revenues. Thus it deducted from total cost those costs which arose from operating below the prescribed load level. Equally it adjusted total revenue so as to compensate for what it regarded as an excessive amount of discounted fares.[30] The difference between total adjusted cost and total adjusted revenue was then related to the industry rate base and if the resulting rate of return was too low a price increase was allowed.

The Board did not however seek totally to insulate the rate of return from fluctuations in the economy. It is crucially important to recognise that the Board would usually suspend price filings which were below the levels implied in the above rate of return calculation. Whilst price competition was precluded, the airlines were free to indulge in non-price competition. As a result they competed by offering more in-flight entertainment, lusher meals, etc. They also put on more flights for the convenience of passengers and as a result load factors fell and aircraft were flying around more or less half empty. Needless to say, all these devices tended to inflate costs. The reader will recollect (see Chapter 2) that Posner identified such behaviour as a property of price-fixing. The reader should bear in mind that the fifty-five per cent/45.5 per cent load factors did not become operative until 1971. It is also interesting to note that in the 1970s the Board sought to deal with the over-capacity problem by seeking to impose even more regulation. To this end it sought to induce the airlines to enter into capacity limitation agreements although, according to Breyer, its strategy failed to work.[31]

It is tempting to argue that the CAB was captured by the airlines. Certainly its tendency to enter into frequent conferences with them was hardly consistent with the arms-length relationship which might be thought to be desirable as between the regulator and the regulated. Regulation is of course likely to produce a protective relationship since the credibility of the regulator is likely to suffer if the firms within its constituency go bankrupt. It is however important to recognise that the relationship which existed between the CAB and the airlines was not one which was purely determined by themselves. Congressional pressures were an additional factor. These had two main objectives. Firstly, they aimed to maintain services on less lucrative routes. Secondly, they sought to keep down the level of subsidies. The CAB policy of restricting entry, together with the equal rates for equal miles principle, had the potential to generate profits on popular routes which could (a) subsidise the less popular and (b) minimise the need for external subsidy. The element of cross-subsidy and the Congressional pressure in effect for it, were a reflection of the influence of local consumer interests. This suggests that airline regulation fitted closely with the Posner view. The reader will recollect (see Chapter 2) that Posner emphasised the concept of taxation by regulation and criticised the idea that regulation was purely a product of producer pressures.

As in the case of motor carriers, the impression which emerges is that the industry was structurally competitive. Economies of scale were not such as to preclude that possibility. The CAB seemed to spend a lot of its time seeking to keep the lid on competition. Sooner or later someone was bound to ask the question—was it really desirable that so much effort should be directed to such an end?

4   FINANCIAL INSTITUTION REGULATION

i Banking

Banking in this context is a shorthand term for deposit-taking institutions. Today the four main forms of deposit-taking institution are commercial banks, mutual savings banks, savings and loan associations and credit unions. Commercial banks are investor-owned. Savings banks and credit unions are mutual institutions owned by their depositors. Savings and loan associations exhibit both kinds of ownership. Historically banking in the US emerged on a dual basis. Those who organised a bank could seek a charter from a state—in which case they would be supervised by that state. Alternatively they could obtain a charter from the federal government and in that case they fell under what was to become a multi-institution federal jurisdiction. Federally chartered banks (i.e. national banks) were required to be members of the Federal Reserve System whilst state banks had the option to be members. Membership carried with it access to the Federal Reserve Board (FRB) lender of last resort facility.

During the 1930s, in response to the Great Depression and the wide-spread bank failures which followed in its wake (more than a third of commercial banks failed between 1930 and 1933), a system of regulation was imposed on the banks. As a result the American banking system became one of the most regulated industries in the US and indeed one of the most regulated banking systems in the world. Incidentally regulation was not an entirely new phenomenon. For example branching was controlled by state laws and national bank branching was regulated under the McFadden Act 1927. The new regulation had a twofold aspect. One element was concerned with preventing bank failures in the first place. Banks were to be rendered more profitable by restricting competition and they were to be debarred from engaging in more risky business. The other element was concerned with bank runs. If, despite the above, a bank failed and its depositors were sent empty away, then depositors at other banks were likely to descend on their banks and the same result might then arise. In order to stop runs from rippling through the system, a system of deposit insurance was to be instituted. Depositors, knowing that their deposits were insured, would cease to panic. Behind this concern about bank runs was the fear that, if there were widespread runs, the supply of money would contract and the whole economic system would come toppling down. The lender of last resort facility, which is usually thought to be an appropriate instrument for keeping systems afloat in times of a crisis of confidence, seems to have been deemed inadequate on its own.

The main regulatory statutes were introduced in each of the years 1933 to 1935. The most important ones were the Banking Acts of 1933 and 1935 (the former is usually referred to as the Glass-Steagall Act). The Glass-Steagall Act introduced the new system of deposit insurance. Banks paid an insurance premium (a fixed percentage of their deposits) and in return the insurer guaranteed individual deposits up to a certain limit. The Glass-Steagall Act created the Federal Deposit Insurance Corporation (FDIC) and virtually all commercial banks came to be covered by it. All national banks were required to insure with it and state banks who were in the Federal Reserve System were likewise obligated. The FDIC also insures most mutual savings banks. Until fairly recently there were no federally chartered mutual savings banks but in 1978 the state chartered variety were given the option of becoming federally chartered. Those that have done so have been insured by a separate body—see below.

In 1933 the Federal Home Loan Board Act was passed. The Federal Home Loan Board (FHLB) took responsibility for supervising federal savings and loan associations and also such state associations as it insured (see below). In 1934 under the National Housing Act the Federal Savings and Loan Insurance Corporation (FSLIC) was brought into existence—it operated under the FHLB. The FSLIC came to be responsible for insuring the deposits of federally chartered savings and loan associations and also those of state chartered associations which applied to it and were found acceptable. In addition it insures the deposits of the new breed of federally chartered mutual savings banks—see above. Credit unions had to wait until 1970 for their insurance arrangements—the National Credit Union Administration (NCUA) operates the National Credit Union Share Insurance Fund. The NCUA regulates and insures federally chartered unions and may also insure the state chartered variety. For completeness it should be added that states have also operated their own insurance arrangements.

A whole panoply of controls was imposed. As we have noted, it is generally argued that these were designed to increase profitability and reduce risk, and thereby to underpin the monetary system and ultimately the whole economy. In short they were prompted by public interest considerations. State banks were controlled by the appropriate state banking authorities. In the case of federally chartered banks four bodies played a regulatory role—they were the Comptroller of the Currency, the FDIC, the FRB and the Securities and Exchange Commission (SEC). As we noted in Chapter 1, their responsibilities have overlapped, and indeed it has been possible on various issues to choose which body to be regulated by. Incidentally the distinction between state and federal competences is in practice somewhat blurred.

We turn now to the actual controls.[32] Whilst some were not new, most were products of the Banking Acts of 1933 and 1935. Given the complexity of the system, we will focus on those which were applicable to commercial banks. Entry was not free. Charters had to be obtained from the relevant regulatory body (in the case of federal banks this was the Comptroller of the Currency). Those who were allowed to enter had to satisfy certain capital asset ratios. On the liabilities side insured banks were precluded from paying interest on demand deposits. Powers were also granted to set a limit to the interest paid on time deposits. These restrictions, it has been argued, were designed to limit competition on interest rates and thus to increase bank profitability and, to the extent that interest rates were kept down, banks would not have to pursue riskier higher return loans and investments in order to make a profit. On the assets side the FRB was given mandatory powers over the reserves to be kept against deposits.

Various restrictions were imposed on lending and investing. Real estate loans were restricted on the grounds that they could not be quickly liquidated to meet depositors' needs in a crisis. Loans to a single borrower were also restricted because of the obvious danger of putting all a bank's eggs in one basket. In the case of investments, the purchase of securities which were predominantly speculative was banned. Only the highest grade securities (they were specified) should be acquired. Undue exposure to the securities of one corporation was also prohibited. Most interestingly and of great importance, ties with investment banking activity were banned—investment banking being defined to cover issuing, underwriting, selling or distribution of stocks, bonds, debentures, notes or other securities. This, it has been argued, was because during the boom of the twenties banks had, directly or via affiliates, become involved in stock issue and underwriting. When the crash came they were vulnerable. Finally banks were also subjected to close inspection of their day-to-day activities.

But were all these controls dictated by a desire to protect the public interest? Some commentators, most notably George Benston, have cast doubts on the matter.[33] They argue that, faced with the pressure for regulation, financial institutions sought to shape it in a way which was in their own interest. Horse-trading took place and a package emerged which served the particular interests of a variety of institutions. Benston is indeed suggesting that a producer interest explanation is appropriate. He points out that the small unit banks wanted federal deposit insurance because many had failed and they feared that people would shift their deposits to larger branch banks. The larger banks did not need deposit insurance but the New York banks in particular had tried to stop the payment of interest on demand deposits but their cartel had failed. As for the investment banks, they had suffered from commercial bank competition and therefore stood to gain from the banning of the investment banking involvements of the latter. Benston also points out that very few banks with investment banking involvements failed. The traditional public interest explanation may therefore be an over-simplistic *ex-post* rationalisation and the truth may not be so unalloyed. As Oscar Wilde observed, 'The truth is rarely pure, and never simple.'

Before we leave this topic we should note that at a later stage special legislation was also passed in respect of bank mergers. Originally it was doubted whether the antitrust laws applied to banks in view of the fact that they were already extensively regulated. However it was eventually decided that the matter should be clarified. In 1960 the Bank Merger Act declared that banks could not merge without the prior approval of the appropriate supervisory authority. In 1966 an amendment was approved which was designed to guarantee that uniform criteria should be adopted by all the supervisory authorities.

ii Security Dealing
Not only did the Great Crash and the Great Depression

produce banking regulation, they also produced reforms in connection with the issue of and dealing in securities of the private corporate sector. This was a response to the abuses which emerged during the stock market boom and the weaknesses which were felt to have contributed to the stock market dive of 1929 and after. The Securities Act 1933 was concerned with the *initial* issue of securities. The Securities Exchange Act 1934 extended control to cover dealings in *existing* securities on the organised stock exchanges.

The first act was purely concerned with investor protection. The earlier speculative excesses were deemed to have proceeded from lack of information. To remedy this defect, those who issued securities in interstate commerce or through the post had to (a) file a registration statement giving relevant information, (b) adhere to prescribed accounting standards, practices and principles and (c) refrain from making fraudulent or deceptive statements. This act is often described as a piece of truth in lending legislation.

The second act brought into existence the SEC which was made responsible for the implementation of both acts. Since the first act was confined to new issues, it failed to protect investors who purchased already existing securities dealt with on the stock exchanges. The new act therefore required stock exchanges to register with the SEC. It was authorised to police trading practices. Certain manipulative practices by corporations as well as security dealers were condemned by the 1934 act. Securities dealt with on the exchanges had to be registered with the SEC together with a statement about the issue and the issuer.

However, unlike the other industries discussed so far, there were no major changes on the economic regulation front. The SEC was overlord of the stock exchanges, but in practice they continued to operate much as before. Price fixing and entry restrictions were long established. Price fixing on the New York Stock Exchange (NYSE), which deals with eighty per cent of the dollar volume of stock traded on the US exchanges,[34] began in 1792. Entry restrictions (i.e. allocation of seats) date from 1817.[35] Price fixing on the NYSE consisted of an agreed minimum commission paid to brokers for transacting the sale or purchase of securities with non-members.

Such an arrangement would appear to have violated the anti-trust laws but the Supreme Court felt that application of those laws would interfere with the operation of the 1934 act. The minimum commission system survived until 1975 when the force of deregulation finally broke through. Prior to that, the only change related to volume discounts. The Department of Justice initiated a probe in 1968, being concerned about the inflexibility of the minimum brokerage system. As a result the SEC ordered a discount on large volume trades. In 1971 this was followed by negotiated rates on portions of orders over $500,000—in 1972 this figure was reduced to $300,000.

5   COMMUNICATIONS

i   Broadcasting

Central to the regulation of broadcasting, particularly during its formative years, was the constraint imposed by the electromagnetic spectrum. Wireless (literally wire-less) communication gives rise to electromagnetic signals which oscillate at a particular frequency. The full range of frequencies from zero cycles per second to billions of cycles per second constitutes the electromagnetic spectrum. Today it is used by radio, television, satellite transmissions and much long-distance telephone communications. Some of it is assigned to federal, state and local use. The rest is available for the kind of private use discussed below.[36]

In the early days the spectrum was a limited resource with no property rights attached to it (and its use had public good properties). Because it was free, everyone could help themselves to it and the possibility that one signal would interfere with another—a disbeneficial externality—was a real possibility. Because private operators were interfering with naval signals, Congress passed the Radio Act 1912 in order to keep them out of certain frequencies.

However as commercial radio developed the problem of overcrowding and jamming in the commercial sector of the spectrum became so serious that Congress was forced to act. In 1926 it declared that the electromagnetic spectrum was public property. As Coase has pointed out,[37] it did not have to do this. Private property rights in the spectrum could have been identified, assigned, traded and defended in the courts like any other. But the federal government decided to proceed down the path of public ownership. In order to allocate the publicly owned frequencies Congress passed the Radio Act 1927 which created the Federal Radio Commission. In 1934, under the Communications Act, it was replaced by the Federal Communications Commission (FCC) which was given control of communications by radio and by wire (e.g. telephone— see below) both interstate and with foreign countries.

The role of the FCC was as follows. Firstly, it allocated the spectrum to various *uses*—i.e. AM (amplitude modulating) and FM (frequency modulating) radio, VHF (very high frequency) TV, UHF (ultra high frequency) TV, etc. Critics say that its allocation was arbitrary—the reason for this will become apparent in a moment.

Secondly, the FCC licensed *users* in each of the allocated bands of the spectrum. Such users were of course radio stations, television stations, etc. It did not license the networks *per se*. They are brokers who on a national basis match up advertisers, programmes and stations—the latter in the main being independent but tied to the networks by affiliation contracts. However the networks did own some stations and they came under the licensing system on that account. Licences were not permanent. Usually they were of three years' duration but were renewable. There were two main issues here. How many stations should be allocated to a particular area? Who among the contenders for a particular station licence should be chosen? One way round the latter problem would have been to hold an auction. This would be a suitable approach to the allocation of a scarce resource since amongst other things it would aid decision making about the optimal use of the spectrum as a whole. However the FCC set its face against such an approach. Because of this it preferred to rely on certain alternative criteria. Candidates for a licence had to be legally, technically and financially qualified and had to show that they would operate in the public interest. Several candidates might satisfy the first three minimal conditions and it is really in respect of the fourth that criteria became important. The sort of criteria which were used were (a) the extent to which the station was locally owned, (b) the extent to which ownership and management would be integrated, (c) the extent to which owners had diverse backgrounds, (d) the extent to which owners had participated in civic affairs, plus at least a further ten. As Breyer has pointed out, having a list as long as this was like not having any criteria at all.[38] It should be added that the absence of any system of allocation by price, together with the limitation on the number of TV stations in an area (see below), meant that those who were originally allocated licences (they were invariably renewed) in the big cities enjoyed substantial economic rents. Clearly a case could have been made for creaming off those rents.

Thirdly, the FCC regulated the industry in a number of other ways. Here are a few examples. Although it did not determine programme content, it did set standards about the maximum time for commercials and the minimum time for public affairs programming. It also required stations to keep records about merit programmes—these were supposed to be relevant when a licence came up for renewal. Under the 1934 act licence holders were required to give equal opportunity to use broadcast facilities to all legally qualified political candidates, and under the Commission's 'fairness' doctrine licensees had to encourage a balanced exposition of public issues. In order to prevent monopolisation of the media (a free marketplace for ideas is important as well as economic competition) rules were imposed limiting the number of stations (TV, radio) that a company could own. Television stations in the largest markets were limited as to number of hours of network programming they were compelled to carry in prime viewing time. The latter was presumably designed to prevent foreclosure of outlets by the established networks, thus creating a possible opening for additional networks. The FCC adopted rules which forbade networks, and television stations in the same market, from owning cable interests—this reflected the fact that they were direct competitors.[39] Rules were also introduced which were designed to restrain the networks in respect of involvement in programme production, and participation in syndication business.

Two contrasts are worthy of mention. Unlike some of the commissions discussed above, the FCC did not get involved in regulating pricing and profitability. Radio and TV were of course largely free—i.e. paid for by advertising. Nor, unlike some commissions, did the FCC have 'primary jurisdiction' over antitrust matters. In other words, FCC approval of anti-competitive acts did not immunise them from the antitrust laws. The Supreme Court did however indicate that the FCC should administer its regulatory power in respect of broadcasting in the light of the purpose which the Sherman Act was designed to achieve.[40]

One notable feature of FCC policy was 'localism'. Let us consider how this affected TV. Given the spectrum allocated to VHF TV, it would have been possible to envisage situations where at least six powerful transmitters could have served a region and provided a commensurate degree of choice. Instead the FCC decided that TV should be organised on local lines—it should reflect local views and respond to local needs. As a result the number of stations in an area was restricted. As an example Beverley Moore points out 'rather than allocating four VHFs to Washington and three to Baltimore, the FCC could have licensed seven stations, with powerful transmitting facilities, *each serving the entire area*'.[41] Localism does not appear to have been an overwhelming success. Most stations were affiliated to one of the three original networks (ABC, CBS and NBC) and took national programming. The restriction on the number of stations in an area produced high profits in the bigger cities and the fact that the number of stations in an area was restricted helped to entrench the position of the networks who substantially sewed up the outlets.

The FCC has also operated what Gujarati has called the FIFS principle—i.e. first in, first served.[42] The proclivity of regulators to protect the older part of their constituency has already been noted in connection with railways versus truckers. The FCC tended to sit on new developments—cable TV, subscription TV, satellites, etc. As we indicated above, its policy also produced handsome profits for the big city stations and the networks. This sounds like capture. However it can be argued that it was not that simple. Rather the FCC protected the industry for two reasons. Firstly, it preferred

stability and feared that change might undermine the commercial viability of the existing system. Secondly, it hoped
that high profits might provide for cross-subsidisation (a well-
known regulatory phenomenon). Profitable popular programmes would subsidise minority offerings.

ii Telecommunications

The origins of the industry (our focus is on the telephone) go
back to the 1860s and 1870s. Just who first invented the
telephone appears to be a matter of some dispute. What is
clear is that Alexander Graham Bell was the first to file a
caveat—in this case a declaration that he was working on an
invention to transmit voice over wire. The following year
(1876) he obtained a patent and it was from this that the Bell
System i.e. AT & T, derived. AT & T was the parent company
which controlled the various constituents of the Bell System.
AT & T came to dominate the telecommunications industry in
the US. The history of telecommunications regulation is to a
large extent the history of the regulation of what Americans
call Ma Bell. In practice until the late fifties regulation was
light and tended to preserve the powerful position enjoyed by
the Bell System notably in long distance communication.

The industry consists of local and long distance networks.
Originally a local system consisted of local loops linked by
wire to a central office with switching facilities which could
link a caller on one local loop to a receiver on another local
loop. In the case of long distance communication the caller on
a local loop was connected to a local office which then by long
distance *wire* was linked to a central office in another city
which in turn switched the message down one of its local loops
to the ultimate receiver. However in due course technological
change provided alternative means of communication notably
at the long distance level. Coaxial (broadband) cable was
added to telephone poles in order to transmit network TV
programmes to local TV stations (see Broadcasting above)—
narrowband was used for telephone and radio transmissions
but was unable to transmit video. More significantly, wire as a
medium was challenged by microwave systems and satellites.
Microwave became an alternative medium notably for the
transmission of TV signals. Microwave technology was

first publicly demonstrated in 1915 although the technology existed well before that date. A microwave is an electromagnetic wave of extremely high frequency—generally it lies between 1000 and 30,000 megahertz (a hertz equals one cycle per second and so a megahertz is one million cycles per second). This form of communication occupies part of the electromagnetic spectrum (see Broadcasting above) and takes place between towers which have to be in line of sight.

How, it may be asked, did the Bell System come to dominate the industry, and how do we explain the emergence of regulation? Its dominance proceeded directly from its patent monopoly. Quite early on this was challenged by the Western Union Telegraph Company—telegraph was the earlier form of longer distance communication. However in 1880 Bell and Western Union concluded a deal. Western Union handed over its telephone patents, sold its telephone exchanges to Bell, agreed to stay out of the telephone business and Bell agreed to stay out of telegraphy.[43] Bell then had a free hand. It did not own local telephone systems. Rather it licensed local companies to use its patents and required them to pay rents on the equipment which they had to acquire from it (this equipment came from Western Electric which Bell acquired from Western Union in the above deal). Protected by its patents the Bell System expanded its city coverage and long lines were established to link local exchanges. However in 1894 the original patents ran out and competing companies quickly emerged. As a result rates fell both in cities where competing companies existed and also in single company cities where potential competition exerted its influence.

Bell's hold on the industry slipped—by 1907 only half the telephones in use were Bell telephones. It sought to hold back the tide of competition by taking over the independents. It refused to interconnect with them unless they merged with it or sold some of their stock to it. Some succumbed to the temptation but others adopted the aggressive tactic of wiring into areas where Bell already had exchanges. At this point Bell president Theodore Vail went on the offensive. In 1907 he drew attention to this wasteful competitive duplication. He argued that if there was to be no competition then there should be public control. In other words, having lost the protection of its patent monopoly, Bell sought protection from competition by means of regulation. This sounds like capture. Between 1907 and 1910 state legislatures seem to have espoused Vail's philosophy. Competition was rejected in favour of exclusive licences and rate of return regulation. Ida Walters argues that this suited Bell admirably since it:

> allowed Bell to continue to use its competitive edge—inter-connecting—to induce competitors to become Bell operating companies, but the independents could no longer offer lower prices to attract subscribers in areas franchised to Bell companies.[44]

In due course Bell's behaviour brought it to the attention of the Department of Justice. In 1913, in exchange for an anti-trust investigation being dropped, it agreed to cease acquiring independents and to provide interconnection with the remaining independents. Although Bell was supposed not to indulge in further acquisitions it did in fact do so. Wilcox and Shepherd point out that by so doing it increased its market share of telephones in use from fifty to ninety per cent although the development of the suburbs tended to favour the independents and as a result its share fell to around eighty per cent in the 1970s.

As is apparent from the above the Bell System did not, prior to the more recent antitrust divestiture, attain a complete monopoly of the whole system. At the local network level there are today hundreds of independent telephone companies, each a monopolist in its own area. They shared the local telephone network segment of the industry with 22 Bell Operating Companies. The Bell System did however come to be a virtual monopolist of long lines activity—but following the 1913 agreement it had to interconnect with the local independents. In addition Bell was vertically integrated backwards. In 1907 it established a research facility which in 1925 became the Bell Laboratories. As we noted earlier it supplied its own equipment via Western Electric.

As we have seen, regulation at local level by utility commissions began in the period 1907–10. The reader will recall that under the Mann-Elkins Act 1910 (concerned primarily with railway regulation) the ICC was empowered to regulate interstate telephone and telegraph communication. How effective was this dual system in the period during which the Bell System was in a protected state?

Federal regulation between 1910 and 1934 was minimal. Petersen points out that only 4 telephone cases were decided by the ICC.[45] Wilcox and Shepherd indicate that during these 24 years the ICC did not introduce one formal proceeding to reduce rates.[46] However, as we noted earlier (see Broadcasting above), in 1934 the FCC was created and it was assigned the task of regulating interstate and international telephone and telegraph communication. Its regulatory stance until the late fifties could be described as light and protective. It is true that between 1936 and 1939 it carried out an initial study of Bell's rate base, cost and price structure. Thereafter there were no formal public hearings on these issues until 1965. Rather the FCC relied on informal discussions with Bell officials—the relationship which existed was similar to that between the CAB and the airlines.

Beverly Moore's description of FCC regulation suggests that some of the concerns expressed in Chapter 2 about the ability of regulators to keep a check on costs are valid.[47] The FCC was not in a position to question Bell's rate base and costs—it simply had to accept the figures it supplied (for a parallel see Petersen's comments above on electricity rate regulation). The rate base was capable of considerable inflation as a result of setting excessive standards of performance, quality and reliability, building in excess capacity, etc. Another possible source of rate base inflation derived from the fact that Bell produced its own equipment via Western Electric which was not formally regulated. The FCC was also supportive of the Bell monopoly. It supported Bell in resisting competition deriving from technical change—there is a parallel here with FCC policy in broadcasting (see above). Bell was allowed to prevent the interconnection of customer-owned telephone instruments. It was allowed to dominate the coaxial cable network. When microwave competition became a real possibility after World War II Bell carried out a crash programme of microwave investment and, by being allowed by the FCC to refuse interconnection to other microwave carriers, was able to enjoy a *de facto* monopoly. At local level regulation was not particularly effective. Utility commissions lacked the resources. Beverley Moore observed 'you can't herd elephants with flyswatters'.[48]

The rate structure is of considerable interest. Local call pricing was not designed to deal with the peak load problem but long distance rates were, and here regulation of the telephone industry appears to have had an edge over the electricity industry in adopting time-of-use pricing. A key feature of pricing was the early decision to establish a universal service—an idea much favoured by Theodore Vail. This was achieved by means of cross-subsidisation—long distance (toll) calls were used to subsidise calls between points where, unaided, low density and high costs would have precluded the establishment of a service. As Petersen points out, telecommunications involved a substantial dose of taxation by regulation.[49] Bell of course was disposed to defend its monopoly position by reference to the need to prevent cream skimming competition in the lucrative markets which provided the source of subsidy.

The reader will have gathered that the AT & T monopoly did not continue to survive. Competition, based on new technology and antitrust restructuring, eventually broke through.

6   PUBLIC OWNERSHIP

In Chapter 1 we briefly glimpsed at the extent and nature of public ownership in the US. Our purpose now is to look at the subject in a little more detail. What then are the areas of public enterprise? One is the postal service which has enjoyed a legal monopoly of the first class mail service. Up to 1970 it was an executive branch of government but in 1970 Congress established the quasi-independent US Postal Service (USPS). Its status thus appeared to be similar to that enjoyed by the UK Post Office from 1969 onwards. The USPS is headed by an eleven man body of governors, of which nine are appointed by the President and the other two are appointed by the nine from the USPS management.[50] This of course is a federal enterprise.

Whilst airlines are privately owned, airports in the main are instances of public enterprise. The federal stake is limited to Dulles International, and Washington National, airports. A few states operate airports—Alaska and Hawaii are two examples. Most airports are in fact owned by municipalities and counties. There are a few examples of private owner-ship—e.g. Burbank, Lafayette and Rochester.[51] Ports too are usually in public ownership, usually on a municipal or state basis. Occasionally ports and airports may be the responsi-bility of one public body, as for example the Port of New York Authority which, on behalf of the states of New York and New Jersey, is responsible not only for port activities but also for several airports. Waterways are also to be found in public ownership—as for example in New York State.

Gas, electricity and water are all areas which are usually associated with the concept of the public utility and, as such, are sectors where in other parts of the world public enterprise is not uncommon. In the US the importance of the public enterprise in these three areas varies very considerably. At one extreme is natural gas. Extraction and transmission by pipeline are private enterprise activities—there is a small municipal element at the distribution stage which accounts for a few per cent of total sales. Electricity is in the middle. Enterprises owned by municipalities are the most common form of ownership among electricity utilities in the US. There are about 2000 municipal utilities and only 500 or so privately owned. However this gives a very misleading picture since many municipal utilities are small and are only engaged in distribution.[52] If we focus on ownership of generating capacity, then twenty-two per cent is publicly owned—the other seventy-eight per cent is therefore investor-owned capacity. Of the twenty-two per cent, state, district and municipalities represent about ten per cent, federal sources (the giant Tennessee Valley Authority and hydroelectricity produced by the Corps of Engineers from dams, etc.) are responsible for a further ten per cent, and rural electricity co-operatives constitute about two per cent.[53] At the other end of the spectrum, water supply is predominantly the responsibility of the 22,000 or so utilities owned by local governments. Private utilities supply only a quarter of the nation's needs.[54]

The state also had a stake in the railways. However in the main this was not by choice. It has in fact been described as public enterprise by default[55]—as we have seen this is a phenomenon which has not been unknown in the UK! It was in fact a product of the decline of the railways in the face of competition from roads and air. The railways made huge losses and allowed their equipment to become out of date and delapidated—eventually the state had to step in. In 1970 Congress passed legislation to create the National Railroad Passenger Corporation or Amtrak. Amtrak took on responsibility for 23,000 miles of intercity passenger train service. It was financed partly by the railroads and partly by Congress. Collectively they injected close to $400 million. Amtrak purchased the rolling stock (which it has since renewed) but left the railbed, terminals, etc. in the hands of the companies. Although it was intended that Amtrak would enjoy a degree of autonomy, it has in fact made sizeable losses and thus has had to ask for subsidies. This has rendered it subject to political pressures in matters such as closure of lines.[56] The other major public enterprise venture is represented by the Consolidated Rail Corporation (Conrail). This was created by Congress in 1974. It advanced close to $2 billion to buy up the freight interests of eight bankrupt eastern railroads.[57] Both these were federal ventures. Whilst on the subject of transport, it is important to note that the Alaska Railroad is federally owned and that mass transit in some large cities tends to be wholly municipally owned and in many others the municipal stake tends to lie in the seventy to ninety per cent region.[58]

Two other public enterprise activities with ownership involvements[59] must be mentioned for completeness. The first is the Naval Petroleum Reserves. These are oilfields operated by the Department of Energy. The other has already mentioned earlier in this chapter, namely the provision of insurance as part of the system of depositor protection.

NOTES

1. 94 US 113 (1877).
2. 291 US 502 (1934).
3. 118 US 557 (1886).
4. Whilst Congress resisted states trepassing on its inter-state jurisdiction, it appears that the federal government has not shrunk from curtailing the powers of state regulators where it felt it was necessary in order to underpin a federal regulatory plan.
5. D. D. Anderson, 'State Regulation of Electricity Utilities' in J. Q. Wilson (ed.), *The Politics of Regulation op. cit.*, pp.3–41.
6. A. Bierce, *The Devil's Dictionary* (Sagamore, New York, 1957), p.107—acknowledgements to Stephen Breyer.
7. H. C. Petersen *op. cit.*, pp.202–3.
8. 169 US 466 (1896).
9. 320 US 591 (1944).
10. Background information derived from D. Gujarati, *Government and Business* (McGraw-Hill, New York, 1984), p.343.
11. S. G. Breyer and P. W. MacAvoy, *Energy Regulation by the Federal Power Commission* (Brookings, Washington, 1974), pp.59–64.
12. *Austral Oil Co* v. *Federal Power Commission*, 428 F 2nd 407 (1970) 416.
13. D. Gujarati *op. cit.*, p.344.
14. S. G. Breyer and P. W. MacAvoy *op. cit.*, p.5.
15. 347 US 672 (1954).
16. B. M. Mitnick *op. cit.*, pp.188–9.
17. A. F. Friedlaender, *The Dilemma of Freight Transport Regulation* (Brookings, Washington, 1969), p.12.
18. Rate-of-return pricing related to the railways as a whole i.e. it was not based on a company-by-company process.
19. D. Gujarati *op. cit.*, p.253.
20. A. E. Kahn, *The Economics of Regulation: Principles and Institutions op. cit.*, p.14.
21. B. Behrman, 'Civil Aeronautics Board', in J. Q. Wilson (ed.), *The Politics of Regulation, op. cit.*, p.84.
22. *Ibid.*, p.85.
23. For CAB powers see D. P. Locklin, *Economics of Transportation* (Irwin, Homewood, Illinois, 1972), pp.797–810.
24. D. Gujarati *op. cit.*, p.293–4.
25. D. P. Locklin *op. cit.*, pp.826–9.
26. S. G. Breyer *op. cit.*, p.205.
27. D. P. Locklin *op. cit.*, p.821.
28. S. G. Breyer *op. cit.*, p.205.
29. H. C. Petersen *op. cit.*, p.291.
30. M. Schnitzer, *Contemporary Government and Business Relations* (Rand McNally, Chicago, 1978), pp.290–2.
31. S. G. Breyer *op. cit.*, pp.218–19.

126   *Evolution of Policy in the USA*

32. K. Spong, *Banking Regulation* (Federal Reserve Bank of Kansas, Kansas, 1983) and C. H. Golembe and D. S. Holland, *Federal Regulation of Banking* (Golembe Associates, Washington, 1981).
33. G. J. Benston, 'Why Did Congress Pass New Financial Services Laws in the 1930s?; An Alternative View', *Federal Bank of Atlanta Economic Review* 67/4 (1982), pp.7–10 and also D. T. Llewellyn, *The Regulation and Supervision of Financial Institutions* (Institute of Bankers, London, 1986), pp.27–8.
34. G. A. Jarrell, 'Change at the Exchange: The Causes and Effects of Deregulation', *Journal of Law and Economics*, 27 (1984), p.277.
35. *Report of Special Study of Securities Markets of the Securities and Exchange Commission*, H.Doc. 95, part 2, 88 Cong., 1 Sess. (1963), p.75.
36. I have greatly benefited from reading I. Walters, 'Freedom for Communications', in R. W. Poole (ed.), *Instead of Regulation*, (Lexington, Lexington, Massachusetts, 1982), pp.93–134.
37. R. H. Coase, 'The Federal Communications Commission', *Journal of Law and Economics*, 2 (1959), pp.1–40.
38. S. G. Breyer *op. cit.*, p.79.
39. There is however a lot of cross-media ownership—e.g. newspapers and television stations—see B. C. Moore, 'The FCC: Competition and Communications' in M. J. Green (ed.), *The Monopoly Makers* (Grossman, New York, 1973), pp.36–46.
40. B. C. Moore *op. cit.*, p.40.
41. *Ibid.*, p.48.
42. D. Gujarati *op. cit.*, p.394.
43. A promise which it soon forgot since it acquired Western Union in 1910 although it was compelled to sell it in 1913.
44. I. Walters *op. cit.*, p.118.
45. H. C. Petersen *op. cit.*, pp.254–5.
46. C. Wilcox and W. G. Shepherd, *Public Policies Towards Business* (Irwin, Homewood, Illinois, 1975), p.438.
47. B. C. Moore, 'AT & T: The Phony Monopoly' in M. J. Green (ed.), *The Monopoly Makers op. cit.*, pp.79–84.
48. B. C. Moore, *op. cit.*, p.82.
49. H. C. Petersen, *op. cit.*, p.255.
50. *Ibid.*, pp.402–7.
51. J. R. Wiley, *Airport Administration* (ENO Foundation for Transportation Inc., Westport, Connecticut, 1981), p.410.
52. H. C. Petersen, *op. cit.*, p.410.
53. P. L. Joskow and R. Schmalensee, *Markets for Power* (MIT Press, Cambridge, Massachusetts, 1983), p.12.
54. *Financial Times*, 5 February, 1986, p.8.
55. H. C. Petersen, *op. cit.*, p.407.
56. This is closely based on an excellent account in H. C. Petersen *op. cit.*, pp.407–10.
57. J. W. McKie, 'Government Intervention in the Economy of the United States' in W. P. J. Maunder (ed.), *Government Intervention in*

the Developed Economy (Croom Helm, London, 1979), pp.84–5.

58. C. Wilcox and W. G. Shepherd *op. cit.*, pp.527, 552.

59. The qualification is made because occasionally public enterprise may involve no asset ownership. The case *par excellence* in the US is COMSAT—the Communications Satellite Corporation created under the Communications Satellite Act 1962. It handles internal and international communications satellite systems. Although the corporation is privately financed (much of it coming from authorised common carriers such as AT & T) some of the board of directors are appointed by the President and confirmed by Senate. It is therefore an example of *quasi* public enterprise without a public ownership stake.

4 Forces for Change

1 INTRODUCTION

The purpose of the first part of this chapter is to try to explain why economic regulation gave place to economic deregulation. In Chapter 1 we noted that deregulation is a potentially misleading word, since it might suggest a total elimination of control whereas what has happened, as we shall see in Chapter 5, is that varying degrees of change have been introduced which collectively may be described as regulatory reform. Nevertheless, whilst bearing this point in mind, the word deregulation will be employed since it is a useful short-hand blanket term.

In Chapter 1 we recognised that it is difficult to pinpoint a particular date when the deregulation process got under way. Nevertheless we suggested the mid-seventies as a useful mile-stone. The Ford administration did propose legislation which sought to eliminate federal price setting in respect of airlines, trucking, banking and gas. Moreover the first deregulatory statute dates from 1975—i.e. that relating to security dealing. This was followed in the late 1970s and the 1980s by a procession of federal deregulatory statutes and also by deregulation at the state level. Not all deregulation was dependent upon statutory change. In some cases the regulatory body itself began to deregulate prior to the deregulatory enactment. In the case of communications (i.e. broadcasting and telecommunications) no deregulatory statute was forthcoming until 1984 (cable TV) but changes, which began to erode the long-standing system of control, can be traced back to the late 1950s. Loosening up of security dealing began in 1968.

It is important to emphasise that when we look to ideas as an explanation of why change takes place, we are really concerned with the influence of perceptions and indeed political convenience, as well as what we may term objective truth. If regulation is conceived to have certain untoward effects then, provided those who share those perceptions have political influence, change may very well occur. The point here is that the dominant perceptions may be disputed by some and indeed subsequently may be found to lack foundation. Nevertheless if at the time they are believed to have substance then they can be influential in bringing about change. Thus if there is a widespread *conviction* that regulation has significantly contributed to inflation, or has materially inhibited technological change and economic growth, then the bases for action exist. Political convenience refers to the fact that regulation may indeed have been a scapegoat. Steiner is of the view that much of the pressure for deregulation came from people inside and outside government who were frustrated by the inability of government to cope with inflation. Regulation was a scapegoat and deregulation was a convenient way of appearing to do something about it.[1] There is undoubtedly something in this argument but, given that some deregulation was intended to lead to price increases, it cannot be the whole of the story. More will be said about the inflation issue later.

Any explanation of why deregulation occurred has to take account of the fact that regulation is to a significant degree indivisible. That is to say, perceptions about regulation are perceptions about social regulation (and possibly antitrust too) as well as economic regulation. If, for example, social regulation is seen to be burdensome, then it is likely that that perception will at least in some degree carry over into the field of economic regulation. Equally, within the field of economic regulation, a failure of regulation in one industry is likely to give rise to doubts about its desirability in other industries. There is no doubt that social regulation came to have a bad press—it came to be regarded as burdensome and indeed ineffective. We have already seen in Chapter 1 that during

President Johnson's Great Society, and in the years immediately after, the US went in for social regulation on a considerable scale. Moreover regulation tended to be additive. The new round of social enactments was not accompanied by a compensating retirement of older forms of regulation. As a result there was what Steiner has called a 'cumulative clogging of the pores'[2] which, to mix our metaphors, proved to be the final straw. To the charge of being burdensome was added the accusation of ineffectiveness. MacAvoy, reviewing the evidence observes:

> The reductions in pollution and in accident and illness rates due to the initiation of regulation by OSHA, NHTSA, and EPA should be observable. However, analysts have been unable to find significant reductions in unhealthful conditions which were to be dealt with by the new regulatory activities.[3]

The deregulation movement was also in part a reaction to Big Government. Steiner is of the view that the reaction was not just about the burden. It was also about the credibility of government. He points out that governments like markets can fail. This, he believes, may have been the longest-lasting impact of Vietnam and Watergate.[4]

2   THE CLIMATE OF IDEAS

How do we explain the phenomenon of deregulation? A considerable amount of academic effort has been devoted to the study of economic regulation. This has thrown up a substantial corpus of ideas and evidence which has suggested that to a greater or lesser extent this form of intervention has not been, or might not be, in the public interest. It is therefore tempting to conclude that academic critiques have led to political action. But is this a legitimate conclusion? There are some writers who have cast doubt upon this thesis. Robert Poole, writing as recently as 1982, was of the opinion that the findings of economists and political scientists have not been reflected in public policy. Whilst their findings had been widely discussed in universities and journals, they had been virtually unknown to most legislators and opinion leaders.[5] This seems to be an indefensible view. Whilst it is important not to exaggerate the influence of academic thinking, there is good evidence to the effect that it played an important role in three senses. Firstly, academic findings have provided much of the basic evidence which was necessary if legislative proposals for deregulation were to stand a chance of Congressional acceptance. Secondly, academics played a direct role in the deregulation process. Thirdly, academics performed a crucial general educative function.

Airline deregulation provides a particularly good example of the first of these two influences at work. Breyer has presented us with a very clear picture of the campaign which led to the 1979 Cannon-Kennedy deregulation bill.[6] Let us consider the first point. He observes that if the deregulation issue was to get off the ground, evidence of the anti-competitive harms of airline regulation had to be thoroughly researched. He therefore points to the crucial role played by the initiating academic studies of Caves,[7] Douglas and Miller,[8] Levine[9] and Jordan.[10] Of course this alone did not suffice. Three other factors were necessary.

(a) Further detailed evidence was required in order to deal with detailed issues which academics, limited in their access to data, were not in a position to deal with thoroughly. For example, what would happen to service to smaller communities?

(b) Even if a powerful case against regulation could be made, it was also important to provide a credible alternative to the existing system and to indicate clearly how the transition to it could be accomplished.

(c) On the political plane it was necessary to make the issue visible, organise a coalition in favour of deregulation and ensure presidential support for such a change.

The hearings held by Senator Edward Kennedy played a key role in all this. Academics such as Levine and Jordan were important in engaging the support of senior government officials. President Ford extended his support and indeed appointed a new chairman of the CAB who was favourable to reform. The issue having been launched in the public eye, Jimmy Carter made it a part of his election campaign and as President supported the passage of the Cannon-Kennedy bill.

In addition, academics played a key role in an even more direct way. When President Carter came to office he appointed as chairman of the CAB an academic economist Alfred E. Kahn, a supporter of legislative reform, who immediately began to take steps to end control of air fares. He and fellow economist Elizabeth Bailey were able to bring to bear new thinking, notably contestable market theory, which was of considerable relevance to the airline deregulation issue. Much the same could be said of the appointment of Darius Gaskins to the chairmanship of the ICC. It should be added that whilst some of the important statutory changes affecting surface transport modes came in the Gaskins era, they were essentially a codification of changes which had been made previously using existing regulatory powers. Here great credit must be given to sitting Commissioner Daniel O'Neal, whom President Carter appointed as chairman of the ICC. Apparently as vacancies occurred President Carter filled them with persons known to be sympathetic to deregulation and some of these were professional economists.

Before we turn to discuss specific ideas which appear to have exerted an influence, it is important to note that those of economists and political scientists associated with Chicago University appear to have been extremely influential. We noted their influence in Chapter 1 in connection with the new learning which has exerted a significant influence on antitrust thinking and policy.

i The Undermining of the Public Interest Theory
Prior to the emergence of ideas and influences which led to the call for deregulation, the dominant philosophy was that regulation was in the public interest. There can be no doubt that whilst the attack on that view may not in itself have led to the deregulation of any particular industry, it did help to undermine the general credibility of regulation. Moreover the concept of capture, however controversial it might be, was one which was easily understood even by those who did not

comprehend the more technical arguments which could be invoked against regulation.

The undermining process proceeded from a variety of sources. One was the development of general models of bureaucratic behaviour. Regulators can be cast as bureaucrats and, as Mitnick points out, such models predict that either the regulatory agency will be captured by the supposedly regulated industry or that regulation will lead to results which are consistently favourable to the industry.[11]

However more specifically influential were the outputs of revisionist economic historians such as Kolko, political scientists such as Bernstein and above all economists notably Stigler and Posner (both of Chicago). The contribution of the latter two was to provide alternative theories to the dominant public interest model and to stimulate others to do likewise. The most powerful of these in terms of its undermining impact was that of Stigler. Prior to Stigler, and hopefully not at the risk of too much caricature, it was possible to envisage regulation as the product of a benign and disinterested state which interfered in the workings of the market solely to protect the general good. After Stigler we were more inclined to see the state not as a benign actor but as a market place where producer groups and politicians traded private advantages— i.e. regulation for political support.

In fairness, it should be said that whilst we have highlighted the significance of Stigler's 1971 contribution, he was not the first economist to cast doubts upon the public interest view. A trenchant denunciation of the role of economic regulation was produced by Horace Gray as early as 1940 in an article entitled 'The Passing of the Public Utility Concept'. Gray's thesis was in essence a simple one. The public utility concept originated as system of social restraint designed primarily to protect consumers from the aggressions of monopolists. However it ended quite differently. Public utility status came to be the haven of refuge:

> for all aspiring monopolists who found it too difficult, too costly, or too precarious to secure and maintain monopoly by private action alone. Their future prosperity would be assured if only they could induce government to grant them

monopoly power and protect them against interlopers, provided always, of course, that government did not exact too
high a price for its favours in the form of restrictive legislation. If political manipulation should fail to remove this
last source of danger, the Supreme Court could be relied
upon to restrain any overly zealous regulatory commission.[12]

Posner's alternative, which is penetrating and admirably
balanced, is of course different to that of Stigler. Regulation is
really designed to achieve internal subsidisation. The
resource implications of the latter render it inconsistent with
the kind of model upon which public interest regulation would
be based and equally it is not consistent with Stigler's private
interest theory since if the regulated capture the regulators
they would not then compel themselves to supply goods at a
loss. The main reasons why, in terms of its undermining
affect, Posner's theory is less powerful than that of Stigler are
twofold. Firstly, Stigler presents a picture of regulation being
dictated by naked self-interest and this is dramatically
opposed to the spirit of the public interest theory, whereas
regulation according to Posner is endowed with a more acceptable social rationale. Secondly, Posner concedes that the
public interest theory could be modified so as to encompass
the provision of subsidies.

Bernstein's crucial contribution was to set the ball rolling in
terms of life-cycle theories of regulatory agency development.
Others were to follow. Bernstein was quite categorical about
the fate of regulatory agencies:

> The close of the period of maturity is marked by the com-
> mission's surrender to the regulated. Politically isolated,
> lacking a firm basis of public support, lethargic in attitude
> and approach, bowed down by precedent and backlogs,
> unsupported in its demands for more staff and money, the
> commission finally becomes a captive of the regulated
> groups.[13]

Kolko's influence lay in his examination of early railway
regulation. His conclusion was that it was designed to serve

the interests of the railway owners, who in his view success-fully sought to use the coercive power of the state for their own ends. He puts the matter thus:

> The railroads realised that they needed the protection of the federal government, and they became the leading advocates of federal regulation on their own terms . . . The federal regulation of railroads from 1887 until 1916 did not disappoint the American railroad industry. If the railroad leaders often disagreed on the details . . . the railroads nevertheless supported the basic principle and institution of federal regulation. And . . . they enthusiastically worked for its extension and for the supremacy of federal regulation over the states . . . Under the benevolent supervision of the Interstate Commerce Commission, the economic conditions of the industry improved sharply, as internecine competition was replaced by rate maintenance and the elimination of rebates, and the railroad system received protection from the attacks of both the states and powerful shippers.[14]

ii The Potentialities of Competition and the Market

The intellectual defence of economic regulation ultimately boiled down to the proposition that in the long run competition was neither feasible nor desirable—i.e. natural monopoly conditions existed or excessive competition would ensue. A decision to deregulate implies that competition is in some degree feasible and is also desirable. Deregulation in the sense of a reform of regulation may manifest itself not merely as an elimination of restrictions, but also as an attempt to introduce features which characterise free market competition—i.e. ingredients which lead to a more efficient use of resources or simply more responsiveness to consumer pressures. It is possible to point to a series of ideas which have weakened the case for regulation by making a case for competition and the free play of market forces. In the most general sense one such source of ideas was the writings of Milton Friedman.[15]

He and writers such as Hayek have emphasised the connection between economic freedom and political freedom, and the insidious nature of government intervention. Friedman attacked various forms of occupational restriction (registration, certification and licensing)—not surprisingly the latter attracted most criticism. [16] He also addressed himself to the phenomenon of natural monopoly which he termed technical monopoly. He recognised that technical considerations might require only one supplier. However when he considered what organisational response would be required in such a situation—i.e. public ownership, unregulated private monopoly or regulated private monopoly—most significantly he indicated a preference for the second. His argument is that in the short run substitutes often exist which act as a controlling influence. In the longer run his objection to regulation was founded on the point that natural or technical monoplies enjoy not just a *de facto* but also a *de jure* monopoly. As a result when technological change renders competition possible the monopolist invokes his *de jure* monopoly to perpetuate his position. Fellow Chicagoan Harold Demsetz however points out that Friedman failed to recognise that economies of scale do not necessarily give rise to a need to impose the traditional form of economic regulation—see below. Friedman also argued that the supposedly regulated may capture the regulators and as a result prices under regulation may be no lower than without it.

Another source of criticism stemmed from the work of Demsetz. His main contribution to the debate was twofold. Firstly, as we noted in Chapter 2, he argued (following Chadwick) that continuing economies of scale do not necessarily dictate a need for traditional rate-of-return regulation. [17] Such economies may require that there should only be one supplier, but that does not preclude the possibility of having a large number of bidders for the privilege of being that sole supplier. Traditional regulation proceeds from the notion that only one producer can be installed. Having been installed, but not having been required to name his terms in advance, he will, if left to his own devices, proceed to exert his monopoly power. Demsetz envisages that bidding for the monopoly franchise will compete away the monopoly profits in the first instance. However, as we noted in Chapter 2, it may not be that simple. A regulatory body still has to exist in order to let the franchise, to deal with windfall profits and losses and to guarantee that service is provided as promised. Demsetz argues that an oft-cited reason for regulation is duplication of distribution facilities. He argues that duplication can be reduced to optimal proportions by charging a price for the use of public places for distribution purposes, by the sale of distribution networks by unsuccessful outgoing suppliers to the successful new ones, or by public ownership of distribution networks. Demsetz's second contribution was his emphasis on the idea that it is sunk costs and not economies of scale which are the main barrier to competitive entry. This, as Elizabeth Bailey points out, was to be a crucial ingredient in the theory of contestable markets[18]—see below.

A third Chicagoan contribution came from R. H. Coase. Within the general framework of regulation, Coase's main contribution has been to emphasise the important part which can be played by property rights. As we indicated in Chapter 2 these provide an alternative means of dealing with externalities such as pollution. But property rights also have a potential role to play in economic regulation, notably in respect of broadcasting and telecommunications. Coase has pointed out the alternative to public ownership of the electromagnetic spectrum and its allocation by the FCC (see Chapter 3) would be to create private property rights in it and to allow those rights to be traded like any other property.[19] This he has argued would have two advantages. Firstly, it would enable more economic use to be made of the limited resource. Secondly, it would enable society to cream off at least some of the rents which have accrued to the lucky recipients of licences under the existing allocation system.

The next development to be discussed has unquestionably had a distinctly practical impact. We are of course referring to contestable market theory associated with the name of William Baumol and others.[20] It is highly relevant to those situations where the number of enterprises in the market is limited. Fewness on a conventional view may suggest that some regulatory control of prices is called for. However the theory of contestable markets suggests that it is possible to have a competitive outcome even if there is only one firm in the industry provided that that firm is constrained in its pricing behaviour by the existence of potential as much as actual competition. The latter influences depend upon the existence of free entry which in turn depends on the existence of free exit. It is not economies of scale that constrain entry but sunk costs (see Demsetz above). There will be freedom of exit if no sunk costs are laid upon entrants. For example, in airline operation terminal slots, baggage handling facilities, etc., give rise to sunk costs. These need to be provided separately. If this is so then an airline can contemplate entering a specific passenger route with equanimity since if the worst comes to pass it can also leave in a relatively costless fashion—i.e. it can switch its aircraft to another route, switch them to freight or simply sell them. In other words, the theory envisages that competitors can hit and run if necessary. As a result of all this, any attempt by an incumbent airline to raise prices above competitive levels, or to allow costs to drift up, will provoke entry. To that extent regulation of prices will not be neces-sary—potential and actual competition will perform the necessary policing role. The theory suggests that airline operation is a likely industry in which to find highly contest-able markets, provided arrangements exist to take care of the sunk cost problem. Similar conclusions could be drawn in respect of surface transport provided track is publicly owned. The theory also suggests that those features of regulation which impede exit, such as refusals to abandon unprofitable routes or lines, will impede entry and are therefore likely to be counterproductive. Baumol and Bailey also emphasise that some sluggishness in the pricing response of incumbents to entry will also facilitate contestability, although such a condition is not absolutely essential. The reader will recognise that this theory, like that of Demsetz, emphasises that the number of firms *in the market* does not determine the extent of its competitiveness—however the two theories reach that conclusion by reference to different factors.

Unlike contestable market theory, our final theoretical influence is a relatively old one, but one which had not taken practical root to the same extent in the US as it had in other countries. We are of course referring to the idea that public utility pricing should aim to replicate conditions which exist in perfect competition equilibrium. In other words price should be based on marginal cost. This prescription, which is discussed in Chaper 2, is particularly associated with Harold Hotelling and Abba Lerner and it was one which attracted Alfred Kahn—see below.

iii Consumer and Environmental Pressure Groups

Consumerist influences have played a significant role in the deregulation process. As we have seen, the consumer movement successfully pressed for more social regulation (e.g. consumer protection), but in addition it chose to attack the restrictions and distortions of competition inherent in the older system of economic regulation. This is reflected in Ralph Nader's study group reports[21] which exerted a nationwide influence, but local groups were also active. The reforming influence of the latter will be discussed later when we come to consider electricity utility regulation.

Environmental pressure groups were also at work. Donald Anderson, discussing electricity utility regulation, has pointed out that historically regulators tended to conceive their function as being the prevention of excess profits, rather than the promotion of economic efficiency through the manipulation of the pricing structure.[22] Consumers for their part were little concerned about either price levels or price structures until the late 1960s and 1970s since, thanks to favourable fuel price trends, and the fuller exploitation of scale economies and other technological advances, monthly electricity bills were stable. Indeed the real price of energy fell markedly over the period from 1950 to 1970. However, in the 1970s the price of electricity moved sharply upwards, partly because fuel prices moved violently in an upward direction and also because the benefits of economies of scale and other advances had largely been exploited. Because of this, electricity rate determination became a controversial issue. As a result increasing attention was given to both the rate level and the rate structure.

Environmentalists had strong views on these matters and succeeded in bringing pressure to bear. They pointed to the pollution resulting from electricity generation and argued that prices needed to be higher—they needed to internalise the externality. In addition the control of pollution required that the rate structure should be modified. Rates tended to be based on the declining block tariff system. In other words a high price per kilowatt-hour (kwh) was charged for the initial block consumed but reduced rates per kwh were charged for subsequent blocks. This tended to encourage consumers to use more electricity. The environmentalists sought to restrict the consumption of electricity and therefore favoured the marginal cost philosophy. Putting the two together we can say that environmentalists favoured a marginal social cost approach to electricity pricing. There was therefore scope for a coalition between reforming economists and environmentalists.

3   GENERAL CRITICISMS OF ECONOMIC REGULATION

Any explanation of deregulation must take account of the impact of certain criticisms which are applicable to the general system of economic regulation.

The first is the phenomenon of regulatory lag. This is important where economic regulation involves rate determination. Regulatory lag in this context refers to the fact that rate determinations only occur at intervals, and may therefore lag behind changes in cost conditions. It is easy to see that such a lag may create difficulties in a period of rapid inflation when rates may fail to keep pace with the inflation of input costs—more will be said on that subject in the next section. However there are arguments on the other side. We have already noted that Baumol and Bailey have argued that a lagged price response by incumbents may facilitate contestability. Then again in a period of input price inflation, regulatory lag may act as an inbuilt source of pressure which forces regulated firms to increase their efficiency as a means of offsetting the rise in input prices. Clearly there is a limit to the scope for such offsetting activity. Regulatory lag may also act as a stimulus to technological change, since if regulators immediately reduced prices when utilities, etc., introduced cost saving innovations, then there would be no incentive to innovate. The parallel with Schumpeter's view of the role of temporary monopoly in stimulating technological progress is very close.[23]

A major criticism of regulatory rate setting is the inability of regulators to exercise any really close control over the various categories of cost. To a large extent they have to take the regulated firm's word for it. Another way of putting it is to say that rate regulation is really a form of cost-plus pricing. Costs have to be taken for granted and regulators largely concern themselves with the task of applying a margin of profit to cost. The possibility therefore arises that costs may be padded—i.e. the existence of X-inefficiency seems a real possibility. Particular attention has been given to the idea that the rate base may be padded. This is the so-called Averch-Johnson (A-J) effect.[24] The effect depends on the possibility that the permitted rate of return will be greater than the true cost of capital. If that is so, a utility will derive an extra margin of profit from any capital that it can insinuate into its rate base. Firms may seek to invest in higher levels of physical capacity, may prefer to buy rather than lease or may choose more capital-intensive technology.[25] The end product is increased profits for the firm. More capital is used to produce any given level of output than would be necessary for cost minimisation. The actual cost of producing output would be increased. The A-J effect is of course a prediction under certain assumptions. Whether it manifests itself in reality is a matter for empirical investigation, although this does not seem to have deterred some economists from concluding that since the theory predicts overinvestment, overinvestment undoubtedly exists. A number of studies (all concerned with electricity generation) concluded that such excessive use of capital did appear to occur, although another study found no sign of it.[26] However Joskow and Noll, reviewing the evidence, point out that in one way or another all these studies were methodologically open to criticism[27] and they quote with approval work by D. McKay which, on the basis of sounder analysis, could detect no A-J effect.[28] Some writers have also argued that electrical equipment users had a vested interest in colluding with electrical suppliers over prices, since this would inflate the rate base. On the other hand, J. Fred Weston argues that a review of the actual purchasing behaviour of the former renders this unacceptable.[29] However, in respect of the admittedly special position enjoyed by the Bell System, it is difficult to resist the conclusion that Bell as a supplier of telecommunication services was under a strong temptation to pay high equipment prices since it owned the equipment supplier (Western Electric)—for more on this see below.

Cross-subsidisation is a well-established by-product of economic regulation. The welfare loss which stems from it is illustrated by Figure 4.1 and is derived from the work of Alfred E. Kahn.[30] In the diagram we show the demand and marginal cost curves (the latter are also supply curves) of urban and rural rail passenger transport. Without cross-subsidy, no rural transport would be supplied but there would be a supply to urban consumers of quantity OQ3 at price OP1. Suppose now that the regulators take it upon themselves to institute a system of cross-subsidisation and the marginal cost of the subsidised service is pitched mid-way between rural and urban costs. The result is a welfare loss. Urban consumers now demand OQ2 and sustain a deadweight loss equal to consumer surplus area ABC. Rural consumers now consume OQ1. The true cost of supply OQ1 is OP3FQ1. The welfare derived from it is the area under the rural demand curve and therefore there is an excess of resource cost over welfare—i.e. area DP3FG. The latter constitutes an additional source of loss. There is of course a redistribution of income as between urban and rural consumers. Rural consumers gain consumer surplus area P2DG. Urban consumers lose a relatively large amount—i.e. for quantity OQ2 they now have to pay P1P2BA extra.

If society did not intend that regulation should be conducted in this manner, then the above welfare loss case against cross-subsidisation would need no qualification. However if society believes that some sort of income redistribution between urban and rural consumers is justified, and is quite happy to forget about the above welfare loss, the fact still remains, as Kahn observes, that cross-subsidisation is a pretty crude way of achieving it. For example, unless all rural consumers of transport are poor and all urban consumers are rich, we are presented with the spectacle of some poor urban consumers subsidising some rich rural ones. It should also be pointed out that cross-subsidisation tends to create conditions of unfair competition. Enterprises which operate in both lucrative and less lucrative markets can skim the cream off the former in order to subsidise sales in the latter. This will put enterprises who operate exclusively in less lucrative markets at a distinctly unfair competitive disadvantage.

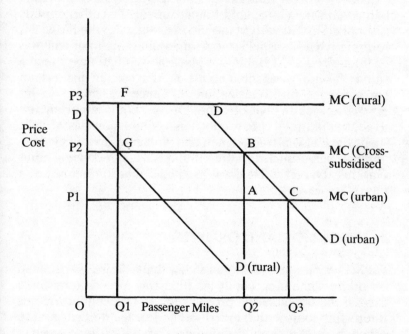

Figure 4.1: Effects of Cross-Subsidy

A final general point relates to the expertise of commissions. Regulation has attracted criticism because the quality of commissioners is variable. Occasionally the political appointment system produces some hilarious results and it is quite impossible to resist quoting two of them. The first, cited by Craig Petersen,[31] concerns an appointment to the FCC. The title of an article in the *Wall Street Journal*, which reported the appointment, escapsulates the episode— 'Mrs X Wanted Only to Sing, but She Ended Up on the FCC'. The lady in question, who before the war sang on a morning radio show, was appointed by President Nixon in 1971. In defence a Republican Senator observed 'Having had a career as a radio vocalist, she is familiar with many of the operations of the broadcast industry from her own unique experience.' The article observed that perhaps the lady's most notable achievement in her seven year term of office was to spend $4,600 of federal funds on installing in her office a private bathroom with a large gold-framed mirror. The other episode is supplied by Edward Mansfield in his study of the FMC.[32] It refers to what Mansfield calls a forgettable appointee who was characterised as 'a Baltimore playboy who had never seen a ship in his life.' Mansfield points out that strictly this was not correct since on confirmation reference was made to his extensive yachting background. Of course it is important not to get this matter out of proportion. Commissions, as we have seen, have also attracted men and women of extremely high ability—names such as Alfred Kahn, Elizabeth Bailey, Darius Gaskins, Daniel O'Neal and Nicholas Johnson being just a few examples.

4   INFLATION AND GROWTH

Earlier we mentioned Steiner's view that a desire to be seen to be doing something about inflation was a motivating force behind the deregulation programme. In that connection it is interesting to note that in 1974 when President Ford came to office, he held a summit conference on inflation and invited to it economists representing every area of the subject. Little or no agreement emerged (which some would say was not entirely surprising) except on one subject—that regulation was in need of reform.[33] The deregulatory recommendations which are relevant to this study were mainly in the field of transport. In trucking, entry controls should be eased or even abandoned, more rate freedom should be allowed and rate bureaux should lose their antitrust immunity. In the case of the railways the latter two should apply. All requests for air fare changes, including discounts, should be automatically approved.

The implication of all this was that economic regulation was viewed as keeping prices up. However, according to MacAvoy, this assessment was more appropriate to the 1950s and most of the 1960s.[34] By the late 1960s it was apparent that regulation was beginning to show signs of holding price increases down. During the 1970s, when inflation began to move ahead rapidly, MacAvoy argues that two forces were clearly at work. Firstly, rates tended to lag behind sharply rising costs. Secondly, because of the fear of adverse publicity, when commissions granted increases they were less than what was warranted by inflation. As a result, profitability tended to decline. The return on equity fell and since this made it increasingly difficult to raise equity capital, regulated firms tended to shift to debt. But because regulation imposed limits on the debt/equity ratio the regulated industries found themselves unable to raise sufficient capital and investment had to be cut back. This had an adverse effect on growth and on the quality of service. MacAvoy concedes that whilst some of the decline in the growth of regulated industries mirrored the general economic slowdown, some was the product of the regulators not adapting to rapid inflation.

The above argument about regulation in the 1970s has focussed attention on its impact on growth. Regulation was indeed increasingly seen as giving rise to a substantial diversion of resources in the form of administrative cost of government (i.e. the cost of running regulatory bodies) as well as the private administrative and compliance costs of industry. Murray Weidenbaum and Robert Defina attempted to estimate these latter private costs of federal regulation.[35] The figure for 1976 was estimated to be $65,000 million and by 1979 it had risen to $102,000 million. Weidenbaum also quotes with approval Edward Dennison's view, that as a result the US lost about a quarter of its annual potential increase of productivity, because of this diversion of investment resources.[36] However it seems that in the main this diversion was the product of social regulation, which required capital investment in worker safety, environmental protection, etc., rather than of economic regulation. It seems reasonable to argue that the main growth-retarding impact of economic regulation (other than the transitory effect of inflation discussed above) was the general blunting of the edge of competition as a stimulator of technological change combined with specific rulings which kept change at bay. More will be said on the latter topic below.

5   FACTORS IN SPECIFIC INDUSTRIES

We now move to a consideration of those factors which have been relevant to specific industries.

In the case of electricity, a variety of changes have been contemplated although not all have been taken up. Firstly, the idea that the electricity industry is naturally monopolistic has been challenged. It has been argued that there is scope for competition at the generation stage.[37] However, at the transmission stage sharply increasing returns to scale are said to exist and it is held that inter-utility competition in distribution would be costly because of duplication. Injecting competition at the generation stage is likely to be frustrated by the fact that generating companies (in many but not all cases) also own the transmission and distribution systems. Such vertically integrated companies are not disposed to handle power which they have not generated (such handling is called wheeling). Various solutions have been suggested.

One would be to restructure private ownership—i.e. the ownership of distribution should be separated from that of generation/transmission. An alternative would be for such a separation to be accompanied by public ownership of transmission (see Demsetz above). In the first case the private owners of transmission systems would have to be willing to interconnect with other suppliers and to act as common carriers. In the second case the fact that the transmission system was publicly owned would presumably guarantee that it was available to all suppliers without discrimination.

Even if there was no restructuring of private ownership, or any public ownership on the lines discussed above, it is still possible to argue that some competition would be injected into the system if private generation/transmission companies were obligated to interconnect and wheel. This arises from the fact that there are some independent distribution companies (investor and municipally owned) who would presumably be willing to exploit such a situation. This latter is of course a more modest proposal since independent utilities are in a minority. All these schemes assume that competition at the generation stage would manifest itself—i.e. what at best would be an oligopolistic structure would not be subject to collusion. Hence the importance of an effective system of antitrust surveillance.

A criticism of regulation, particularly in the field of electricity, has been the existence of cost padding and in particular the notorious A–J effect. The latter has arisen so often in policy discussions that it is difficult to resist the conclusion that it must have undermined the credibility of the traditional approach to electricity rate regulation. Here our earlier point about perceptions is important since, whilst the A–J effect seems to have been regarded as a real problem, the empirical evidence (at least in the case of electricity), does not as we have seen bear out that concern. It should be added that even if it is a real problem, it is not apparent that anyone has come up with a practical remedy.[38]

Regulatory lag has been another problem which has affected electricity rate regulation, although it is not peculiar to that industry. However, unlike the A–J effect, solutions have been devised.

If we are really looking for the shortcomings which have actually led to reform then we need to focus on price structures. Traditional structures have attracted criticism for two reasons. Firstly, they have failed to face consumers with the true economic cost of the electricity they have consumed—hence the increased interest in ideas such as marginal (social) cost pricing. Secondly, some interest groups have been concerned about the impact of electricity prices on poorer consumers—hence lifeline tariffs. Both will be discussed in Chapter 5.

When we try to explain the deregulation of natural gas we are really concerned with what Breyer calls regulatory mismatch.[39] In other words, the system of regulation adopted was inappropriate to the problem. The reader will recollect that originally regulation was applied to retail prices but was progressively extended backwards to pipeline companies and finally to producers. The reader will also recall that the FPC

attempted to apply cost of service rate making to gas production but the administrative task proved overwhelming. It
had to resort to nationwide ceilings and these were very
inflexible.

This approach would not have created any problems if the
regulated price had also been the market clearing price—i.e.
the price at which supply and demand are equal. But of course
there is no reason why these two should coincide, since one is
based upon cost alone whereas the other is determined not
only by cost factors but also by demand considerations. In fact
what happened was that the demand for natural gas was very
buoyant. It was originally relatively cheap, thanks in part to
regulation, and so consumers and industry turned towards it
and having done so were locked into it as an energy source.
The growth of demand was also stimulated by the fact that the
price of alternative sources of energy began to rise (this was
most dramatic after 1973 as a result of the OPEC oil price
hike). On the other hand, the low price imposed by regulation
discouraged the search for new gas, reserves were depleted
and supplies coming to market failed to keep pace with
demand. Since interstate prices were regulated but intrastate
prices were not, some distortion was likely. Producers endea-
voured to sell gas intrastate and considerable resource costs
were incurred as industrial users shifted to gas producing
states to take advantage of supply availability. This diversion
of supplies did not however prevent intrastate price levels
from rising above the interstate controlled level. The fact that
demand exceeded supply forced the FPC to add yet more
regulation to the existing control of prices. The latter is a
familiar phenomenon—see the discussion of the CAB in
Chapter 3. Instead of allowing prices to rise in order to ration
what was available, the FPC, rather like the FCC in respect of
the unpriced electromagnetic spectrum, devised public
interest criteria to allocate the limited supply. The crisis,
which undoubtedly helped finally to precipitate deregulation,
occurred in 1977 when an exceptionally severe winter exacer-
bated the existing shortage. Factories closed and consumers
had to suffer discomfort.

Breyer points out that in the conditions of the 1970s, regulation sought to deal with the problem of the rents which

would have accrued to producers if a free market had been in existence. Cost of service rate making had the effect of transferring rents to users but at the expense of a shortage. An alternative would have been to allow prices to rise and to cream off some of the rent via the tax system.[40]

Rather than consider railways separately from trucking we will look at them together since there is an obvious connection. A variety of criticisms were levelled at the regulation of surface freight transport and these have been admirably summarised by T. Gale Moore.[41] We will focus on four of them—its effects in creating inefficiencies within modes, in misallocating traffics as between modes, in restricting traffic carried and in inhibiting technological change within modes.

Firstly, we should take account of the fact that the cost of producing a good or service when competition does not exist may well exceed the lowest attainable cost. Moore correctly points out that second-best problems do not arise here since it is always preferable in Paretian terms to save resources and thus generate additional goods. It is apparent that ICC control largely inhibited price competition. Just how much effect this had would have been a matter for speculation, were it not for the fact that in the mid-1950s, by virtue of a series of court decisions, poultry and frozen food and vegetables were exempted from the Interstate Commerce Act and therefore from regulation. The subsequent experience in this segment of the market provided a sharp contrast. (It should be noted that such fortuitous contrasts, either within the US or internationally, have been extremely influential). As a result of those court judgements, rates for fresh poultry, frozen poultry and frozen food and vegetables fell— by thirty-three per cent, thirty-six per cent and nineteen per cent respectively—without noticeable loss of service quality. The lower intrastate rates in those states which did not submit trucking to regulation provided yet further evidence in favour of deregulation.

Moore also points out that when price competition is precluded, competition tends to take place in service, although this is not a complete loss to society. It is also important to recognise that regulation was not merely a matter of controlling entry and price. A whole farrago of restrictions were

imposed which increased costs—e.g. backhauls were prohibited, the serving of intermediate points on routes was
disallowed and sometimes carriers were required to follow
roundabout journeys. The waste of fuel to which these restrictions gave rise attracted particular criticism following the
OPEC oil boycott and price hikes. In the case of railways, a
great deal of criticism was levelled at the effect of regulation in
creating and maintaining excess capacity—much of the latter
was due to ICC refusals to allow the closure of unprofitable
lines. Mergers which were a means of rationalising the rail
network had been subjected to inordinate delays by the
ICC.[42]

Secondly, the reader will recollect that value of service rate
making was a well-established feature of the ICC railway rate
system. When trucking came under its wing, trucking rates
were based on rail rates and the value-of-service principle was
therefore further extended.[43] A whole series of studies has
pointed out that by adopting this system, instead of relating
rates to the costs of particular modes, traffic has been mis-
allocated—traffic was not allocated to the mode best suited to
it.

A third source of loss was the static welfare loss that arose
since some commodities were not transported because prices
were hoisted above competitive levels—this is the familiar
deadweight welfare loss.

The fourth source of loss was the reduction in the incentive
to innovate. This stemmed from two sources. (a) The ICC
itself exhibited great inertia in allowing new technologies. The
'Big John' case, in which the ICC resisted a Southern Railroad
rate filing in connection with newly developed large, eco-
nomically-operated hopper cars, is a classic instance. (b) In
addition the ICC price umbrella reduced the pressure to
innovate in order to survive.

The losses due to the first three factors have been quanti-
fied. The annual loss during the 1960s ranged from a low
estimate of $3,800 million to a high estimate of $8,900
million.[44]

Clearly a more flexible approach to pricing, and a more
accommodating treatment of route closure and indeed rationalising mergers, was called for in the case of railways. In the

case of trucking, increased competition was a desirable development. Economies of scale did not preclude it in an industry
which bore the hallmarks of contestability. As for the fear of
destructive competition, it was possible to point to experience
in the UK, Australia and other countries where deregulation
had not been accompanied by the disasters predicted by the
excessive competition thesis.[45]

We turn now to the airlines. The system of regulation
exercised by the CAB was discussed in Chapter 3 and we will
not recapitulate the details. What inspired the decision to
abandon this elaborate system of control? Firstly, the
blockaded entry and control of price, together with a system
of allocating new routes which was designed to stabilise
market shares, all helped to protect less efficient airlines and
keep prices up.[46] Secondly, and great emphasis was laid on
this point, the cartel which the CAB operated in conjunction
with the airlines was imperfect. It ruled out competition on
price but not on service.[47] It was in the latter area that competition manifested itself (e.g. in-flight entertainment, more
frequent services, etc.). As a result costs and thus prices were
escalated and the inflation of costs ate into the profits which a
more perfect cartel would have produced.

The effect of the CAB system would have been much more
difficult to discern if all US airlines had been under the aegis of
the CAB. Again fortuitously, a controlled experiment existed
because intra-state airline operation in California (a massive
market) and Texas were not touched by the CAB system and
indeed to all intents and purposes were free of regulation.
Credit for drawing attention to this must go to Michael
Levine[48]and its properties (in California) were analysed in
depth by William Jordan.[49] Great emphasis was laid on two
factors. Firstly, for similar distances, the unregulated airfares
were much lower than CAB rates. For example, in 1972
Californian interstate fares for very short hauls, short hauls
and short-medium hauls were respectively 1.4, 1.8 and 1.9
times the level of California intrastate fares.[50] Secondly,
unregulated carriers achieved dramatically better load factors
than the trunklines.

Two other points were important. The CAB system ruled
out rate-structure experiments by individual airlines. But

unregulated carriers were free to experiment and introduced peak/off-peak structures which were undoubtedly beneficial. The tendency for regulation to lead to overinvestment (which has been doubted in the case of electricity) was a well attested property of the CAB system. When a new aircraft emerged which offered more rapid service, airlines rushed to acquire it, since competition could only manifest itself in service. It did not follow that this was what consumers wanted. They might have preferred lower prices rather than more rapid transit. In short the existing planes could have enjoyed a longer life—the latter was a feature of the unregulated segment. At rock bottom, one of the major drawbacks of the CAB system was that it did not allow consumers a proper choice between price and service.

The advocates of deregulation had of course to dispose of a number of objections. Firstly, market chaos and destructive competition would ensue. But the experience of California and Texas indicated no tendency to chaos. Destructive competition implied monopolisation and/or the jeopardising of safety standards. But unregulated experience did not point in either direction. Economies of scale were not pronounced and so there was no prospect that one firm in pursuance of that benefit would drive out all the rest and then be able to keep them out. Indeed airline operation had the potentiality to be highly contestable. Safety standards had not been sacrificed in California and Texas and in any case the FAA was there to prevent such a possibility.

Secondly, there was the problem of service to small communities which was assumed to depend on cross-subsidies. However the scope for indulging in the latter was susceptible to overestimation. Such a practice depends on profits being made on some activities and we have noted that service competition tended to eat into profits and therefore undermined the potential for cross-subsidisation. It should be added that during the Kennedy hearings a close examination of the evidence revealed that the extent to which service to small communities would be curtailed had in fact been greatly exaggerated.[51] It should further be noted that the CAB system had not prevented the abandonment of services to the most unprofitable cities but this had not been a problem because the gap had been filled by commuter airlines.[52]

The justification for regulation may be undermined by the passage of time. Three things can happen. (a) It may come to be realised that regulation was based on a misreading of the situation which gave rise to it. (b) Even if the original situation was correctly interpreted, conditions can change and may render the regulation irrelevant or even perverse. (c) Experience may prove that the regulatory instruments are less than perfect. All this seems to have happened in banking.

The specific issues which have stimulated the deregulation debate are as follows:

(a) The banking industry has been highly regulated but much of that regulation was not necessary because the original analysis was wrong. Macroeconomic instability was not caused by the instability of the banking system—the former caused the latter and owed much to the kind of forces which were identified by Keynes, combined with a perverse response on the part of the monetary authorities. A less regulated and more competitive system was called for.

(b) Interest rate ceilings were increasingly bypassed, gave rise to costs and weakened some institutions. The Regulation Q ceiling on time and savings deposits originally only applied to commercial banks. In 1966 it was extended to mutual savings banks, savings and loan associations and credit unions. However with the passage of time this control became less effective since competition developed outside the deposit taking institutions—notably from money market mutual funds. Not only that, but the depository institutions had a vested interest in keeping down the interest which they had to pay—it swelled their profits and cushioned their inefficiencies.[53] In periods of high interest rates a tendency for the ceiling to lag behind market realities could lead to financially embarrassing withdrawals (i.e. disintermediation).

(c) Regulation stemming from the depression era also created anomalies as between the deposit taking institutions. Commercial banks could offer cheque accounts and could make short term consumer and commercial loans. The savings and loan association could do neither—on the assets side they were confined to longer term housing-related loans and here interest rates tended to be low. The latter restrictions greatly weakened these thrift institutions. In times of stress they needed to be able to switch their assets to more profitable activities and to be better able to match their assets to their liabilities (traditionally they had tended to borrow short and lend long). Moreover there was a case for creating more competition between institutions rather than reserving certain classes of business to certain types of institution. Much the same could be said about the Glass-Steagall Act which substantially prevented commercial banks from being involved in investment banking.

(d) Particularly following the spectacular failure of thrift institutions during the early 1980s, more thought needed to be given to deposit insurance. The flat rate insurance premium was an encouragement to institutions to undertake riskier and more profitable business. It was described as a 'heads I win, tails you lose situation'.[54] Premiums needed to be related to the riskiness of an individual institution's portfolio.

The main features of the regulation of the NYSE were described in Chapter 3. For more than a century and a half minimum brokerage commissions had been fixed, and entry restricted. When the SEC came into existence in 1934 it is not surprising, given the anti-competitive temper of the times, that it did not seek to remove these restrictions. Indeed they remained undisturbed until the late 1960s. Why did deregulation eventually break through?

Two instrumentalities can be identified. Academics had long criticised the minimum brokerage system—the critics included Stigler and Demsetz. It led to commissions above the competitive level. It therefore encouraged inefficiency and lined the pockets of the brokers at the public's expense.[55] Some indication of the latter was the high prices paid for seats on the NYSE. These were rents arising from the limit on entry and represented the capitalised value of the supernormal profits of doing business on the exchange.[56] It was also argued that customers were not able to chose the combination of brokerage and ancillary service which best suited them. However, whilst these studies indicated that the system was indefensible (and others rejected the bogy of destructive competition[57]), they were not the immediate cause of its demise.

The immediate cause was associated with the growth of institutional trading. Between 1960 and 1976 the institutional share of NYSE business more or less doubled—by the latter date it was fifty-four per cent by value and forty-four per cent by volume of all NYSE transactions. The fixed commission system discriminated against the large block trading of the institutions since brokers' revenues increased in proportion to the size of orders but costs did not go up *pro rata*. Brokers therefore made huge profits on these large deals—in a free market brokerage would have fallen to reflect the lower unit cost of these larger trades. Institutions were able to obtain some rebates through the medium of what were called 'give-ups'. A broker would transact a block of shares for an institution and then surrender part of the commission to a broker who rendered some service for the institution. The second broker would then rebate the price of the service to the institution.

Despite such alleviations, the institutions found the NYSE unsatisfactory and this led them to seek other ways of reducing brokerage costs. In some degree they succeeded in doing so by switching deals to the so-called Third Market— i.e. the over-the-counter market—and also by buying into the brokerage business. The latter was forbidden on the NYSE but was allowed outside New York. In themselves these strategies did not cause deregulation. They were however symptomatic of the growing dissatisfaction with the NYSE and as a result the attention of the SEC, the Department of Justice and ultimately Congress was attracted. The response of the SEC in moving towards deregulation (i.e. outlawing the minimum commission system) has been characterised as a shift towards a new politically effective interest group and thus away from the old NYSE constituency. Barry Weingast however points out that the SEC was not the only actor. Re-election minded politicians on the relevant Congressional committees were also instrumental, since eventually they too were persuaded that there was political mileage in supporting the change desired by the new constituency.[58]

Deregulation in broadcasting has largely been a product of

technological change. The idea that the allocation of the electromagnetic spectrum might be subject to the price mechanism had, as we have seen, been advocated but was not a factor leading to change. The main cause was the fact that television signals could be imported into the home via cable and satellite—thus bypassing the restriction which the allocation of the spectrum had imposed on the range of programmes available in any area by conventional broadcast means. The almost inevitable first reaction of the FCC was to seek to maintain the viability of the existing system which it had helped to foster—in other words it sought to hold back these new developments. Its desire to maintain the *status quo* was the product of a number of factors. Firstly, the existing system enshrined the desired philosophy of free broadcasting (i.e. paid for by advertising). Secondly, it was supposed to serve the needs of localism. Thirdly, by restricting competition, the profitability of the network-owned and affiliated stations was maintained, and this held out the promise of the inevitable regulatory phenomenon of cross-subsidisation. In this case the subsidised element was public affairs and other merit programming.

The networks and the affiliates were of course not likely to welcome the alternative sources of programming provided by the cable and satellite systems, since they would draw away viewers and therefore undermine the advertising potential of traditional broadcast TV. They therefore pressed the FCC to oppose change. Inevitably however, the pressure of the public to take advantage of cable and satellite etc. as a means of providing greater choice, was bound to force the FCC eventually to cease its regulatory protection of the older system, and to allow these newer technologies to establish themselves.

However greater choice was not the only factor. Technological change was also capable of providing the benefit of greater efficiency. Thus in 1981 a Congressional study pointed to the societal interest in accommodating '. . . the vast changes in technology that have occurred over the last several decades so that their enormous productivity-enhancing powers may be fully reaped.'[59] Whilst this referred to telecommunications, it was obviously applicable in some degree to broadcasting. There is a further point which, whilst it is something of a hypothesis, seems likely to have been an important factor if UK policy is any guide. Here we refer to the tendency, which we have just noted, of the regulated interests (the networks and their affiliates) to exert pressure on the regulators to resist change. This was bound to have an adverse effect upon American jobs and exports since other countries were likely to accept change and countries like Japan would be in a position to supply the technology. Without a home market US industry would be at a disadvantage. On the other hand if change was embraced domestically the vast US market would provide (a) a base for amortising the initial R & D cost and (b) scale economies in production. Finally we should note that the greater number of channels which the newer technologies provided tended to render regulation concerning programme balance and commercial frequency increasingly unnecessary.

The utterly dominating position held by the Bell System in US telecommunications was discussed in Chapter 3 and we will not repeat the details. That position was also one which the FCC initially sought to protect. Subsequently, as in broadcasting, its stance began to change. What forces generated a disposition to accept the need for change? It has to be said that the case for change was less clear cut than some we have discussed. Diametrically different views were held about what should be done to the Bell System.

Those who called for change drew attention both to the properties of the system of regulation and to the nature of the industry's structure. It has been argued that the FCC never exercised any really close control over rate making (and much the same was said about state regulatory bodies). It was also alleged that Bell was in a position to inflate its rate base and that little effective control was exercised over it. Inevitably the question of the industrial structure comes into the picture since, as we have seen, Bell was integrated backwards into equipment manufacture (via Western Electric). Some critics alleged that the rate base was inflated not simply because of the excessive quantity and quality of equipment used, but also because of the excessive price which the unregulated Western Electric could charge the rest of the Bell System and indeed the system as a whole. However the excessiveness of Western's profits has been the subject of much dispute. Beverley Moore cites a California Supreme Court judgement which agreed that Western's rate of return was modest if it was subjected to the risks of competition. But since it was part of a regulated monopoly and did not face such risks its rate of return ought not to exceed that of the Bell Operating Companies.[60] On the other hand, Almarin Phillips points to the judgement in the case of *US* v. *AT & T* (1974) which stated that Western's profits were lower than those of other manufacturing firms.[61] Critics also pointed out that even if local telephone systems were natural monopolies (and some were disposed to dispute this point although not always with accompanying evidence), it was not clear why such natural monopolies should be owned by Bell. If they were independent then the foreclosure of the equipment market would be terminated.

Criticism was also levelled at the idea that the Bell System as a whole was a natural monopoly and that it should there-fore be left in charge of the telecommunications business. Some cast doubts on its original naturalness, pointing out that it had been built up by a series of what may best be described as monopolising tactics (sometimes in cooperation with the regulators). Others were disposed to accept that, however built up originally, it had come to have a character of a natural monopoly, but with the emergence of microwave and satellite technologies competition was now possible and should be allowed. On the other hand Almarin Phillips has vehemently argued that the Bell System is subject to increasing returns to scale—therefore allowing interlopers into the industry made no sense.[62] Moreover, telecommunications is subject to beneficial externalities and as a result is likely to be under-supplied. Phillips appears to argue that cross-subsidisation (to which some critics object), as part of a policy of universal service, helps to counteract this tendency. If competitors do enter they tend to choose the profitable heavy density markets and Bell objected that this cream-skimming eroded the resources which were necessary if light density services were to be maintained.

Phillips admitted that a policy of perpetuating Bell's natural monopoly only made sense if it was willing to embrace tech-nological change. This is really the nub of the problem. Critics allege that AT & T was reluctant to accept change (more about that later). It therefore seems likely that the FCC drew the conclusion that whilst there was advantage in substantially preserving the core of the telecommunications natural monopoly and its static scale benefits, from a dynamic point of view it was desirable that Bell should be kept on its toes by allowing competition from new technology to play, and not merely threaten to play, around the edges.

6   PRIVATISATION

In contrast to the UK, the retreat of the US government from involvement in industry has focussed on deregulation rather than privatisation. There are two reasons for this. Firstly, public enterprise is relatively less important in the US than in the UK economy. Secondly, much of the public enterprise in the US is to be found below the federal level and it is at the federal level that the pressure to privatise via asset sales has been most evident.

Whilst ideological considerations may not have been absent, the federal programme of privatisation seems, as we noted in Chapter 1, to have been primarily a product of budget deficit politics—*force majeure* imposed a need to reduce the federal budget deficit. At the end of 1985 matters came to a head in the shape of the Gramm-Rudman-Hollings budget reform law of the December of that year. It required a sizeable reduction in the federal budget deficit by fiscal 1987, otherwise the General Accounting Office would be free to slash expenditure in order to achieve the required reduction. As we pointed out earlier, since President Reagan did not want to raise taxes but did want to increase defence spending, the only alternative was to cut other programmes, such as welfare, and to exploit other devices, such as a asset sales, to the full. Although a central feature of the Gramm-Rudman-Hollings law was found to be unconstitutional by the Supreme Court in July 1986, the law was not rendered ineffective. In any case the need to tackle the budget problem, despite possibly helpful revenue effects of the separate tax reform legislation, remained.

At the beginning of 1986 a shopping list of possible federal privatisations was being considered. One candidate was Conrail which the reader will recollect was the product of a federal 'lame duck' rescue of the freight interests of certain eastern railroads. The Gramm-Rudman-Hollings law did not precipitate the idea of selling off Conrail although it gave it greater urgency. From the very beginning it was intended that ultimately Conrail should be privatised or, if by 1983 it had not come back to profitability, it should be sold off piecemeal. In fact by 1983 Conrail was reported to be back in profit and by 1984 offers were being considered. The Bonneville, Alaska, Southeastern and Western area Power Marketing Administrations were also identified and indeed were included in the list of official budget proposals for 1987. These were electricity utilities which collectively sold six per cent of the electricity produced in the US and handled the hydroelectric power produced by the Corps of Engineers at government owned dams. Rather daringly some commentators included the Tennessee Valley Authority as a possible candidate for privatisation. Naval Petroleum Reserves were also identified as a possible target. These consisted of two oilfields—Elk Hills in California and Teapot Dome in Wyoming—which were run by the Department of Energy. These too were included in the official list of 1987 budget proposals. It was also suggested that Washington's Dulles and National airports, built with federal funds, should be sold off.

NOTES

1. P. O. Steiner, 'The Legalisation of American Society: Economic Regulation', *Michigan Law Review*, 81 (1983), pp.1285–306.
2. *Ibid.*, p.1290.
3. P. W. MacAvoy *op. cit.*, p.94.
4. P. O. Steiner *op. cit.*, p.1288.
5. R. W. Poole (ed.), *Instead of Regulation op. cit.*, pp.viii–ix.
6. S. G. Breyer *op. cit.*, pp.317–40.
7. R. Caves, *Air Transport and Its Regulators* (Harvard University, Cambridge, Massachusetts, 1962).
8. G. W. Douglas and J. Miller, *Economic Regulation of Domestic Air Transport: Theory and Policy* (Brookings, Washington, 1974).

9.   M. Levine, 'Is Regulation Necessary? California Air Transportation and National Regulatory Policy', *Yale Law Journal*, 74 (1965), pp.1416–47.
10. W. A. Jordan, *Airline Regulation in America* (Johns Hopkins, Baltimore, 1970).
11. B. M. Mitnick *op. cit.*, p.132.
12. H. M. Gray, 'The Passing of the Public Utility Concept', *Journal of Law and Public Utility Economics* 16 (1940), p.281.
13. M. H. Bernstein, *op. cit.*, p.90.
14. G. Kolko *op. cit.*, pp.231–3.
15. M. Friedman, *Capitalism and Freedom* (University of Chicago, Chicago, 1962), notably Chapters 8 and 9.
16. Friedman's views on occupational licensing seem to have stimulated the work of T. Gale Moore on the same subject. The latter's 'The Purpose of Licensing', *Journal of Law and Economics*, 4 (1961), pp.93–117 is regarded as a precursor of Stigler's work in undermining the public interest theory and suggesting a private interest explanation.
17. H. Demsetz *op. cit.*
18. E. E. Bailey, 'Deregulation of Contestable Markets: Application of Theory to Public Policy' in T. G. Gies and W. Sickel (eds), *Deregulation: Appraisal Before the Fact* (University of Michigan, Ann Arbor, 1982), p.3.
19. R. H. Coase 'The Federal Communications Commission' *op. cit.*
20. See W. J. Baumol, J. C. Panzar and R. D. Willig, *Contestable Markets and the Theory of Industry Structure* (Harcourt Brace, San Diego, 1982); W. J. Baumol, 'Contestable Markets: An Uprising in the Theory of Industry's Structure', *American Economic Review*, 72/1 (1982), pp.1–15; E. E. Bailey and W. J. Baumol, 'Deregulation and the Theory of Contestable Markets', *Yale Journal on Regulation*, 1 (1984), pp.111–37; E. E. Bailey, 'Contestability and the Design of Regulatory and Antitrust Policy' *American Economic Review*, 71/2 (1981), pp.178–83; K. J. Button, 'New Approaches to the Regulation of Industry', *Royal Bank of Scotland Review*, 148 (1985), pp.18–34.
21. See M. J. Green (ed.) *The Monopoly Makers op. cit.*; R. C. Fellmeth (ed.), *The Interstate Commerce Omission* (Grossman, New York, 1970).
22. D. D. Anderson *op. cit.*, p.18.
23. On the subject of regulatory lag see S. H. Archer, 'Regulatory Lag', *Economica Aziendale* 2 (1983), pp.175–84.
24. H. Averch and L. Johnson, 'Behaviour of the Firm Under Regulatory Constraint', *American Economic Review*, 52 (1962), pp.1052–69.
25. C. Wilcox and W. G. Shepherd *op. cit.*, p.385.
26. Studies finding such an effect include R. Spann, 'Rate of Return Regulation and Efficiency in Production: An Empirical Test of the Averch-Johnson Thesis', *Bell Journal of Economics and Management Science*, 5 (1974), pp.38–52; L. Courville, 'Regulation and Efficiency

in the Electric Utility Industry', *Bell Journal of Economics and Management Science*, 5 (1974), pp.53–74; H. C. Petersen, 'An Empirical Test of Regulatory Effects', *Bell Journal of Economics and Management Science*, 6 (1975), pp.111–26. Studies finding against include W. J. Boyes, 'An Empirical Examination of the Averch-Johnson Effect', *Economic Inquiry*, 14 (1976), pp.25–35.

27. P. L. Joskow and R. C. Noll, 'Regulation in Theory and Practice: An Overview' in G. Fromm (ed.), *Studies in Public Regulation*, (MIT Press, Cambridge, Massachusetts, 1981), pp.1–65.

28. D. McKay, *Has the A-J Effect Been Empirically Verified? Social Science Working Paper 132* (California Institute of Technology, 1976).

29. J. F. Weston, 'Comment' in H. M. Trebing (ed.), *New Dimensions in Public Utility Pricing* (Michigan University, Lansing, Michigan, 1976), pp.609–10.

30. A. E. Kahn *op. cit.,* pp.190–1.

31. H. C. Petersen *op. cit.*, pp.309–10.

32. E. Manfield *op. cit.*, p.63.

33. F. Thompson and L. R. Jones *op. cit.*, p.1.

34. P. W. MacAvoy *op. cit.*, pp.31–80.

35. M. L. Weidenbaum and R. Defina, *The Cost of Federal Regulation of Economic Activity*, (American Enterprise Institute, Washington, 1978).

36. A. R. Ferguson and M. L. Weidenbaum, 'The Problem of Balancing the Costs and Benefits of Regulation: Two Views' in J. F. Gatti (ed.), *The Limits of Government Regulation* (Academic Press, New York, 1981), p.147.

37. L. W. Weiss, 'Antitrust in the Electric Power Industry' in A. Phillips (ed.), *Promoting Competition in Regulated Markets op. cit.*, pp.135–74 and W. J. Primeaux, 'A Reexamination of the Monopoly Market Structure for Electric Utilities' *ibid*, pp.175–200. More recent thinking has cast doubts on the idea that economies of scale have been exhausted at the generation level. Joskow and Schmalensee draw attention to economies of scope and vertical integration and argue that because of these factors *integrated* generation and transmission may be a natural monopoly—see Joskow and Schmalensee *op. cit*. They also cast doubts on the more simplistic deregulation scenarios and suggest that arrangements which allow for wholesale power to be pooled and loads to be coordinated—i.e. as in European grid systems—may be the best way forward.

38. W. H. Melody, 'Comment' in H. M. Trebing (ed.), *New Dimensions in Public Utility Pricing op. cit.*, p.206.

39. S. G. Breyer *op. cit.*, pp.240–60.

40. *Ibid.*, pp.258–60.

41. T. Gale Moore *op. cit.*, in A. Phillips (ed.), *Promoting Competition in Regulated Markets op. cit.*, pp.55–98.

42. D. Smith, 'The Evolution of Rail Merger Policy', *Transport Research Forum*, 24 (1983), p.560.

43. A. F. Friedlaender *op. cit.*, pp.16–27.

44. T. Gale Moore *op. cit.*, p.71.
45. T. Gale Moore, *Trucking Regulation Lessons from Europe* (American Enterprise Institute, Washington, 1976).
46. G. W. Douglas and J. C. Miller *op. cit.*, p.141.
47. G. C. Eads, 'Competition in the Domestic Trunk Airline Industry: Too Much or Too Little', in A. Phillips (ed.) *Promoting Competition in Regulated Markets op. cit.*, pp.13–54.
48. M. Levine *op. cit.*
49. W. A. Jordan *op. cit.*
50. P. W. MacAvoy and J. W. Snow, *Regulation of Passenger Fares and Competition among the Airlines* (American Enterprise Institute, Washington, 1977), p.42.
51. S. G. Breyer *op. cit.*, pp.332–4.
52. P. W. MacAvoy and J. W. Snow *op. cit.*, pp.15–24.
53. An excellent summary of the need to reform banking regulation is to be found in A. S. Carron, 'The Political Economy of Financial Deregulation' in R. G. Noll and B. M. Owen (eds), *The Political Economy of Deregulation* (American Enterprise Institute, Washington, 1983), pp.69–83.
54. J. R. Barth, R. D. Brumbaugh, D. Sauerhaft and G. H. K. Wang *op. cit.*, p.15.
55. G. J. Stigler, 'Public Regulation of the Securities Markets', *Journal of Business* 37 (1964), pp.117–42; H. Demsetz, 'Perfect Competition, Regulation and the Stock Market' in H. G. Manne (ed.), *Economic Policy and the Regulation of Corporate Securities* (American Enterprise Institute, Washington, 1969), pp.1–22; R. R. West and S. M. Tinic, 'Minimum Commission Rates on New York Stock Exchange Transactions', *Bell Journal of Economics and Management Science*, 2 (1971), pp.577–60; W. F. Baxter, 'NYSE Fixed Commission Rates: A Private Cartel Goes Public', *Stanford Law Review*, 22 (1970), pp.675–712: I. Friend and M. E. Blume, 'Competitive Commissions on the New York Stock Exchange', *Journal of Finance*, 28 (1973), pp.795–819.
56. J. L. Hamilton, 'Deregulation in the Securities Brokerage Industry', in T. G. Gies and W. Sichel (eds), *Deregulation: Appraisal Before the Fact op. cit.*, pp.81–2.
57. H. M. Mann, 'The New York Stock Exchange: A Cartel at the End of Its Reign' in A. Phillips (ed.) *op. cit.*, pp.306–12.
58. B. R. Weingast, 'The Congressional-Bureaucratic System: A Principal Agent Perspective with Applications to the SEC, *Public Choice*, 1 (1984), pp.147–200.
59. Sub-Committee on Telecommunications, Committee on Energy and Commerce, *Telecommunications in Transit* (US House of Reps., 3 November, 1981) p.27.
60. B. C. Moore, 'A T & T: The Phony Monopoly' *op. cit.*, p.78.
61. A. Phillips, 'The Impossibility of Competition in Telecommunications: Public Policy Gone Awry', in M. A. Crew (ed.), *Regulatory Reform and Public Utilities* (Lexington, Lexington, Massachusetts, 1982), p.23, citing Civil Action No. 74-1698 (U.S.D.C., D.C., 1974).
62. *Ibid.*, pp.7–33.

5 Deregulation and Privatisation

1 DEREGULATION

In the previous chapter we discussed forces for change. In this chapter we seek to describe the changes that have actually occurred. Much of the discussion will concern deregulation at the federal level, but it is important to recollect that, as we pointed out in Chapter 1, parallel systems of regulation often exist at the state (and indeed municipal) level. Here too deregulatory moves have been apparent. However, a detailed analysis of change at the state (and municipal) level is beyond the scope of this book, but we will draw attention to instances which give at least a flavour of what has been happening lower down.

Although some radical structural changes have been proposed by academics, which would inject some competition and efficiency into the electricity industry (see Chapter 4 and endnotes thereto), in practice the structure does not appear to have been fundamentally disturbed. It should however be noted that under the Public Utility Regulatory Policies Act 1978, enhanced interconnection powers and a new power to require wheeling were granted to the FERC[1] (the latter succeeded the FPC in 1977). Nevertheless regulation rather than competition has continued to be the prime method of control over potential market power. In so far as changes have occurred, apart from those just mentioned, they have taken the form of modifications to the system of regulated pricing.

We have noted that in the inflationary conditions of the 1970s regulatory lag gave rise to considerable financial difficulties for utilities, including those in electricity. That problem was eased by a number of procedural changes. Firstly, commissions became increasingly willing to allow proposed rate increases to take effect before the actual rate decision was reached—this was subject to a requirement to repay increases which were subsequently found to be in excess of the justified level. Secondly, as a response to changed conditions in capital markets from the mid-1970s, commissions began to allow for increases in interest and equity costs. Thirdly, they became increasingly disposed to allow construction in progress to be included in the rate base. Fourthly, they began to consider not merely historical cost data but also estimates of future costs.[2]

The other detailed changes related to modifications of traditional price structures. The unprecedented requests for rate rises in the 1970s focussed increased public attention on this matter. Two developments occurred. Firstly, the virtues of marginal cost pricing attracted increased interest. Marginal cost pricing had made substantial headway in Europe in the 1950s and 1960s but did not come to the US until the 1970s. Peak load pricing has the virtue of bringing home to consumers the true cost of the electricity they consume at different times of the day, etc., and, by discouraging consumption at peak periods and diverting it to the usage trough, it reduces the need for extra capacity. As we pointed out in Chapter 4, a marginal social cost approach was also preferred by environmental groups—e.g. the Environmental Defence Fund (EDF)—since it was likely to reduce consumption and therefore pollution, as compared with a declining block tariff.

One of the early successes of the EDF was the decision by the Wisconsin Public Service Commission in 1973 to embrace marginal cost as the basis for its pricing structure. This was the first such decision. The EDF then focussed its attention on the New York Public Service Commission (NYPSC) where it found a willing ally in Alfred Kahn who was both chairman and a keen supporter of the marginal cost approach. A peak load structure was adopted by the NYPSC in 1977.[3] The virtue of time of use pricing (which embodies seasonal as well as daily variations) subsequently attracted Congressional attention. In 1978 Congress passed the Public Utility Regulatory

Policies Act to which we referred earlier. That act required commissions to hold public hearings on the subject of rate structures. The act was opposed to the declining block system and favoured time of day and seasonal rate systems. According to Leonard Weiss, by the late 1970s several states were making explicit use of marginal cost pricing, and most had moved some way in that direction.[4]

The second development related to lifeline rates. These were introduced by the California Public Utilities Commission (CPUC) in 1975. In this case it was advocates of the consumer interest who took a key role. They were organised in the Citizens Action League (CAL). CAL decided that CPUC was a suitable campaign target. Again it was the large increases in electricity rates—in this case allowed by CPUC without public hearings—that precipitated action. CAL was able to attract the support of gubernatorial candidate Gerry Brown. CAL proposed that CPUC should hold down the price of an initial amount of electricity which the average domestic user needed for basic requirements such as heating and lighting. CPUC was staunchly opposed to the idea, which was described by some as having the character of the well-known and non-existent free lunch. However when Gerry Brown became governor he appointed commissioners favourable to the lifeline concept and a state law was also passed requiring CPUC to designate a lifeline amount of electricity. In practice the effect was that the burden of increases fell on commercial and industrial users.[5]

Statutory deregulation of natural gas was a product of the Carter years, although the Ford administration did itself propose the abolition of federal price setting in gas production. However some changes in natural gas regulation preceded the statute. Firstly, as we noted in Chapter 3, the problem at the wellhead end of the industry was that traditional cost-of-service ratemaking, which often tended to be conducted on an enterprise by enterprise basis, proved to be unworkable. As a result the FPC was forced to move to a regional and then a national price ceiling system. Secondly, regulation tended to hold down prices and as a result shortages emerged—MacAvoy reports that in the early 1970s shortages were equal to twenty per cent of total demand.[6] The depression of prices also led to a deterioration in the reserve/ output ratio. Some rate increases were instituted in the early 1970s, but fears of adverse consumer and political reactions prevented prices from increasing to market clearing levels.

In 1976 however the FPC took the bold step of approving a substantial increase which involved forward–looking estimates of the price needed to bring new sources of supply on stream. The new move was disputed, but was approved by the Supreme Court in *American Public Gas Company* v. *Federal Energy Regulatory Commission (FERC)*.[7] MacAvoy points out that the 1976 initiative is a good example of a commission setting the deregulation process in motion prior to Congressional action.[8] The latter followed in 1978 during the Carter administration, when the Natural Gas Policy Act was passed. This was to put it mildly an extremely complicated piece of legislation. Basically what the act did was this. (a) It granted regulatory control over intrastate as well as interstate wellhead prices. (b) The regulatory body was the FERC which, as the reader will recall, replaced the old FPC in 1977. (c) It was necessary to raise wellhead prices substantially in order to encourage the search for new gas supplies (the meaning of 'new' gas was defined in the statute). However a too rapid price shock had to be avoided. The act therefore allowed a phased increase in the prices of new (and high cost) gas—they were allowed to rise at the rate of inflation together with a further annual escalation factor. The latter meant that over time a substantial real price increase would occur. After 1985 control was to cease. By contrast the price of old gas in interstate trade (previously regulated by the FPC) was only allowed to increase at the rate of inflation and was not destined to be deregulated in 1985. This treatment of old gas was obviously designed to curtail what would otherwise have been an unjustified windfall. However, other things being equal, all price controls were to cease in 1989.[9]

We turn now to transportation, where a substantial programme of deregulation has been introduced. Presidential acceptance of the need for more reliance on competition and less on regulation was not new—we noted earlier that such a call was made by President Kennedy. During the Ford administration the Council of Economic Advisers advocated transport deregulation—a suggestion supported by President Ford. Deregulatory bills were indeed introduced during President Ford's period of office although the majority of the proposals which reached the statute book were products of the Carter era. However, as in the case of gas, we shall see that statutory deregulation in transport was sometimes proceeded by agency instituted change.

On the railway front Congress adopted two statutes. In 1976, during the Ford era, it passed the Railroad Revitalisation and Regulatory Reform Act (4R Act). The aim of the act was primarily to improve the financial health of the carriers—it was therefore different from the airline and trucking measures (see below) which were more concerned with consumer choice and efficiency.[10] The 4R Act was important in two respects. Firstly, it provided for greater rate setting freedom for railways. Secondly, it sought to facilitate mergers and route abandonments. In respect of the latter issue more liberal rules were introduced and a tight time schedule was prescribed for merger decisions.

This dose of deregulation was however found to be inadequate and the Staggers Rail Act was therefore introduced in 1980. This statute limited ICC jurisdiction over rates to those where railroads exercised market dominance, and it narrowed the definition of what dominance meant as compared with the 4R Act of 1976. T. Gale Moore has pointed out that as a result about two thirds of railroad rates were freed of maximum rate regulation.[11] The act also gave railroads more scope to reduce rates by providing that the ICC could not reject a rate reduction unless the cut gave rise to a rate below variable cost. In addition the act extended the authority originally granted under the 4R Act to exempt particular forms of traffic from all rate controls. It curtailed the activities of rate bureaux and provision was made for a more expeditious application of the liberal rules on route abandonments which had been introduced in 1976.

In both trucking and airlines the regulatory agency began to deregulate prior to the formal deregulating statute. It has indeed been argued that, notably in the case of trucking, deregulatory statutes were largely a codification of changes that had already been introduced.[12] As we pointed out earlier, this process of change in agency policy was facilitated by President Carter's action in appointing chairmen and commissioners known to be favourable to regulatory reform—the appointments of Daniel O'Neal to the chairmanship of the ICC and of Alfred Kahn to the chairmanship of the CAB are often cited, but there were of course others.

The Motor Carrier Act 1980 was an exercise in partial deregulation. Firstly, restrictions on entry, which had not been important in railways, were crucial in trucking. The act changed the entry conditions radically. It enlarged the types of transportation which were totally exempt from regulation, and in respect of those which continued to be subject to regulation it substantially relaxed the system. A service could now be supplied if (a) the applicant was fit, willing and able, and (b) a useful public purpose was served. The burden of proof was now shifted. Previously it was the applicant who had to show that the licence was required by public convenience and necessity. Now the act required the protestor to show that a licence was inconsistent with it. Moreover only those truckers who already had a licence to operate the service in question could protest, and the fact that the new competition would divert traffic from the protestor was not in itself a sufficient objection. Secondly, in respect of rates the act prescribed a generous zone of freedom within which they could rise or fall, and the ICC normally lost the power to control such rates provided that they were set by individual as opposed to collective action. Thirdly, the antitrust immunity enjoyed by collective rate making was substantially cut back. Fourthly, the act authorised the ICC to eliminate many of the restrictions which gave rise to circuitous routes, prohibited service to intermediate points, prevented backhauls, etc.[13] Other states followed the deregulatory path including Florida, Maine, Alaska, South Dakota and Wisconsin. In the same year deregulation of household goods transport was accomplished under the Household Goods Transportation Act. In 1982, by virtue of the Bus Regulatory Reform Act, many parts of the Motor Carrier Act 1980 were extended to motor carriers of passengers. Barriers to entry and exit were relaxed, an interim zone of rate freedom was prescribed, all rate regulation was to cease after three years and much of the state control of fares and service was pre-empted.[14]

The most dramatic instance of deregulation occurred in 1978 under the Air Passenger Deregulation Act. This was an exercise in total economic deregulation, on a phased basis, although control of safety was to continue under the aegis of the FAA. The act differed substantially from that of 1938 by emphasising the need for efficient, low priced service and to that end it placed maximum reliance on market forces and actual and potential competition. It also sought to protect service to smaller communities by guaranteeing an essential service subsidy for ten years. During a transitional phase entry to interstate routes was to be progressively opened up—within limits, existing intrastate as well as interstate carriers could enter routes. There were also routes which various airlines were certificated to operate but which they did not fly on a regular basis. If these services were not started other airlines could enter. A substantial zone of rate freedom was also established. As time passed control was to cease over rates, then over routes and mergers (the latter was to pass to the Department of Justice under existing antitrust statutes). It was also envisaged that from 1985 the CAB would itself disappear. For completeness we should mention the Air Cargo Deregulation Act 1977—it adopted a free competition approach to air cargo. Fitness was to be the sole criterion for entry. Operators could establish any rate they chose and were freed from the necessity to file tariffs. All restrictions on the size of aircraft were removed.

Deregulatory influences also spread to US policy in respect of international airline operation. The first manifestation of this was a Presidential document of 1978 entitled *International Air Transport Negotiations*. It spelled out the changes which the United States desired in its bilateral air services agreements with other governments—more will be said about this from a UK standpoint in Chapters 6 to 8. The document indicated that the United States would call for more opportunities for competitive pricing, for the elimination of restrictions on capacity, frequency and route operating rights, and for the possibility that more than one US airline would be able to operate on routes between it and the other party. It also envisaged the approval of more gateway points for direct flights into the US. The objective of placing maximum reliance on competitive market forces was incorporated into the International Air Transport Competition Act 1979. The influence of this new thinking became apparent in 1978 when the United States renegotiated its bilateral agreement with the Netherlands. The new US–Netherlands bilateral incorporated a number of competitive features—each country could put as many airlines on a route as it wished, capacity and frequency restrictions were removed and each state determined the fares for journeys starting from its end.

The new deregulatory mood was also apparent in the United States approach to the determination of air fares. These had been agreed within the traffic conferences of the International Air Transport Association (IATA)—an international cartel. Traditionally these fares were subsequently approved by governments. More will be said about this system—again within a UK context—in Chapters 6 to 8. However during the 1970s competitive influences—to be discussed in those chapters—began to undermine the IATA system. In 1978 it was further undermined when the CAB demanded that IATA should produce reasons why it should not lift the antitrust exemption, which the price fixing conferences had up to that point enjoyed. In order to avoid court actions, American airlines left IATA, although they rejoined when President Reagan put an end to the legal threat. Nevertheless the United States pressure had the effect of weakening the influence exerted by IATA—for example, it was agreed that airlines could be members of IATA without being bound by fare agreements. Of great significance were the 1982 discussions between the United States and a group of European countries, which led to the introduction on the North Atlantic routes of a more flexible system of reference fares and zones of reasonableness around them.

One final point needs to be made. Since the CAB was due to be wound up in 1985, and it has played a major role in connection with international airline operations, it was essential that a new body should be assigned any residual regulatory tasks. It was in fact agreed that access to routes and air fare matters should from the sunset of the CAB be handled by the Department of Transportation.[15]

Deregulatory statutes in banking were a feature of the early 1980s. In 1980 the Depository Institutions Deregulation and Monetary Control Act was introduced. It provided for a six year phase-out of deposit interest rate ceilings. It equalised conditions of competition by requiring that all financial institutions offering similar types of deposits should operate under the same reserve requirements. The act also began to break down the barriers which insulated some institutions from the competition of others. Savings and loan associations were allowed to invest up to twenty per cent of their assets in consumer loans, commercial paper and corporate debt securities, and mutual savings banks were allowed to make commercial, corporate and business loans up to five per cent of their assets.

This was followed in 1982 by the Garn-St Germain Depository Institutions Act. A good deal of this statute was concerned with coping with the difficulties experienced by savings and loans associations. However there were also provisions which increased interinstitution competition. On the liabilities side, savings and loan associations were allowed to introduce a new Money Market Deposit Account (MMDA) in order to compete more effectively with the rapidly growing money market mutual funds which we mentioned earlier. In 1983 they were also allowed to operate Super-NOW accounts for the same reason. Like the MMDA, the Super-NOW accounts have no interest rate ceiling but, unlike the MMDA, Super-NOW accounts are not restricted in terms of the number of cheque transactions allowed. Federally chartered savings and loan associations were also allowed to offer demand deposits to persons or organisations with which they had a loan relationship—previously only commercial and mutual savings banks could offer demand deposit facilities. On the assets side, federally chartered savings and loans associations, and federally chartered mutual savings banks were given expanded commercial and consumer lending powers. It should however be noted that the commercial banks were not at this stage successful in their desire fully to break into the investment banking business from which they had been largely debarred by the Glass-Steagall Act. The 1982 act also required that an investigation should be carried out into the deposit insurance system.

Three other developments are worthy of note, and help to bring this account up to date. Firstly, as we have just noted, the Glass-Steagall Act largely debarred commercial banks from getting involved in investment banking business. However in recent years the FRB has been in favour of relaxing this restriction[16] and indeed in 1986 and 1987 the federal Court of Appeals and the FRB ruled in ways which have strengthened the hand of commercial banks wishing to play a greater role in securities business. In addition the system of state banking has had a liberalising influence. Thus the New York state equivalent of the Glass-Steagall Act has been interpreted in a more liberal fashion, and this has undoubtedly put pressure on the federal authorities to keep pace. Federal reform in this area seems highly likely since the Reagan administration has become increasingly anxious about the relative smallness of American banks when compared with the muscle exerted by conglomerate rivals abroad.

Secondly, deregulatory influences have also been at work, not just in relaxing the rules which govern the legitimate range of business, but also in breaking down the geographical frontiers in the banking structure. Branching is one way in which banks can spread their tentacles and this kind of activity has long been regulated at state and federal level—the federal regulator being the Comptroller of the Currency and the federal legislation going back to the McFadden Act 1927. However it was not in respect of branching but in connection with the ability of banks to spread themselves geographically through the agency of bank holding companies that the main change has been taking place. Originally bank holding companies largely escaped from regulatory surveillance. This was remedied by the Bank Holding Company Act 1956. The 1970 Douglas Amendment to the latter declared that the interstate acquisition of a bank by a bank holding company was prohibited, unless specifically authorised by the state of the target bank. According to Kenneth Spong, since states had no such laws, interstate banking expansion was prohibited, although there were some interstate banks already in existence whose position was 'grandfathered'—i.e. their existing structure was not disturbed.[17]

More recently however this geographical confinement of bank expansion has been modified by virtue of the fact that states have introduced laws which permit interstate banking. Some of these laws have taken a reciprocal form as between states. It should also be noted that some such interstate banking pacts were constructed in a way which excluded eastern (i.e. New York) banks. This was challenged, but in 1985 the Supreme Court declared that this exclusionary element did not violate the constitution—this has undoubtedly encouraged the inter-state banking movement.

Thirdly, we noted that in 1980 by virtue of the Depository Institutions Deregulation and Monetary Control Act thrift institutions (savings and loan associations) were allowed greater flexibility in the range of their permitted business. This liberalising tendency has also been apparent in state regulation as, for example, the Californian legislature which in 1983 passed the Nolan Bill which allowed thrift institutions to broaden their investment activities.

The reader will recollect that federal regulation of security dealing was a product of the 1930s and was a response to the stock market crash of 1929 and after. Under the Securities Exchange Act 1934 the SEC was given a supervisory power over the stock exchanges. In practice this gave rise to a system of self-regulation since for many years the SEC largely left matters of internal conduct to the exchanges themselves and exercised only a general oversight. However the SEC did possess specific controlling powers and, as the reader will also recollect, in 1968, following a Department of Justice probe concerning the inflexibility of the NYSE minimum brokerage system, the SEC stepped in. As a result of its pressure a volume discount was introduced together with negotiated rates on portions of orders over $500,000. In 1972 the latter figure was reduced to $300,000. Then in 1975 the SEC made explicit use of its rule making power to abolish the fixed commission system. In the same year Congress passed the Securities Acts Amendments, which required a national market system in which competitive forces would play a much bigger role—rate fixing was banned.[18]

Until 1984 deregulation in radio and TV was not accompanied by a deregulatory statute. Instead the regulatory agency, the FCC, which initially protected the *status quo*, eventually accepted the newer technologies and removed many of the restraints which had been imposed upon them. It should be added that the process of deregulation was further assisted by the courts, which refused to accept some of the rulings which had been imposed on the newer technological developments.

The *status quo* was the system of over-the-air broadcasting by TV and radio. The most interesting issues arose in connection with the former. The new technologies which challenged the broadcast TV system (in which the networks and their stations plus the affiliated stations had a vested interest) were CATV (Community Antenna TV—cable for short), subscription or pay TV (STV for short) and direct to home satellite broadcasting (DBS for short).

Let us begin with cable. During the 1950s cable TV was uncontroversial. There were areas where for one reason or another reception was poor or non-existent or choice was limited. Cable could perform a valuable role in picking up signals in good reception locations and piping them into deprived geographical areas. The broadcasters could have no objection to this since it would increase audiences and advertising revenue potential. However cable had other possibilities. It had a considerable signal carrying capacity and apart from carrying local signals, it could also import distant signals, thus increasing viewer choice. These distant signals could be imported by microwave (and in due course would be beamed down by satellites and then hooked up to a local cable distribution network). The greater choice which cable's distant signals provided was likely to attract audiences away from the advertising revenue offerings provided by broadcasters, and therefore they sought to restrict its development.

The politically powerful broadcasters adopted a two-pronged attack. Firstly, they sought to challenge cable in the courts on the grounds that the importing of distant signals infringed the copyright of programme producers. Secondly, they pressed the FCC to restrict the development of cable.

However they hit two snags. In *United Artists* v. *Fortnightly Corporation* (1966) the district court handling the case held that importing distant signals without a licence was a violation of the 1909 Copyright Act, but on appeal the Supreme Court reversed the ruling. It held that a transmission by cable was not a performance and therefore did not infringe copyright.[19] In the case of the FCC the original snag was that it declined to exercise a regulatory role in respect of cable. However in its *Carter Mountain Transmission Corporation* decision it changed its mind, and decided to assert a jursidiction over common carrier microwave systems serving cable companies. This was followed in 1965 by the adoption by the FCC of rules governing the grant of microwave authorisation to be used in connection with the relaying of TV signals to cable systems. Then in 1966, with some hesitancy as to its exact authority, it decided to assume regulatory authority over the cable TV system itself[20] and, responding to the pressures of the broadcasters, it imposed substantial restrictions on the fledgling industry. The attitude of those who were in the ascendant in the FCC was that cable was merely a supplementary service—the prime need was to protect the existing broadcasting system. The new rules were as follows. A cable system had upon request to carry the signals of all local stations in its vicinity. The FCC in effect froze all cable systems in the top 100 markets since, whilst existing imports of distant signals were permitted, further importations were banned without a hearing. The FCC also took the view that a failure to pay royalties for distant signals caused economic injury to broadcasting.[21]

As we indicated in Chapter 4, the cable system held out considerable attractions for the public and its possibilities caught the public imagination. According to Bruce Owen, another factor which portended change was the growing political strength of the cable interests.[22] Eventually some sort of compromise, which would allow cable to make an increasing mark, was inevitable, and in 1972 new rules to that effect were promulgated. Whilst they heralded the beginning of the opening up of TV to greater competition, they did not involve a complete liberalisation.

Elaborate rules were laid down which guaranteed the position of the networks and limited the number of signals which could be imported from independents. Thus in the top 50 markets the following had to apply. A cable system had to take all the local stations. It had to carry all non-local stations which were significantly viewed. It could import independent distant signals but the end result had to satisfy the condition that there were at least three network stations plus three independents. The imported signals were subject to an anti-leapfrogging rule which required cable systems to take the nearest qualifying distant signal. This was supposed to be designed to encourage localism—a topic we discussed in Chapter 3. There was also an exclusivity rule—if a local station had exclusive rights then that programme had to be blacked out of any importations. Rules were also prescribed concerning own programming and public interest programming. The position of copyright was ultimately resolved under the Copyright Act 1976—a cable transmission was deemed to be a performance. Cable systems were granted a compulsory licence and had to pay a percentage of their revenues as a fee for importation.

As we have already seen, the 1970s were characterised by a growing mood in favour of deregulation. In 1979 the Supreme Court upheld a lower court ruling of 1978 removing the own programming and public interest rules imposed on cable. Even the FCC was not unresponsive to the change of atmosphere. In 1980 it took two steps when it abolished the restrictions on the importation of distant signals and the exclusivity rule. However not all restrictions were removed—for example, the requirement to carry all local stations remained in place. It should be noted that the declining effective resistance to change on the part of traditional broadcasting interests was probably influenced by the fact that they could and did themselves enter into cable activities, although that too was subject to restrictions designed to preserve competition—see Chapter 3.

In 1984 Congress passed the Cable Telecommunications Act which gave the cable interests much of what they wanted in terms of a free hand including the phasing out of rate regulation. However, not everything was immediately swept away since the requirement that cable operators had to carry all local TV signals persisted although, as Jeremy Tunstall points out, within a year this rule had been struck down by the Federal Court of Appeals.[23] The deregulatory mood also extended to direct to home satellite broadcasting of which the FCC officially approved in 1981.

Another development to which the FCC was originally opposed was STV. Conventional TV stations can broadcast a scrambled signal and charge viewers for using the technology to decode it—viewers can be periodically billed or can use coins in a slot. The preference of the FCC for a free system was referred to in Chapter 4. Up to 1968 the FCC had refused to authorise any STV system except on an experimental basis.[24] However in 1968 it granted a general authorisation but then once more 'committed infanticide by regulation'.[25] This took the form of the imposition of rules which entirely banned the broadcast for pay of series programming, commercials, virtually all major sports events and, with few exceptions, any theatrical feature film that had been released more than two years previously.[26] In 1970 similar rules were also applied to cable! These 'antisiphoning' provisions helped to prevent STV and cable companies from bidding for films and sports events and therefore kept down the price to broadcasters. They were in due course challenged by the Department of Justice and those affected in *Home Box Office* v. *FCC*. The Court of Appeals for the District of Columbia Circuit decided that they should be rescinded.[27] Another barrier to change had gone down.

The most recent competitive influence has been DBS. Satellites in communications are not new. Their original major role was in international telecommunications. The US COMSAT was a majority participant in the *international* telecommunications satellite organisation INTELSAT, and interestingly AT & T was a major shareholder in COMSAT. (In passing it should be noted that AT & T had a dominant position in international terrestrial communications—i.e. ocean cable). The next stage in the development of the satellite was its application to *domestic* telecommunications. A major step in this field was taken by the FCC in 1972 when it decided that domestic satellite activities should be based on competition, and indeed by 1984 it is reported that seven separate groups were engaged in commercial operations.[28]

As we have seen, the networks in TV (and radio) have generally been opposed to the opening up of the system to competition. However, when in 1972 the FCC opted for satellite competition, the networks were all in favour since they saw satellites as a cheaper method of relaying their TV signals than the microwave system supplied by AT & T. Satellite systems of course came to play an important role in cable, and ultimately they made a powerful impact by virtue of the fact that technology (which had been in existence since the 1960s) enabled signals to be bounced off satellites directly down into homes which possessed the requisite dish antenna. The latter had been deregulated by the FCC in 1979—Jeremy Tunstall points out that this equipment had facilitated pirated (i.e. unpaid) reception from satellites.[29] In 1980 the FCC was approached by the Satellite TV Corporation—a subsidiary of COMSAT—to provide a DBS service. The FCC in a highly deregulatory mood in fact granted no less than 13 applications—slots were to be allocated later. The first DBS service became available in 1983. During that year the FCC authorised additional satellites and in 1984 completely deregulated domestic satellite services. Operators could alter rates and services without having to get FCC approval.

Mention should also be made of certain deregulatory moves in programme content regulation in both radio and TV. In 1979 rules regarding commercials and public affairs content in radio were dropped and in 1983 a similar move was made in respect of TV. Jeremy Tunstall has also pointed out that ownership rules have been relaxed—e.g. the number of VHF TV stations allowed to a single owner has been increased and the rules relating to broadcast ownership of cable have been relaxed. Franchise periods have been lengthened and renewal procedures have been modified in ways which favour the incumbent. According to Tunstall, many more commercial TV stations have been licensed, particularly independent ones who in the past helped to undermine the system, and hundreds of additional radio stations have appeared on the scene.[30] Multiplicity and possibly greater choice, thanks in considerable measure to the outpourings from DBS, appear now to be the order of the day. The emergence of a fourth network—Fox—should also be noted.

The course of events in telecommunications was in some degree similar to that in TV broadcasting. Technological changes occurred, some of which were also operative in broadcasting, which threatened the *status quo*—the latter of course being in the main the dominating position held by the Bell System. The initial reponse of Bell, aided and abetted by the FCC, was either to resist such changes or to embrace them and thus to preempt competitive entry. However in due course competition was allowed to make incursions into Bell's position but without the aid of a deregulatory statute. A major difference from broadcasting is that more recently there was a major antitrust restructuring of the dominant enterprise.

The reader will recollect that the vertically integrated Bell empire was not an absolute monopoly. Nevertheless via the Bell Operating Companies it played a very powerful role in the local telephone system. It was dominant in the long lines business and was vertically integrated backwards into equipment manufacturing via Western Electric.

The reader will also recollect that telecommunications has thrown up a major problem for regulators and for those who have wished to see more competition. The problem, as we noted in Chapter 4, was whether the Bell System as a whole was a natural monopoly. Almarin Phillips, it will be recalled, claimed that Bell is subject to increasing returns and it was therefore folly to allow new entrants provided Bell was willing to embrace new technology. A study of the history of Bell's response to new ideas (see below) can leave the reader doubting whether Bell would have been disposed to embrace change if it had not been forced by competition to do so. That then posed the question of how, if the Bell system was a natural monopoly, it was nevertheless possible to keep it on its technological toes. A permanent queue of potential entrants sounds attractive but if they had never been let in Bell would have almost certainly have ceased to regard them as a credible threat. Moreover if they had never been let in it is likely that they would have eventually lost heart. This suggests that if there was doubt about Bell's willingness to innovate, whilst it enjoyed a dominating position, then some actual competitive entry was necessary. There was also another issue. Bell was disposed to resist every change—even the apparently relatively innocuous (see below). However it was possible to imagine that some areas could be subjected to competition without really endangering the static natural monopoly core.

We will begin by considering the regulatory response in two areas—the long distance section and terminal equipment. Originally, as we pointed out in Chapter 3, long line communication took place by wire. Subsequently microwave technology came on the scene and it together with satellites came to dominate the stage. After the second World War a number of firms constructed microwave facilities in order to transmit TV signals. Bell then responded with a crash programme of facilities, and was able to dominate the industry by virtue of a number of factors.

Firstly, it appears to have persuaded the FCC that TV signals should be carried by common carriers whenever common carrier capacity was sufficient to provide the service. The competitors were therefore eventually forced to exit from the industry. Secondly, it severely incommoded its main common carrier rival, Western Union, by refusing to interconnect with it and the FCC did not overturn this policy. Bell argued that a monopoly was necessary if a nationwide service was required and cream skimming on profitable routes would undermine its ability to carry out the necessary rate averaging policy.[31]

By the early 1960s a number of firms were pressing to enter the private microwave business—they argued that they could provide a service at costs considerably below common carrier tariffs. In 1959 the FCC responded to a request by two North Dakota TV stations to be allowed to construct microwave facilities *for their own use*. In a historic decision, the FCC acceded. The commission decided that there were sufficient frequencies above 890 megacycles to provide for the present and future needs of private users as well as the common carriers. This is usually referred to as the *Above 890 Decision*. As we have emphasised, the decision merely allowed firms to provide a service for themselves.

It was inevitable that firms would then begin to press the

FCC to be allowed to provide facilities for other business users—in other words to become common carriers. One such firm, Microwave Communications Inc. (MCI), sought permission to operate a private line service between St. Louis and Chicago. Bell opposed the request but the FCC, after six years delay, granted it in 1969 and also required Bell to interconnect. In so doing Commissioner Nicholas Johnson is reported as saying 'I am still looking, at this juncture, for ways to add a little salt and pepper of competition to the rather tasteless stew of regulatory protection that this Commission and Ma Bell have cooked up.'[32] This is a good indicator of a changed disposition on the part of the regulatory body. Other firms were subsequently allowed to provide what are called specialised common carrier services by virtue of the *Specialised Common Carriers* decision of 1971.

It will come as no surprise to learn that Bell did not take all the microwave developments lying down. It filed cut-price tariffs which in turn provoked investigations by the FCC concerning their fairness—a highly technical matter. After some delay Bell was forced to make modifications.[33]

Other deregulation initiatives occurred in the 1970s and 1980s. In the early 1970s the FCC decided that most combinations of communications services and computing were not common carriage of the kind subject to the Communications Act 1934. It allowed communications carriers to provide computer services on an unregulated basis provided that they did so through 'fully separate' subsidiaries. In 1980 the FCC devised a computer service solution in respect of the Bell system. In the same year it also decided that non-dominating communications carriers ought not to be subjected to rate, service, entry and exit regulation—as a result regulatory requirements were greatly reduced or eliminated.[34]

Bell also opposed developments on the terminal equipment front. It had always opposed interfacing with equipment which it did not provide. It objected to a device called a Hush-a-Phone which was attached to the telephone mouthpiece in order to provide privacy in communication. The FCC supported Bell but in 1956 a federal appeal court rejected the restriction. Despite this Bell continued to adopt a restrictive attitude and matters were brought to a head in the 1968

Carterfone decision. Without electrical connection the Carterfone device linked up a telephone handset with a local two-way radio. Bell opposed it as an 'alien attachment' but the FCC found that the device did not adversely effect the telephone system. This, together with the *Hush-a-Phone* decision, helped to allow entry into the terminal equipment industry. Follow-up decisions in the 1970s further liberalised the terminal equipment market. To facilitate the process the FCC devised technical standards which would protect the national telephone system from harm. Equipment which had been registered with the FCC and certified as not harmful could automatically be attached.

A major development was the recent antitrust action against AT & T (i.e. Bell) which led to the 1982 consent decree. This involved a significant restructuring. A Sherman Act suit was launched by the Department of Justice in 1974—the suit sought to force AT & T to divest itself of both Western Electric and the local telephone companies (i.e. the Bell Operating Companies). In practice what happened was that the local operating companies were separated off—they will continue to offer local services on a regulated natural monopoly basis. Bell will continue as a 'competitive' equipment supplier and as a regulated long lines (interstate and intrastate) operator. The fact that the local operating companies are separated off means that they will have no automatic requirement to use AT & T's long lines service or to buy Western Electric's equipment.

Finally mention must be made of a significant change which has been occurring in recent years. We refer to unbundling, whereby separate charges are made for individual products and services. When prices are not unbundled consumers are not aware of the costs of individual items. Apart from assisting consumers it also helps to facilitate competition.

2 PRIVATISATION

At the time of writing, only one of the privatisation measures at federal level mentioned in Chapter 4 has been carried through—namely Conrail. In 1984 it was reported that Transport Secretary Elizabeth Dole had accepted an offer of £1.2 billion for an eighty-five per cent stake from a rival railway—Norfolk Southern. However this sparked off a series of objections inside and outside Congress. It was objected that the bid was too low—expert analysts felt that it was worth substantially more. It was also pointed out that competition would be reduced if a rival railway was able to take Conrail over. This particular move having been blocked, it was decided to proceed by way of an offer to the public. This was accomplished in 1987, the government, taking advantage of a bull market, was able to raise a net $1.6 billion. As for the two federally owned airports (Washington's Dulles and National), they were reported to be badly in need of modernisation and federal funds were not likely to be forthcoming. The FAA originally proposed that they should be sold off to a regional body which would be able to issue bonds in order to raise modernisation cash. This proposal, although it would have raised funds for the federal government, was not a privatisation but a transfer of assets within the public sector. In fact the proposal was not proceeded with—instead the airports are to be leased.

NOTES

1. H. Dym and R. M. Sussman, 'Antitrust and Electricity Utility Regulation', *The Antitrust Bulletin*, Spring (1983), pp.74–6.
2. P. W. MacAvoy *op. cit.*, pp.107–11.
3. D. D. Anderson, 'State Regulation of Electric Utilities' in J. Q. Wilson (ed.), *The Politics of Regulation, op. cit.*, pp.32–8.
4. L. W. Weiss, 'State Regulation of Public Utilities and Marginal-cost Pricing' in L. W. Weiss and M. W. Klass (eds), *Case Studies in Regulation* (Little, Brown, Boston, 1981), pp.285–90.
5. D. D. Anderson *op. cit.*, pp.26–32.
6. P. W. MacAvoy *op. cit.*, p.112.
7. 555 F2d 852, 1977.
8. P. W. MacAvoy *op. cit.*, p.114.
9. R. R. Braeutigam, 'The Deregulation of Natural Gas' in L. W. Weiss and M. W. Klass (eds), *Case Studies of Regulation, op. cit.*, pp.142–86.
10. M. T. Farris, 'Evolution of the Transport Regulatory Structure of the US', *International Journal of Transportation Economics*, 10 (1983), p.191.

11. T. Gale Moore, 'Rail and Truck Reform—the Record So Far', *Regulation*, Nov/Dec 1983, p.34. See also B. J. Allen, 'Nature and Implications of the "Partial Deregulation" of the Railroad Industry in the United States', *International Journal of Transport Economics*, 10 (1983), pp.373–84.

12. The flavour of such changes in airline and trucking regulation respectively can be derived from E. E. Bailey, 'Deregulation and Regulatory Reform of U.S. Air-Transportation Policy' in B. M. Mitchell and P. R. Kleindorfer (eds) *Regulated Industries and Public Enterprise* (Lexington, Lexington, Massachusetts, 1980), pp.29–56; T. E. Keeler, 'The Revolution in Airline Regulation' in L. W. Weiss and M. W. Klass (eds), *Case Studies of Regulation, op. cit.*, pp.6–9; M. Alexis, 'Progress and Prospects of Regulatory Reform in Surface Transportation in T. G. Gies and W. Sichel (eds), *Deregulation: Appraisal Before the Fact. op. cit.*, pp.51–74.

13. D. L. Flexner, 'The Effects of Deregulation in the Motor Carrier Industry', *The Antitrust Bulletin*, 28 (1983), pp.185–200.

14. M. T. Farris *op. cit.*, p.193.

15. US Department of Transportation, *CAB Sunset Seminar: Future Administration of the International Aviation Functions of the CAB*, Vol. 2, (Washington, 1983).

16. E. G. Corrigan, 'A Look at the Economy and Some Banking Issues', *Federal Reserve Bank of New York Quarterly Review*, 10/1 (1985), p.5.

17. K. Spong, *Banking Regulation: Its Purposes, Implementation and Effects* (Federal Reserve Bank of Kansas City, Kansas, 1985), pp.110–13.

18. H. R. Stoll, 'Revolution in the Regulation of Securities Markets: An Examination of the Effects of Increased Competition', in L. W. Weiss and M. W. Klass, *Case Studies of Regulation, op. cit.*, pp.12–52.

19. 392 U.S. 390 (1968).

20. W. B. Emery, *Broadcasting and Government*, (Michigan State University Press, Michigan, 1971), pp.200–1.

21. D. Gujarati *op. cit.*, p.419.

22. B. M. Owen, 'The Rise and Fall of Cable Television Regulation', in L. W. Weiss and M. W. Klass, *Case Studies of Regulation, op. cit.*, pp.86–101.

23. J. Tunstall, *Communications Deregulation* (Basil Blackwell, Oxford, 1986), p.139.

24. S. M. Besen, T. G. Krattenmaker, A. R. Metzger and J. R. Woodbury, *Misregulating Television* (University of Chicago Press, Chicago, 1984), p.11

25. *Ibid.*, *loc. cit.*

26. *Ibid.*, *loc. cit.*

27. D. C. Cir. Ct. No. 75–1280, *et al.*, 25 March 1977, *cert. den.*, 46 USLW 3190 (1977).

28. J. Tunstall *op. cit.*, p.69.

29. *Ibid.*, p.77.

30. *Ibid.*, pp.146–7.

31. B. M. Owen and R. Braeutigam, *The Regulation Game: Strategic Use of the Administrative Process* (Ballinger, Cambridge, Massachusetts, 1978), p.208.
32. Quoted in L. W. Weiss and A. D. Strickland, *Regulation: A Case Approach* (McGraw Hill, New York, 1976), p.195.
33. B. M. Owen and R. Braeutigam *op. cit.*, pp.208–30.
34. D. I. Baker and B. G. Baker, 'Antitrust and Communications Deregulation', *The Antitrust Bulletin*, Spring (1983), pp.4–6.

Part III
Evolution of Policy in the United Kingdom

6 Public Enterprise and Economic Regulation in Practice

1 THE SCOPE OF PUBLIC ENTERPRISE

In Chapter 1 we provided a brief sketch of the growth of public enterprise. In this Chapter we begin by tracing that growth in more detail in order to identify the individual components of the public enterprise sector which were in principle available for privatisation by the post 1979 Thatcher governments. As we indicated earlier, some public enterprise existed prior to the bout of nationalisation in the immediate post-war period. Some of it was associated with the municipalities and emerged in the 'gas and water socialism' era which was a feature of policy in the late nineteenth century. The rest was, as we pointed out earlier, largely a product of a relatively new organisation called the public corporation. The nature of that body and the controls which the state placed upon it will be discussed later in this chapter.

Immediately pre-war about a third of gas supply was the responsibility of municipal undertakings, as opposed to private companies.[1] The situation in electricity was more complicated since the industry falls into three parts—production, transmission and distribution. At the production end the municipalities' share of sales was about fifty-seven per cent and their share of capacity was about sixty-six per cent.[2] Transmission was dominated by the Central Electricity Board (CEB) which was created under the Electricity Supply Act of 1926. It constructed a grid which interconnected power stations. Under the Board's aegis, power generation was concentrated in the hands of the large and more up-to-date stations (both municipal and private). The Board bought power from the generators and sold it in bulk to the distributors (both municipal and private).[3] By the 1930s about eighty per cent of water supply was in the hands of local government, local water boards, etc.

The public corporation seems to have made its modern debut in 1908 with the creation of the Port of London Authority.[4] Important further developments were the creation in 1926 of the British Broadcasting Corporation (BBC) and the CEB (discussed above). In 1933 the whole complex of transport in Greater London, comprising the underground railways, the Metropolitan Railway, the bus, trolley-bus and tram services (both public and private), were handed over to a public corporation, the London Passenger Transport Board (LPTB).[5] The architect of the scheme was Herbert Morrison,[6] whose views on the role of public enterprise were in due course to be highly influential. We must also mention the British Overseas Airways Corporation (BOAC) which was created in 1939.

It was under the Attlee Labour government of 1945–51 that public ownership, under the aegis of the public corporation, came to exercise a really significant role in the British economy. Labour took into public ownership (nationalised) the Bank of England, together with the coal (under the National Coal Board (NCB)—now referred to as British Coal), electricity and gas industries—in all instances paralleling French experience. It is worth mentioning at this point that in later years the gas industry shifted from the production of town gas to the importation of liquid gas, and eventually to the extraction of natural gas and oil mainly under the North Sea. The railways, their docks, ships, hotels and restaurants, together with canals and inland waterways, were likewise nationalised. All this, together with the LPTB, was vested in the British Transport Commission (BTC). It was also required to take into public ownership all enterprises predominantly engaged in long distance road haulage. As if this was not enough, the BTC was further required to take over the extensive interests which the railways had acquired in road passenger transport (buses and coaches), and it was given power to acquire further such undertakings. This was to be Morrisonian co-ordination with a vengeance! The iron and steel industry was also taken into public ownership in the form of the Iron and Steel Corporation. Airline nationalisation was extended to include internal services—some of the external services were divided between the BOAC and the short-lived British South American Airways Corporation. Internal and European routes were the province of British European Airways (BEA). Later internal and international services were merged within British Airways.

Prior to coming to power in 1951, the Conservative party, both by its action in Parliament and by means of its election manifestos, indicated its dedicated opposition to nationalisation. However it did not propose totally to roll back the frontiers of the state. Rather it declared that it would undertake no further nationalisation and would denationalise steel, road freight transport and the purchase of raw cotton.[7] The nationalisation of steel had been bitterly contested. Whilst the Conservatives had not been happy about the other acts of public ownership, they had to recognise that some of the industries involved were already partly publicly owned, had in some cases been subject to significant state interference, or had been thought of as possible candidates for nationalisation by various committees which had no doctrinal axe to grind. Perhaps the party also recognised what had become apparent to ministers, namely that some of the nationalised industries were a 'poor bag of assets'[8] for which the former owners had been handsomely compensated. However, except in the mind of the Labour Party and its supporters, steel had not been regarded as a prime candidate for nationalisation. The nationalisation of steel was indeed regarded as the thin edge of the wedge—if steel could be nationalised, where would it all end? The Conservatives therefore denationalised steel in 1953, although they provided for a degree of control over price and investment policies by creating a supervisory Iron and Steel Board.[9] In the same year an act was passed to denationalise the BTC stake in road haulage. As things transpired only part of the industry was disposed of by the specially created Road Haulage Disposal Board and, following a change of mind, a further act was passed in 1956 putting an end to further haulage denationalisation. The unsold rump of road haulage stayed with the BTC as British Road Services.

Whilst the Conservatives were doctrinally opposed to further nationalisation, they did go on to create yet further public corporations—notable among these were the Atomic Energy Authority (AEA), the Independent Television Authority (ITA), both created in 1954, and the Sugar Board, established in 1957. The AEA was to be responsible for the acquisition, production and disposal of radioactive substances, and for the designing of prototype nuclear power stations.[10] The ITA was to preside over the provision of television services alongside the BBC. Its function was to provide broadcasting facilities, and could if necessary produce programmes itself although in practice this role was assigned to private programme contractors whom it regulated.[11] The Sugar Board was the culmination of a long history of state intervention in the British sugar beet industry. The British Sugar Corporation (BSC) had been established in 1936 as a result of the amalgamation of a number of sugar beet companies. Whilst the Board came to be classed as a public corporation, BSC was a limited company with private shareholders. Interestingly, the chairman and two directors were nominated by the government and the articles of association provided (a) for government control of the activities of the company and (b) for financial assistance to be provided by the Board.[12] When the National Economic Development Office (NEDO) reported on the nationalised industries in 1976, the Treasury were shown to be holding 11.2 per cent of the voting capital of BSC.[13]

The return of Labour between 1964 and 1970 did not greatly extend the scope of public ownership *as compared with that achieved by the Attlee government*. In 1966 the British Airports Authority (BAA) was brought into being. But it did not extend the boundaries of public ownership since the main initial task of the Airport Authority Act 1965 was to transfer four airports from direct state control to the BAA (they were Heathrow, Gatwick, Stanstead and Prestwick). In addition several regional airports were transferred from central government to local authorities.[14] Likewise the Transport Act 1968, which created Passenger Transport Executives (classified as public corporations) was not designed to transfer assets to the public sector. Rather what the act did was to create Passenger Transport Authorities, who took over the municipal bus fleets in their areas of operation, and co-ordinated them with the operation, in and out, of National Bus[15] and the private bus companies. The actual execution of policy was in the hands of the executives who also handled the control of fares and subsidisation which might extend to local rail passenger services.[16]

Nor did changes at the Post Office involve any extension of public ownership. Although the Post Office formally became a public corporation in 1969, all that happened was that the assets, previously managed by a government department under a minister responsible to Parliament, were transferred to the new and separate corporation. It should be added that those assets included those concerned with the postal service (the latter goes back to 1840 when the Penny Post was intro-duced) and also those concerned with the telegraph service (taken into public ownership in 1870) and the telephone service (taken into public ownership in 1912). It is also worth mentioning in passing that in 1961 the Post Office had been allowed greater freedom of action and was thereafter classi-fied as a public corporation.[17] The only major contribution of the Labour party to changing the balance between private and public activity was the decision to renationalise the steel industry in 1967 and to take into public ownership via the Transport Holding Company some road haulage and road passenger enterprises. In the case of steel the leading fourteen firms were taken back into public ownership, thus giving rise to the British Steel Corporation—some smaller firms were left in private hands.[18]

The Heath Conservative administration of 1970–74 made it clear that it wished to disengage from industry. Some indi-cation of this view was manifested in its decision to abolish the Industrial Reorganisation Corporation. This body had been created by the previous Labour government to sponsor mergers (and it was this aspect which dominated its activities) but it also had powers which could have led to significant state investment in industry.[19] The initial Heath posture could also have heralded widespread denationalisation but in the event it did not go down that path. The government did sell off its stake in Carlisle and Scottish public houses as well as two travel agents (Lunn-Poly and Thomas Cook and Sons). However this could hardly be regarded as a meaningful attempt to push back the frontiers of the state! The government also announced that it would not rescue 'lame ducks' but was then faced with financial crises at Upper Clyde Shipbuilders (UCS) and Rolls Royce and was forced to make a U-turn in policy. UCS was itself the product of a rationalisation merger of three rival shipbuilding companies. The merger had been forced upon the companies as the price for receiving aid from the Shipbuilding Industry Board under the previous Labour administration. UCS was soon in difficulties again, was given further aid by the Heath government and (reconstructed as Govan Shipbuilders) was ultimately nationalised—see below. The aero engine aspect of Rolls Royce was taken into public ownership—the government acquiring a 100 per cent stake in Rolls Royce (1971).

Mention should also be made of the Water Act 1973. It transferred responsibility for supplying water from local authorities, local water boards, etc., to regional water authorities which from 1974 were categorised as public corporations. The old statutory water companies remained in existence and therefore there was no transfer of assets from private to public.

Under the succeeding Labour government (1974–9) more public corporations and more public ownership entered on the scene. In 1975 the government set up a new interventionist body—the National Enterprise Board (NEB). This public corporation was originally conceived as a state holding company which would 'introduce public ownership into the strongholds of private industry'[20]—clearly there was to be a parallel here with French and Italian experience. It was anticipated that the NEB would seek a commercial rate of return on its participations. In other words it would be seeking to invest in success. In the event a good deal of the government resources made available to it were tied up with enterprises rescued by the Labour government and the previous Conservative administration. These included 100 per cent equity stakes in Rolls Royce (1971), British Leyland, Ferranti, Alfred Herbert and Data Recording Instruments as well as minority shareholdings in a number of other companies including International Computer (Holdings).[21]

In addition Labour had to cope with the consequences of the international recession as it affected international trade and therefore the demand for ships. The British shipbuilding industry, which was in difficulties prior to the recession, now reeled under the impact of a shortage of orders and intense competition.[22] The response of the government was contained in the Aircraft and Shipbuilding Act 1977—it chose to nationalise the major shipbuilding, ship repairing and marine engineering companies. Twenty-seven companies were named in the schedule to the act including famous names such as Cammell Laird, Govan, Scott Lithgow, Swan Hunter, Yarrow and Austin Pickersgill. There thus came into existence British Shipbuilders. The 1977 Act also created another nationalised concern in the shape of British Aerospace. The latter absorbed the aircraft, guided weapons and space engineering interests of the British Aircraft Corporation, Hawker Syddeley Aviation, Hawker Syddeley Dynamics, Scottish Aviation and Sperry Gyroscope. In addition the government established the British National Oil Corporation (BNOC) in 1976. BNOC was formed to explore for and extract oil and gas in the North Sea, to discharge a regulatory role, and to collect royalties from other oil companies.[23] All these were public corporations, fully owned by the government as opposed to equity participations in limited companies.

As we noted earlier, in 1976 NEDO produced a study of UK nationalised industries. It listed the public corporations then in existence and these are laid out in Appendix Table 1. It estimated that they contributed eleven per cent of the Gross Domestic Product (GDP) and were responsible for eight per cent of employment. It should be added that whilst NEDO was aware of the decisions to nationalise shipbuilding and aerospace, the data contained in the appendix table do not include their contribution. Nor does Appendix Table 1 show that there were quite a number of limited companies (other than those in which the NEB was involved) where the government had, directly or indirectly, equity stakes. Apart from the British Sugar Corporation, which we have already mentioned, the Treasury had a 48.2 per cent stake in the equity of British Petroleum, the AEA had a 100 per cent stake in British Nuclear Fuels and the Radiochemicals Centre and a thirty per cent involvement in the National Nuclear Corporation, whilst the Northern Ireland Office had 47.6 per cent of Harland and Wolff. There were others.[24]

By virtue of taking account of items not included by NEDO, Richard Pryke estimated the GDP contribution of public enterprises in 1977 as being 12.7 per cent and the employment share as 9.4 per cent.[25] It should be added that these corporate assets were not the only ones which were available for privatisation. In addition various government departments were involved in productive activities which could be sold off—e.g. the Royal Ordnance Factories and the Royal Dockyards. All this, with some exceptions, constituted the bulk of the potentially privatisable inheritance of the post 1979 Thatcher governments.

2   THE NATURE OF THE PUBLIC CORPORATION

Public enterprise is an overall term for public ownership. It includes both public corporations wholly owned by the state and public limited companies (Companies Act companies) in which the state has a stake, often a controlling one. As we have seen, the public corporation was the overwhelmingly dominant vehicle of public ownership in the post-war period.

Since our main focus is upon the public corporation, we may begin by asking what have been its main characteristics?

i   It is established by statute and cannot cease trading without Parliamentary approval. In other words it cannot be declared insolvent and wound up as is the case with a Companies Act company.

ii   It is managed by an independent board appointed by the sponsoring minister. The board members are not civil servants. Moreover they are appointed for fixed periods, whereas civil servants may hope to have tenure in their profession. Equally the public corporation's employees are not civil servants.

iii A public corporation will normally have no private

shareholders. The assets are in public ownership. Robson's way of putting it was that 'The equity is owned by the nation'.[26]

iv   Robson, in his analysis of post-war public ownership up to the mid-1960s, stressed the freedom which the founding fathers hoped public corporations would enjoy from political interference, notably in their day-to-day activities. This did not mean that the public corporation would be totally free from political interference. Ministers could exercise some control, Parliamentarians could ask questions and get ministerial answers to some of them, and Parliament could discuss general policy.

v   Robson also drew attention to the characteristic of disinterestedness *on the part of the early post-war nationalised industries*. A public purpose was specified in the nationalisation statute and the serving of the public interest rather than a narrow pursuit of profit was central to the ethos of the public corporations. Maximisation of profits was no part of its function. Rather a minimalist philosophy was adopted whereby the revenues of the nationalised concerns should be sufficient to enable them to pay their way taking good years with bad. The detail of this arrangement is discussed below as is its modification over time in favour of a more commercial approach.

vi   Robson also drew attention to the corporation's self-contained finances. They were divorced from the general budget. That does not however mean that there was no ministerial or Treasury control in matters such as borrowing.

We must now deal with some distinctions which are largely semantic. Firstly, it appears that all nationalised industries were public corporations but that not all public corporations were nationalised industries. Nationalised industries were public corporations which were engaged in trading activities of some kind and derived their revenues, or a major part thereof, from the sale of goods and services to customers rather than from government grants. Thus in 1968 the House of Commons Select Committee on Nationalised Industries, whilst accepting that both the Bank of England and the BBC were public corporations, noted that the Bank of England derived its revenue from interest paid by customers etc., whereas the BBC did not derive a licence income *directly* from the public. The Bank of England was therefore deemed to be a nationalised industry whereas the BBC was not. If, as Rosemary Levacic points out, the BBC had sold its licences directly to the public it would have qualified as a nationalised industry.[27]

The other semantic point relates to activities such as the Royal Ordnance Factories and the Royal Dockyards. The former came to be financed by a trading fund under the Government Trading Funds Act 1973—indeed some commentators refer to such activities as trading funds. The Royal Dockyards were not given this status. In the final analysis these two bodies were parts of government departments and were under the management of civil servants. Clearly they did not satisfy the public corporation criteria listed above. Nevertheless, as Rosemary Levacic points out, *for statistical purposes* they were classed as public corporations.

There is one other point which needs to be clarified. On page 196 above we drew attention to the public corporations, equity stakes in Companies Act companies, trading funds and other departmental activities in existence in the mid-1970s, and observed that they constituted 'with some exceptions' the bulk of the privatisable inheritance which awaited the post-1979 Thatcher governments. The qualification 'with some exceptions' refers primarily to the fact that whilst most of the above had a trading potential which made them possible bases for private enterprise activity, some public corporations did not fall into that category. We are of course drawing attention to the few public corporations that performed administrative/coordinating/regulatory roles—an example being the Passenger Transport Executives.

3 THE STATE AND PUBLIC ENTERPRISE

The original stance of the state in its relationship with public enterprise was one of maintaining an arms-length relationship. The architect of the immediate post-war nationalisation programme was Herbert Morrison. His views about the proper relationship of the state to its public industries was revealed in his book *Socialisation and Transport* (1933).[28] His philosophy arose out of his experience in searching for an appropriate organisation for London's transport—a quest which, as we noted earlier, ultimately led to the setting up of the LPTB. Morrison rejected inter-modal competition as wasteful—his arguments are not wholly convincing but that is another matter. Rather he looked towards a solution based on coordination—a division of labour which would arise by means of administrative action, when all the competing assets were vested in one public corporation, rather than from the process of competitive selection. Morrison also believed that public corporations should be managed by men of proven business experience. Having established such an expert board, the government should let them get on with the job. Morrison's emphasis on the need for professionalism at board level also led him to reject the idea that boards should be forums for the representation of various interest groups—e.g. trade unions, consumers, etc.

It has to be admitted that much as Morrison favoured a hands-off approach to public corporations, the corporations established in the immediate post-war period were subject to more political control than those created prior to 1939. The subsequent history of public corporations—for the most part they were of the nationalised industry type—reveals that this process of subjecting them to closer political control did not end in the 1945–51 period. In an attempt to increase their accountability and to improve their performance, more scrutiny and more control was progressively brought to bear by governments of both the main parties.

The emergence of the privatisation philosophy in the Conservative Party can be said to be intimately related to this changing relationship. Firstly, despite the closer surveillance and control, the performance of the nationalised industries failed to satisfy the Conservatives. The Conservative government of 1979, whilst committed to some denationalisation, was disposed to try its hand at improving their performance; but ultimately it appears to have decided that nothing less radical than privatisation would do the trick. Secondly, one of the reasons for privatisation was government interference itself. The Conservatives came increasingly to the view that political control and efficiency were incompatible. Politicians, *of whatever hue*, would always succumb to the temptation to subvert nationalised industry policy to the political needs of the moment. Efficiency tended to be sacrificed for the sake of political expediency. Only when freed from political interference would these industries be able to reach their full potential. We are of course anticipating some of the argument which will unfold later in this chapter and in the next, but it is necessary to do so in order to justify what comes next.

What comes next is indeed a brief survey of the growth of scrutiny and control. Nationalised industries have been subject to ministerial control and to Parliamentary scrutiny. Prior to 1939 political control over nationalised industries was weak. Ministers possessed few powers, and the ones that they did have at their disposal were limited to specific matters. In the post-war period nationalised industries were subjected to closer control. Constitutionally the industry boards were directly accountable to ministers, and of course in turn ministers were answerable to Parliament. Ministers could give boards directions of a general character in relation to the performance of their functions in matters which were felt to affect the public interest. In addition ministers were granted powers over specific matters which varied from industry to industry. The consent to the Treasury as well as ministers was necessary when boards wished to borrow.

The directions which were given by ministers might be overt but more usually were in some degree covert. Robson makes it clear that certainly in the fifties and sixties the power to issue directives was of far less importance in relations between government and the nationalised industries than the influence which was exercised covertly by discussion, negotiation and downright pressure.[29] This was bound to give rise to contention, since nationalised industry performance might suffer because of the need to accommodate the political needs of ministers or of government policy as a whole. Ministers would achieve their objectives, but because the pressure they exerted was concealed from the public gaze, the nationalised industries were left to 'carry the can'. There are many instances on record where it is apparent that as a result of overt or covert pressure, nationalised boards were deflected from policies which suited their own commercial interests. Thus BEA and BA were required to buy and operate British aircraft irrespective of their merits. The CEGB was required to use more expensive coal produced by the NCB. The nationalised railway system was called upon to keep open unprofitable lines. During the first half of the 1970s, the nationalised industries as a whole were subjected to pressure to hold down prices as part of government macroeconomic strategy, and even the post 1979 Conservative government found it electorally advantageous to repeat the process.

One of the most obvious ways of influencing the policy of a nationalised industry board was to select chairmen and board members who were believed to hold similar views to the minister. But this power through appointments system may not always work, since it is always possible for apparently reliable appointees to 'go native'.

Parliamentarians also attempted to exert their influence, particularly in respect of complaints from constituents. However a convention was established which reflected the desirability of leaving nationalised industries free to run their day-to-day business. Because of this, ministers were not disposed to answer Parliamentary questions on matters of detail. Rather they were inclined to ask the chairmen of the corporations to write to the MP concerned. As Redwood and Hatch point out, it was difficult totally to prevent matters of detail being probed, since MPs could devise questions in which departmental policy and detailed nationalised industry business were intertwined.[30] Parliament as a whole was of course free to debate nationalised industry policy (as for example when the corporations produced their Annual Reports and Accounts), and in an attempt to facilitate Parliamentary scrutiny a Select Committee on Nationalised Industries was set up in 1952. In 1979 the select committee was disbanded. That did not mean that select committee surveillance ceased. A new system was established whereby a series of select committees shadowed the various departments of state. Moreover each select committee could investigate the nationalised industries which fell within the shadowed department's field of sponsorship. As a result the chairman and senior officials of a nationalised industry could be required to give evidence to the relevant select committee. In addition two other select committees also occasionally dealt with nationalised industry matters, namely the Public Accounts Committee and the Treasury and Civil Service Committee. The first is concerned with the use of funds granted to departments by Parliament and acted as a watchdog on the public purse. The second scrutinised Treasury affairs and thus could look into the financial provision made for nationalised industries. It should be mentioned that the former committee was of the opinion that the books of the nationalised industries, indeed of all public corporations, should be open to inspection by the Comptroller and Auditor General (C & AG). This was not accepted, but as Redwood and Hatch point out the C & AG does 'have access to the main public accounts which include the expenditure of public funds in connection with nationalised industry purposes.'[31]

In addition to Parliamentary scrutiny and *ad hoc* ministerial (departmental) interventions, the nationalised industries were also subjected to a system of controls, broadly uniform in character, which became progressively tighter. The Morrisonian nationalised industries were not subjected to detailed guidance on matters such as pricing, the return on assets generally, and new investment in particular. As we have implied, nationalised industries applied to their sponsoring departments and through them to the Treasury for finance for investment. It is also apparent that the government departments had not established any means of assessing the profitability of investments, and therefore the relative merits of projects, in one sector of the nationalised economy as compared with another, and more broadly the relative merits of public as opposed to private investment.

The general rule for Morrisonian nationalised industries was that their revenues should, taking an average of good and bad years, be not less than sufficient to cover the costs they incurred plus interest, together with provision to cover depreciation, redemption of capital and the building up of reserves. In practice they were not held to this. Depreciation was calculated on a historical cost basis although boards recognised that it would be prudent to make supplementary provision to cover the likely excess of replacement over historic cost. In reality retained income to cover normal depreciation, supplementary depreciation, capital redemption and reserve accumulation was not sufficient even to replace existing assets. In 1961 a White Paper (*The Financial and Economic Objectives of the Nationalised Industries*)[32] was issued by the then Conservative government which instituted a tougher regime. Over a five year period revenue should be sufficient to cover costs including interest, depreciation on a *replacement* cost basis and to allow for an allocation to general reserves which would enable the enterprise *to make a contribution towards their own capital development*. In addition the government decided to publish financial targets. Each industry, depending on its circumstancs, would be set a financial target which would in most cases take the form of an overall rate of return on its net assets. Such a return would obviously help to facilitate more self-financing of development, and would at least go some way to tackling the problem of achieving a better overall allocation of capital resources within the economy. No real guidance was given on pricing.

In 1967 another White Paper was issued (*Nationalised Industries: A Review of Economic and Financial Objectives*)[33]-this time by a Labour government. It dramatically extended the range of controls, since it proposed to institute investment appraisal and contained specific prescriptions on pricing. The main ingredients were as follows. Firstly, the existing system of financial targets was to be retained. In practice during the first half of the 1970s, under the succeeding Conservative government, they were largely suspended since nationalised industries were requested to hold prices down as part of a macroeconomic strategy. To enable them to do so massive subsidies were made available. The financial target system was however revived in the later 1970s. Secondly, a more commercial approach was to be injected into investment appraisal. The government stressed its desire to see an increase in the profitability of new investment throughout the economy and the nationalised industries were to be no exception. The government indicated that it intended to treat them as commercial bodies. Investment projects would therefore have to show a satisfactory rate of return in commercial terms. To this end the Discounted Cash Flow (DCF) method of investment appraisal should be applied to all investment projects and a common Test Discount Rate (TDR) of eight per cent, later raised to ten per cent, was to be adopted. Projects which did not meet this requirement would normally be rejected. However the government recognised that wider social considerations might justify a project which would fail on a narrow commercial calculation. If therefore a nationalised industry was required to undertake a project which could not be justified by commercial criteria, then a subsidy would be paid in compensation. Thirdly, the need to achieve an optimum allocation of resources also required that some prescription should be made in respect of pricing. The policy makers latched on to the deceptively simple welfare-maximising properties of marginal cost pricing. They decided as a general principle that prices should be aligned on long run marginal cost. There might be certain circumstances where short run marginal cost was more appropriate—as would be the case if excess capacity existed and prices did not need to provide for the maintenance of capital. Also prices might be allowed to rise above long run marginal cost in order to choke off demand which was in excess of existing capacity.

In 1975 the financial screw was further tightened. In order to control the growth of public expenditure the new Labour government attempted to introduce a policy of strict financial control. Cash limits were imposed on government expenditure programmes. In the case of nationalised industries, the policy took the form of placing a limit on each nationalised industry's net external borrowing from central government—these were referred to as External Financing Limits (EFLs). Tighter EFLs could obviously be justified on the grounds that they assisted in keeping down the subsequently well-known concept of the Public Sector Borrowing Requirement (PSBR) and that this in turn helped to control the supply of money—

the latter was beginning to attract more attention as a key variable.[34] The EFLs were of course possible tools for enforcing a better performance from nationalised industries, since one possible reaction to a tightening of them was to improve the internal use of resources and to dampen down wage expectations. Equally however nationalised industries might seek ways around them by putting up prices or postponing investment.

In 1978 another White Paper emerged (*The Nationalised Industries*)[35]—again the originator was a Labour government. The common TDR was abandoned. Apparently where the nationalised industries had used the DCF technique, they had concentrated on expansion plans and had not applied it to those investments which were designed to maintain the existing system, and which were regarded as being so essential that no formal appraisal was needed. A new system called the Required Rate of Return (RRR) was introduced. The government declared that nationalised industries should take the opportunity cost of capital as being five per cent in real terms before tax. The industries should therefore earn at least five per cent on their new investment as a whole and not just on projects suitable for individual appraisal. Individual projects could still be subject to a TDR but the government did not specify the rate to be employed. The nationalised industries would have to consult government departments about the appropriate rate including allowances for risk and appraisal optimism. The rate of individual projects would obviously have to be such that the overall RRR of five per cent was achieved. On the subject of prices it was recognised that marginal cost pricing had not been followed, partly because of macroeconomic policy of price restraint and partly because of the inherent difficulty of implementing such a system. The White Paper recognised the virtues of the marginal cost approach but it was given less emphasis. It emphasised the need to relate prices to the costs of supplying particular goods and services and to avoid cross-subsidisation.

One interesting feature of the 1978 White Paper is the degree to which Labour had changed its view about the 'hands off' approach. The 1978 view was that it was desirable that a minister should be able to give directions to a board, *which were either general or specific*, on matters which affected the public interest.

Controls on the activities of nationalised industries did not however end with the prescription of returns on assets and new investment, statements about pricing and EFLs. The 1967 White Paper said that government departments should develop, in consultation with the industries, indicators of performance which would enable the latter's success in containing costs, increasing efficiency and economising on manpower and capital resources, to be judged. The NEDO report of 1976[36] indicated that little had been achieved. The 1978 White Paper recognised that long term performance criteria were needed. It appreciated that whilst a nationalised industry might meet its financial target, live within its EFL, etc., much depended on how it did so. As we have noted an EFL could be ducked by pushing up prices. It was therefore desirable to establish *real* as opposed to financial criteria. This process was indeed put in hand.[37]

When the Conservative government came to power in 1979 it decided, as we indicated earlier, to lean more heavily on EFLs. It also adopted a number of other approaches to the stimulation of nationalised industry efficiency. Some of these will be discussed in the next chapter against the backdrop of the growing Conservative conviction that privatisation was the ultimate solution. However two devices will be mentioned here. Firstly, in 1980 under the Competition Act the new government took powers to subject nationalised concerns to what may be termed value for money audits. Under the 1973 Fair Trading Act nationalised corporations could be investigated, but there was a need to satisfy the condition that a monopoly existed within the meaning of the act. Under section 11 of the 1980 act the Secretary of State for Trade could directly and without the need to demonstrate the existence of a monopoly, refer nationalised concerns to the Monopolies and Mergers Commission for an investigation of their costs, efficiency, service, etc. Secondly, statutory monopolies were relaxed, so that new entrants could offer competition to the previously protected state enterprises.

4 THE NATURE AND SCOPE OF ECONOMIC REGULATION

Economic regulation has been relatively less important in the UK than in the US. As we have seen the prime instrument of government micro-intervention in the UK has been public enterprise rather than regulation. When the Thatcher government came to power in 1979 the principal sectors of the UK where regulation operated was limited to road haulage (lightly regulated), road passenger transport (express coaching and buses), airline passenger transport (both domestic and international), security dealing (e.g. operations on the Stock Exchange), other financial institutions (in particular the banks, building societies and insurance companies), broadcasting (notably independent television and independent radio) and the professions. In addition membership of the European Community meant that steel, surface transport modes and agriculture, were subject to Community regulatory regimes, and intra-European airline operation was a potential candidate.

It should be noted that these regulated areas were not populated exclusively by privately owned businesses—large public enterprises fell within the ambit of the regulatory system (e.g. the National Bus Company and British Airways). It should be added that public corporations sometimes acted as the regulatory body—e.g. the Civil Aviation Authority. More recently economic regulation has extended its scope to include newly privatised industries such as telecommunications, natural gas, airports and newly emerging industries such as cable TV. More will be said on these aspects in Chapters 7 and 8.

i Road Haulage and Railways
In the case of road haulage capacity restrictions via the licensing activities of Traffic Commissioners were originally introduced as a result of the Road Traffic Act 1933. The system, which ran until 1968, was a response to the increasing competition which the railways felt from the growth of road freight transport. The railways complained that they were burdened by regulation whilst the road hauliers were free of

restraint. Whilst this was true it is also true to say that the railways were burdened by their own bureaucratic systems. Licensing was also introduced in order to protect wages and safety standards—it was alleged that these had suffered as a result of the intense competition between road and rail.[38] There is of course an obvious parallel here with US experience. In 1963 the government set up a committee on carriers' licensing which in due course gave rise to the Geddes Report.[39] It quite simply recommended the abolition of all restrictions on capacity, although it did propose that permits should be issued which could be revoked in case of unsafe operation. The Transport Act 1968 reflected these liberalising views and in effect substituted quality for quantity regulation. For vehicles under 3½ tons' gross weight, all that was necessary was the possession of a normal vehicle licence together with a general driver's licence for the operator. In the case of larger vehicles, whether for hire and reward or for own account operation, an 'O' licence had to be obtained. In order to qualify for such a licence the applicant merely had to be a fit person and to have made satisfactory arrangements concerning (a) the observance of laws relating to driving hours and (b) the maintenance of the vehicle in a fit and serviceable condition.[40] Following UK membership of the EEC in 1973 the road haulage industry came within the ambit of the Common Transport Policy. More will be said about the impact of that policy in Chapter 8.

A notable absentee from regulation was the railways. From their inception they were regulated by individual Acts of Parliament in respect of rates and under common law had to act as common carriers. From the mid-nineteenth century onwards, general legislation was imposed which prohibited discrimination (the phrase used referred to the showing of undue preference), and later permanent central machinery was established to deal with complaints and fix maximum rates. As we noted earlier the railways were nationalised in 1947 but nevertheless they continued to be regulated. In 1953 by Act of Parliament they were released from certain charging restrictions, in that they were no longer required to avoid undue preference. However maximum rates had to be published and were subject to an Appeal Tribunal which could and did impose lower rates. It was only in 1962, under another Transport Act, that the railways were finally free to charge what price they chose and to pick and choose traffics. It should be noted that from 1973 the railways were subject to the EEC Common Transport Policy. The latter followed a similar approach by emphasising the need for commercial freedom and compensation when public service obligations were imposed upon the railways.

ii Coaches and Buses

We turn now to areas where regulation was still very much the order of the day when the Thatcher government came to office. Firstly there was road passenger transport. Regulation of this sector substantially began in 1930 with the Road Traffic Act. Passenger transport activities were divided into various categories including local (stage) services and long distance (express) services. Traffic Commissioners were appointed whose job it was to regulate the industry. In order to operate a route, a licence was required from the Commissioners which also specified fares and timetables. Existing operators on a route were given priority in operating it, and local and long distance services which overlapped geographically were protected from each other. It was a system in which competition played a minimal role. All this, together with subsequent amalgamations and take-overs, eventually led to what Ian Savage has described as 'territorial monopoly franchises' for bus operators, in which protection from interlopers was granted in return for the maintenance of networks in which profitable services cross-subsidised the unremunerative ones.[41] In the case of express coaching few routes were served by more than one operator.[42]

Three other developments are of importance. Firstly, from the mid-fifties onwards the bus industry went into secular decline. Secondly, reflecting the weakened state of the industry, County Councils were charged with the task of granting subsidies in order to maintain networks.[43] Thirdly, as we saw earlier, under the Transport Act 1968 Passenger Transport Executives were formed in various parts of the country. They took over the municipal bus fleets and co-ordinated their services with those provided by nationalised bodies (such as the National Bus Company) and those provided by privately owned bus enterprises.

iii Airlines

Airline regulation, like other forms of transport control goes back to the 1930s when licences to provide public air services were granted by the Civil Aviation Department of the Air Ministry. The main criteria were qualitative, particularly those relating to safety. In 1938 an independent regulatory body—the Air Transport Authority—was established, but the war intervened and this put a stop to attempts to organise the industry. After the war, as we have seen, the industry was nationalised with three public corporations carving up the business on a territorial basis. Nevertheless the immediately post-war Labour government did recognise that there was a place for independents. In 1960 the Civil Aviation (Licensing) Act created the Air Transport Licensing Board. It not only handled licensing but also determined fares. In respect of licences the by then two nationalised corporations were given no priority in principle, although in practice they were dominant. The emergence of the independents also created a powerful reason for regulation, namely the need to provide some control over the nationalised enterprises which by virtue of their size, access to government finance and power to secure special privileges (e.g. access to airports) would otherwise have been able to offer unfair competition.

The regulatory system took its present form in 1971 under the Civil Aviation Act of that year. The major influence behind the legislation was the Edwards Committee which reported in 1969 and came down firmly in favour of a multi-airline policy and the creation and maintenance of a competitive environment.[44] To this end it suggested the consolidation of private aviation companies in order to create a more effective 'second force' airline. This idea was embodied in the Civil Aviation Act and was subsequently implemented when British United Airways and Caledonian Airways merged to form British Caledonian. The act also created a new regulatory body—the Civil Aviation Authority which has since then been concerned with access to routes and fares.

The reader will be aware that the above account of the

Authority's role relates to domestic services. In the case of international traffic the UK government was unable to act unilaterally. Rather access to routes for scheduled services was determined by government to government—i.e. bilateral—air services agreements. Under such arrangements the two governments determined the number of airlines which could operate on routes between the two countries. In most cases only one airline from each country was permitted to operate. Very occasionally two (dual designation) were allowed from each country. These agreements did not name the airlines—it was up to each government to decide who should act as the designated airline. On occasions permission was granted for an airline from a third country to carry traffic along a route—this is known as 'fifth freedom traffic'. Rigas Doganis cites the UK–Singapore bilateral as an example. Under it the Singapore designated airline was granted fifth freedom rights between Athens and London on its services between Singapore and London. However the Athens–London rights could only be exercised if Greece agreed to it in its air services agreement with Singapore.[45]

In addition to normally restricting access to one from each side, capacity limitations (e.g. restrictions on the number of flights offered) were often written into the agreements, and even if not written in might nevertheless be insisted upon. Tight capacity control was a notable feature of the market in Europe. It was quite common for the designated airlines to operate a revenue-sharing pool in which revenue was shared out in proportion to capacity supplied. Again this was a common feature of European routes.[46] Airfares were not regulated by governments. Rather they were determined by airlines within the traffic conferences operated by the International Air Transport Association (IATA). Governments subsequently approved them. Up to 1979 a fairly rigid framework for price fixing existed which also covered service quality—e.g. seating, meals supplied, etc. That system was however being subjected to competitive stresses and challenges—more will be said on that subject in Chapter 8.

By contrast non-scheduled (i.e. charter) activities were treated in a more liberal fashion. Doganis points out that originally countries insisted on the need for prior approval for incoming non-scheduled flights, but in 1956 members of the European Civil Aviation Conference decided to waive this requirement and that fact, together with the failure of IATA to regulate charter fares, created a situation of relative freedom from international regulation. Nevertheless it did not preclude governments from imposing their own controls. Thus in the case of the UK, when charter operators flew the same route as those supplying scheduled services, they were precluded from offering scheduled service conditions. For example, they might only be allowed to offer return trips including accommodation.

iv Financial Institutions

Security dealing was governed by the rule book of the Stock Exchange. The latter was regulated by a non-statutory body—the Council of the Stock Exchange. Such self-regulation was and still is a typical feature of the UK financial system as will become apparent later. Under this particular self-regulatory arrangement a number of restrictions were imposed. Since 1908 a single capacity system had been in operation. That is to say stockbrokers were confined to buying and selling as agents for their clients. Stockjobbers were confined to making markets for brokers. From 1912 a fixed scale of minimum brokers' commissions had been applied. Jobbers of course made their profits by selling stock for more than they paid for it. Direct entry was also restricted, and members of the Stock Exchange enjoyed a virtual monopoly of security trading. As an alternative outsiders were allowed to buy limited stakes in members. In 1969 a limit of ten per cent was set but this was raised to 29.9 per cent in 1982, with the proviso that outsiders could not have a stake of more than five per cent in a second firm. Three other non-statutory bodies must be mentioned. Firstly, the Take-over Panel was established in 1968 to interpret and administer the City Code on Take–overs and Mergers. Secondly, the Council of the Securities Industry, established in 1978, supervised standards of conduct in the securities industry.[47] Thirdly, there was the security dealers' own trade association—the Association of Licensed Dealers in Securities.

The regulation of other financial institutions (notably

banks, building societies and insurance companies) has by contrast been a relatively diverse matter in which environmental regulation, legal regulation, regulation based on the moral suasion of the Bank of England, together with self-regulation and restraint have all played a part. Our account will merely seek to identify the main features of the situation as it existed in the period leading up to the coming to power of the Thatcher government.

By environmental regulation we refer to the fact that financial institutions, the banks in particular, were constrained by the government's monetary policy—e.g. controls on bank lending, hire purchase controls, exchange controls (which were also very important for the Stock Exchange) and the famous corset which had the effect of making balance sheet growth beyond certain limits less profitable.

Legal regulation had only a limited impact on the British financial scene—there is a contrast here with the US banking system, which as we saw earlier has been subjected to tight legal control. A good deal of the legally based regulation which did exist in the UK was primarily motivated by a desire to protect consumers (depositors, policy holders, etc.). Typical examples were the Insurance Companies Act 1974, the Policy Holders Protection Act 1975, the Banking Act 1979 and the Building Societies Act 1962. The first followed in the wake of insurance company insolvencies. Under the act business was restricted to insurers authorised by the Secretary of State (currently the Secretary of State for Trade and Industry). No authorisation would be forthcoming unless certain safeguards were satisfied. One related to margins of solvency. Another related to the adequacy of re-insurance arrangements. The act also laid down strict requirements in respect of the rendition of accounts, periodic actuarial investigations and audits. It should be added that certain requirements have had to be observed in connection with the Right of Establishment in the European Economic Community.

Interestingly, the Secretary of State could refuse to sanction the appointment of persons who he deemed to be unfit to be directors, controllers or managers. Under the Policy Holders Protection Act a scheme was imposed which was funded by a levy on all authorised insurance companies. Here the aim was that if an authorised company should become insolvent, individual policy holders would be protected by the fund. The banking industry was originally regulated under the Protection of Depositors Act 1963. However this was less than satisfactory. Moreover, whilst in all countries it is typical that those who wish to conduct banking business must first be authorised or licensed, the arrangements in the UK were in this respect weak. However in 1979 the situation was substantially improved when the Banking Act came on the statute book. By virtue of its provisions the Bank of England became the exclusive licensor of both deposit takers and banks, and when licensed they fell under its scrutiny and control. The act also foreshadowed the introduction of deposit insurance. Finally, as a result of the Building Societies Act, the building society industry had been placed under the watchful eye of the Chief Registrar of Friendly Societies.

Unlike the US, legal controls were markedly absent in matters such as the acceptable range of business. Originally the Trustee Savings Bank had been strictly circumscribed but in 1975 those inhibitions were lifted. Only the building societies were constrained by law.

Moral suasion refers to the role of the Bank of England. David Llewellyn has pointed out that the supervisory role of the Bank in relation to the banking system emerged through what he calls an 'implicit deal'. In return for liquidity support via money market operations the banks accepted the supervisory role of the Bank. He goes on to say 'In this way the Bank was able to exercise a greater amount of authority over the details of the banks' business than it formally had legal powers to enforce.'[48] The supervisory arrangements, which became increasingly formal after the banking crisis of 1974, related to such matters as capital adequacy, liquidity, foreign currency exposure and large loan exposure.

v Broadcasting

In the period leading up to the Thatcher government the dominant elements in over-the-air TV and radio broadcasting were the services of the BBC (itself a public corporation financed by a licence fee), the Independent TV companies and the Independent Radio companies. The regulatory element applied to the latter two, and the regulator was the Independent Broadcasting Authority. We will concentrate on the broadcast TV element although the principles in radio were somewhat similar. The Authority did not produce programmes—that was the task of independent programme contractors—although it could arrange for programmes to be supplied if there was a shortage of contractors. It should be added that the Authority owned the transmission system although the studios in which the programmes were made were the responsibility of the contractors.

The regulation of Independent TV broadcasting in the UK has afforded an example of the franchising principle at work. The limit on electromagnetic spectrum space led to a series of monopoly regional programme suppliers, although they were in due course complemented by a national supplier in the form of Channel Four. Franchising involves competition for a monopoly. This may be achieved by an auction, in which the successful bidder pays a price for the privilege of being a monopolist, and that price is creamed off into the public coffers for the general good. Alternatively it may take the Chadwick–Demsetz form in which the franchise is granted to the firm which offers to supply the good or service at the lowest price, in which case the public benefits directly in the price paid. Neither process was adopted by the Authority. The Chadwick–Demsetz approach was in any case ruled out since there is no price—Independent TV was supplied free, being financed by advertising. Instead programme contractors were asked to bid for spectrum space, and the Authority's choice was based upon the quality and merit of the proposed programme schedules. Within a region the successful bidder was not in truth a monopolist—he had to compete with BBC and subsequently Channel Four TV, with BBC and independent radio, and more generally with all other forms of entertainment. It should also be noted that successful bidders competed with each other in order to get their programmes on the national network. On the other hand, the ITV companies collaborated in owning Independent Television News which provided them all with a television news service.

The Authority charged contractors a rental to cover the cost of the transmission system and of regulation. In addition a super-tax was levied by the Authority on the profits derived from the use of the public's spectrum—the proceeds were paid to the Exchequer. Contracts ran for a fixed term but could be extended.

In addition, the Authority was responsible for the regulation of the independent programme contractors. Under the various Broadcasting Acts it, like the BBC, was charged with a public service obligation—i.e. to inform and educate as well as entertain and to provide a wide range of broadcast material. The main features of its regulatory functions under those Acts were as follows.

(a) It set limits to advertising density.
(b) It regulated programme content. To that end contractors were required to submit programme schedules in advance so that it could carry out its monitoring function. Generally it had to be satisfied that programmes did not offend good taste, were impartial, contained a proper proportion of UK content (by origin and performance) and that a suitable proportion appealed to local tastes. More specifically, the contractors had to supply news programmes, and requirements were laid down in matters such as the supply of children's, school's and religious programming. Codes of practice were also devised in relation to violence where young children were concerned and in relation to advertising standards.
(c) Rules were also laid down in respect of ownership. Thus a TV contractor could not also be a radio contractor in an area. Non–EEC individuals and companies were also ruled out, as were those who had interests in advertising. Controls could also be applied when it was felt that newspaper involvements in contracting were likely to be contrary to the public interest.[49] More will be said about cable and satellite TV in Chapters 7 and 8.

vi The Professions

Three other major instances of economic regulation need to be mentioned. Firstly, as we noted in Chapter 1, what are broadly referred to as the professions have been subjected to regulation—largely these systems have been of a self–regulatory kind.[50] As Utton points out, the typical procedure in the UK is for a Registration Council or similar body to be set up by statute, which then ensures that all practitioners have passed specific examinations and have the requisite experience.[51] Normally it is an offence for any unrecognised person to practise the profession or at least to use the title. The latter is the case in respect of architects. The former more typical situation applies in the optical profession—under the Opticians Act 1958 only opticians registered with the General Optical Council could test sight and dispense spectacles (although doctors could carry out the testing function).

Sometimes other restrictions are added as when rules were laid down which prevented effective advertising by opticians, including the display of prices in windows. This led to a virtual elimination of overt price competition.[52] The restrictions practised by the professions have been defended as a form of consumer protection and they may so act although, as Milton Friedman has pointed out, this defence would be more credible if they required periodic re-examination. The latter does not appear to happen. The suspicion indeed arises that the prescription of standards of competence may indeed be motivated by a desire to restrict supply, and thereby raise fee income. Ancillary restrictions of the type discussed above tend to give rise to the same effect. It should be added that in the UK professions there are two layers of regulatory oversight. The restrictive activities of the professions are referrable for investigation by the Monopolies and Mergers Commission. However in the case of the General Optical Council a legal technicality meant that if its activities has been referred the minister would not have had a power subsequently to order remedies, since in this particular instance the Optical Council's rules could only be changed by the Privy Council. As we shall see therefore (see Chapter 7) the matter was instead investigated by the Office of Fair Trading. It should be added that when the Price Commission was in operation, as part of the anti-inflation policy of the 1970s, the prices charged for optical products were investigated by that body.

vii The European Community Dimension

The other two cases of regulation derive from the fact that since 1973 the UK has been a member of the European Community. As a result it must now conform to the regulatory systems arising notably from the Rome Treaty (1957), which gave rise to the European Economic Community (EEC), and the Paris Treaty (1951), from which emerged the European Coal and Steel Community (ECSC).

Membership of the EEC did not imply that thereafter UK agriculture would for the first time have to submit to regulation—quite the contrary, it had been regulated before membership. What it did mean was that the EEC system, enshrined in the Common Agricultural Policy (CAP), had to be introduced in place of the radically different approach previously adopted in the UK. Whilst the broad nature of the CAP was discussed in Chapter 1 it is necessary that we add a few details. The policy had a number of objectives including the achievement of a fair standard of living for the farming community, an increase in efficiency of production, stable markets, security of supply and fair prices for consumers. These by no means consistent objectives were all to be achieved by manipulating the price of agricultural produce. Given the relatively low price of agricultural produce on the world market, it was essential to prevent imports from undermining the relatively high price which was necessary if the farm income objective was to be achieved. Typically therefore variable levies were imposed on imports of agricultural produce.

If the price so engendered led to an excess of supply over demand, then a second instrument was brought to bear—support buying took place. Surpluses were either bought into intervention or disposed of on the world market at a loss. The European Agricultural Guidance and Guarantee Fund financed both these operations. For some products market price had to fall only a little before the agencies stepped in to support the market. This was typical of temperate products. In the case of Mediterranean products (fruit, wine and vegetables) prices could fall a good deal before *official* support measures were activated. It should be added that where the Community had entered into international agreements not to tax imports, the support system took the form of subsidising Community produce so that it could compete with low-priced imports rather than taxing imports so that their price rose to the relatively high Community price level.[53]

Membership of the ECSC brought the UK steel and coal industries within the ambit of the more *dirigiste* powers available under the Paris Treaty. We will focus on steel. The Paris Treaty has given rise to specific rules on the method of making competitive price offers (based on a limited power to align down below published basing point prices) and to a weak system of indicative planning in respect of investments in steel-making capacity. More important are the reserve powers to impose price and quantity controls. These powers remained dormant until the structural crisis which followed in the wake of the oil price increase of 1973 and after. Intervention was first based on the idea of applying voluntary sales quotas, in order to underpin prices and profitability and enable firms to enjoy a breathing space within which to restructure—see Chapter 1. The system was progressively tightened as minimum price controls were applied selectively, import competition was restricted and in 1980 the climax occurred when a 'manifest crisis' was declared and mandatory sales quotas were introduced. In alliance with Eurofer, a producer cartel, the EC Commission in effect assumed a monopolistic control over the industry. Subsidies, which are prohibited under the Paris Treaty, were in fact allowed but latterly only on a restructuring basis and for a limited duration.[54]

NOTES

1. W. A. Robson, *Nationalized Industry and Public Ownership* (Allen and Unwin, London, 1966), p.34.
2. L. Hannah, *Electricity Before Nationalisation* (Macmillan, London, 1979), pp.126–7.
3. Robson *op. cit.*, p.36.
4. *Ibid.*, p.47. Many docks and harbours had been in the hands of public port trusts and commissions—these go back to at least the seventeenth century.

220   *Evolution of Policy in the United Kingdom*

5.   *Ibid.*, p.32.
6.   For his justification of the socialisation of London Transport see H. Morrison, *Socialisation and Transport* (Constable, London, 1933).
7.   L. J. Tivey, *Nationalisation in British Industry* (Johnathan Cape, London, 1966), pp.190–1.
8.   A. Cairncross, *Years of Recovery: British Economic Policy 1945–51* (Methuen, London, 1985), p.471.
9.   W. P. J. Maunder, 'Government Intervention in the Economy of the United Kingdom', in W. P. J. Maunder (ed.), *Government Intervention in the Developed Economy*, (Croom Helm, London, 1979), p.135.
10. Robson *op. cit.*, pp.54–5.
11. *Ibid.*, p.56.
12. *Ibid.*, p.58.
13. National Economic Development Office, *A Study of UK Nationalised Industries, op. cit.*, p.8.
14. A. Nash, *The British Airports Authority* (Kitcat and Aitken, London, 1985), p.6. Subsequently the BAA acquired Edinburgh airport from the Department of Trade and Industry in 1971, Aberdeen airport from the Civil Aviation Authority (CAA) in 1975 and Glasgow airport from Glasgow Corporation in 1975. The Highlands and Islands airports were taken over by the CAA when it was formed in 1971.
15. See below Appendix Table 1, Note 4.
16. J. Hibbs, *Transport Studies* (John Baker, London, 1970), pp.67–8.
17. M. J. Daunton, *Royal Mail* (Athlone Press, London, 1985), pp.342–3.
18. W. P. J. Maunder, *op. cit.*, p.135.
19. For a study of its activities see D. Hague and G. Wilkinson, *The IRC—An Experiment in Industrial Intervention*, (Allen and Unwin, London, 1983).
20. Quoted in M. C. Fleming, 'Industrial Policy' in W. P. J. Maunder (ed.), *The British Economy in the 1970s*, (Heinemann, London, 1980), p.148.
21. National Economic Development Office *op. cit.*, p.8.
22. J. Redwood, *Public Enterprise in Crisis* (Basil Blackwell, Oxford, 1980), pp.160–4.
23. *Ibid.*, pp.181–3.
24. National Economic Development Office *op. cit.*, p.9.
25. R. Pryke, *The Nationalised Industries op. cit.*, p.2.
26. Robson *op. cit.*, p.66.
27. R. Levacic, 'Introduction: the History of Government–Nationalised Industry Relations' in T. J. G. Hunter (ed.) *Decision Making in a Mixed Economy* (Open University, Milton Keynes, 1983), p.169.
28. Cited above at 6.
29. Robson *op. cit.*, p.142.
30. J. Redwood and J. Hatch, *Controlling Public Industries* (Basil Blackwell, Oxford, 1982), p.35.
31. *Ibid.*, p.39.
32. Cmnd 1337.

33. Cmnd 3437.
34. Cash limits and monetary targets were in vogue before the Thatcher government took office—they were a key feature of Chancellor Denis Healey's strategy from 1976 onwards.
35. Cmnd 7131.
36. National Economic Development Office, *A Study of UK Nationalised Industries, Their Role in the Economy and Control in the Future,* (London, 1976), p.33.
37. See Redwood and Hatch *op. cit.*, pp.104–20.
38. *Road Haulage Operators' Licensing Report of the Independent (Foster) Committee of Inquiry* (HMSO, London, 1978), pp.6–7.
39. *Report of the Committee on Carriers' Licensing* (HMSO, London, 1965).
40. T. G. Moore, *Trucking Regulation. Lessons from Europe* (American Enterprise Institute, Washington, 1976), pp.7–8.
41. I. Savage, *The Deregulation of Bus Services* (Gower, Aldershot, 1985), pp.4–7.
42. E. Davis, 'Express Coaching since 1980: Liberalisation in Practice', *Fiscal Studies* 5/1 (1984), p.77.
43. S. Glaister and C. Mulley, *Public Control of the British Bus Industry,* (Gower, Aldershot, 1983), pp.6–7.
44. *British Air Transport in the Seventies* (HMSO, London, 1979).
45. R. Doganis, *Flying Off Course op. cit.*, p.27.
46. M. Ashworth and P. Forsyth, *Civil Aviation Policy and the Privatisation of British Airways* (Institute of Fiscal Studies, London, 1985), p.32.
47. M. J. B. Hall, *Reform of the London Stock Exchange: The Prudential Issues,* Loughborough University Banking Centre Research Paper No. 24, 1986, pp.3–4.
48. D. T. Llewellyn, *The Regulation and Supervision of Financial Institutions* (Institute of Bankers, London, 1986), p.32.
49. On the whole subject of TV regulation see S. Domberger and J. Middleton 'Franchising in Practice: The Case of Independent Television in the UK', *Fiscal Studies*, 6 (1985), pp.17–32; *Report of the Committee on the Future of Broadcasting* (HMSO, London, 1977), Cmnd. 6753; *Report of the Committee on Financing the BBC* (HMSO, London, 1986), Cmnd. 9824.
50. P. Smith and D. Swann, *Protecting the Consumer* (Martin Robertson, Oxford, 1979), Chapter 5.
51. M .A. Utton, *The Economics of Regulating Industry* (Basil Blackwell, Oxford, 1986), pp.59–61.
52. Price Commission, *Dolland and Aitchson Group—Prices, Charges and Margins for Optical Products* (HMSO, London, 1979), pp.2–3.
53. D. Swann *The Economics of the Common Market, op. cit.*, Chapter 8.
54. D. Swann, *Competition and Industrial Policy in the European Community* (Methuen, London, 1983), and D. Swann, *The Economics of the Common Market op. cit.*, Chapter 10.

7 Forces for Change

1 INTRODUCTION

The focus of this chapter is on the question why policies of privatisation and deregulation were introduced—for the most part by the post–1979 Thatcher governments. It is important to stress that at this stage we are only interested in the reasons why, which is not the same as entering into judgements as to whether, in the light of economic analysis, they can be defended or justified. Whether such policies are well conceived and what effects have flowed from them are matters which will for the most part be reserved until Chapter 9.

In any attempt to explain why policies have been introduced, it is important to distinguish between the professed and other, possibly concealed, motives. Politicians tend to advance public interest type arguments in justification of what they do or propose to do. Whilst these may afford a true account, it is possible that there are other explanations which may not be revealed by politicians. Politics is after all about the use of power, and politicians are individuals who seek it—perhaps for its own sake. Therefore the policies they devise may well be those which they feel will most likely deliver that power to them. Then again, as Heald and Steel point out,[1] politicians may espouse policies that best suit their own constituency. In this case both privatisation and deregulation offered possible profit-making opportunities for groups which might normally be expected to vote Conservative. In practice a mixture of motives is possible. Putting on one side the notion of power for power's sake, much emphasis has been placed on Thatcherite conviction politics (in this connection the phrase 'economic evangelicals' has been used[2]) which suggests that there has been a genuine attachment to these policies, although that does not rule out an awareness of their attractiveness in the eyes of the Conservative party's natural constituency.

2 PUBLIC OWNERSHIP

The starting point for any explanation of the emergence of the policy of privatisation must be 1974. The Conservative government which came to power in 1970 subsequently got involved in a battle with the National Union of Mineworkers (significantly a *public sector* trade union). The strike, which contributed to a shortage of energy and a three day working week in industry, eventually resolved itself into a contest over who governed Britain. The Conservative government went to the people in an election in which this was the dominating issue. It lost. A political stalemate emerged, but a further election later in the year placed the Labour party in a position to govern. It did so until 1979 when it lost and was replaced by the Conservative party under Margaret Thatcher.

Up to 1974 a degree of consensus was apparent in economic policy. This was clearly so in the case of the public enterprise sector. Apart from the flurry over steel and the partial denationalisation of road haulage, the nationalised industries were tolerated by the Conservative administrations of 1951–64. That of course did not preclude criticisms of their alleged inefficiency and lack of concern for consumers. When the Heath government came to power in 1970 there were some signs and expectations that it would follow a more right-wing path. This was certainly the message which was derived from the announcement in 1970 by John Davies, the then Secretary of State for Trade and Industry, that the government would not 'prop up lame ducks'—i.e. bail out firms in difficulty. However the Heath government in due course performed a U–turn. Lame ducks were indeed rescued (including being taken into public ownership), whilst on the macroeconomic front the government became vigorously interventionist by virtue of introducing statutory incomes and statutory price control policies. It could indeed be argued that the Heath government was not merely back on the consensus path, but had strayed into the kind of interventionist territory which was more likely to be occupied by a Labour government.[3] However after the 1974 defeats, Conservative party policy shifted markedly to the right. New doctrines such as monetarism were taken on board, which ultimately had profound implications for the public sector and indeed public enterprise. Such ideas were entirely new to Conservative party policy. As William Keegan has pointed out, monetarism did not feature in that party's 1970 election manifesto and neither Sir Keith Joseph nor Mrs Margaret Thatcher made any fuss over it in cabinet in the period 1970–74.[4] New doctrines were accompanied by a new Leader—Edward Heath was dropped and Margaret Thatcher took his place.

Why did the policy (and for that matter the leadership) change take place? The proximate factor was electoral defeat. This provoked a policy re-think, and the Conservative party being in opposition had more leisure to carry it out. Such a re-think could have led to a reaffirmation of previous policies. However there was a powerful reason why that might not happen, namely that the previous policy had failed the crucial test—that of appealing to the electorate and delivering power to the Conservative party.

Central to the re-think process (one commentator has described it as the 'hi-jacking of a political party'[5]) was Sir Keith Joseph, who also helped to set up a 'think-tank', dedicated to a more right-wing approach to policy generally, in the form of the Centre for Policy Studies. During 1974 and 1975 Sir Keith delivered a series of lectures. These were published, and in the preface Sir Keith made the remarkable statement that it was only in April 1974 that he was converted to Conservatism.[6] Having been a long-standing member of the party and having held office as early as 1959, this could only imply that the Conservatism to which he had been converted was different from that which had been involved in the previous consensus. It would of course be wrong to single out Sir Keith as the sole author of the new approach. Equally it is important to recognise that not all that was taken up was a by-product of new thinking. A number of bodies had been in existence for a considerable period—e.g. the Institute for Economic Affairs and Aims of Industry—which had been busily propounding a less centralist, more market-oriented approach to economic policy.

In bald terms the Josephian critique was as follows. Britain's economic performance had declined markedly in comparison with that of its neighbours in North West Europe. Since the Conservative party had held office for 17 of the post-war years, this was an indictment of them as well as of Labour. In relative terms incomes were low, taxes were high and the level and quality of social service provision gave cause for concern. Much of this was due to excessive government, which also threatened freedom, and to the trade unions. Excessive government meant excessive state expenditure, including that on the nationalised industries, and this acted as a burden on the productive private sector. Excessive government also manifested itself as interventions which inhibited the wealth generating powers of the free market system—the latter needed to be released. The environment was also hostile to entrepreneurship and to the values of the free enterprise system, and profitability had fallen to a dangerously low level. Inflation was also seen as undermining the economy. It was the product of excessive monetary growth (in which governments connived) and only a strictly monetarist approach would provide the basis for a cure. Governments attempted to deal with unemployment by bursts of monetary growth, but this was only a short-term solution, and was a cruel deception of the unemployed. A purely *laissez-faire* approach allied to a monetarist stance would not however suffice. Some intervention would be necessary in order to deal with those factors which inhibited the adaptability and mobility which were essential features of a more dynamic economy.[7]

We are of course not concerned with the whole gamut of the Thatcher government's economic policy but only, at this stage, with the privatisation element. In that connection it is necessary to anticipate the subsequent argument in order to emphasise a point of crucial importance, namely that the new policy which emerged after 1974 did not immediately embrace a full-blooded policy of privatisation. Indeed the policy documents which were issued between 1976 and 1979 suggest that privatisation (the word had not been invented in 1976) did not feature at all significantly in Conservative thinking.

In 1977 a group of leading Conservative thinkers (Geoffrey Howe, Keith Joseph, James Prior, David Howell and Angus Maude) published *The Right Approach to the Economy*.[8] It emphasised the need to reinstate a rate of return on capital for all nationalised industries, to cost and finance uneconomic activities separately and to protect management from constant Whitehall interference. It also referred to the vague long-term aim of reducing the preponderance of state ownership, but no industries were specified. In 1978 the Ridley Report (a product of the Conservative party's policy group on nationalised industries under the chairmanship of Nicholas Ridley) was leaked in *The Economist*.[9] Again privatisation was not the main theme. Two of the key suggestions were to impose inflexible rates of return on nationalised industries and to open them up to competition by terminating statutory monopolies. The possibly of denationalisation was considered, but while not rejecting the idea it envisaged surprisingly few opportunities for sell-offs—the BNOC appeared to be the only unequivocal candidate. Samuel Brittan has also pointed out that the 1979 Conservative party manifesto devoted very little attention to privatisation.[10] Indeed the only corporate sell-offs were to be aerospace, shipbuilding and the NFC. The proposal concerning aerospace was hardly startling since it was not part of the core of utilities which are typically publicly owned. The promise to privatise shipbuilding was not as significant as it sounded, since a lack of competitiveness and the depressed state of the world market rendered the non-defence section of limited interest to the private investor.

The actual course of events indicates that the Conservative party's appetite for privatisation subsequently became much more pronounced and that raises the question why? One clue was revealed by Sir Geoffrey Howe, the new Chancellor of the Exchequer. He pointed out that the problem of applying financial discipline to the nationalised industries was much more formidable than they had imagined in opposition.[11] In other words, they were increasingly driven to the conclusion that only more radical policies such as privatisation and/or termination of statutory monopolies would do the trick. We shall return to this point when we come to discuss Mrs. Thatcher's tussles with the nationalised industries. Another factor was the continuing failure of the post-1979 Conservative governments to achieve their stated aim of reducing public spending and taxation as proportions of the GDP. As Samuel Brittan has pointed out, both these ratios were higher in 1985 than they had been in 1979.[12] He points out that privatisation was technically easier and politically more acceptable, and was therefore promoted as a partial ideological substitute.

A third factor was the accumulation of evidence which could be cited in support. It was only when in office that a full perspective was available to the party concerning performance of the nationalised industries during the seventies in matters such as the return on capital, the movement of earnings (and prices) in the public as compared with the private sector and the productive and allocative efficiency of public as compared with private enterprise. The real rate of return in the first half of the 1970s had been depressed as a result of the nationalised industries being forced to hold prices down as part of macroeconomic strategy. Subsequently the rate recovered, but by the end of the decade it was apparent that the progressive decline, which had been taking place prior to price control, was continuing to operate.[13] In fairness it should be said the return in the private sector had also fallen, but it remained positive whereas, excluding subsidies, the nationalised sector rate was negative from 1972 onwards.

On the earnings front, when Edward Heath left office in 1974 the nationalised industry wage index was running at 115 per cent of the private industry one. Under Labour the ratio fell to 108 per cent. However within two years under Mrs. Thatcher's government it was back to 115 per cent.[14] Added to all this were the findings of nationalised industry scholars such as Richard Pryke. In 1971 he had produced an impressive and substantial survey of the nationalised industries' performance, which pointed to a highly creditable comparative record in matters such as the increase of total factor productivity during the period 1958–68, and he looked forward to further favourable developments.[15] However in 1981 he returned to the subject and produced a highly critical report on their performance in the period after 1968. He concluded:

> Although the picture is not wholly black, most of the industries display serious inefficiency because they do not use the minimum quantities of labour and capital to produce the goods and services that they provide. Furthermore, resources are being misallocated because of the failure to pursue the optimum policies for pricing and production. Far too many of the nationalised industries produce at a loss, engage in average cost pricing or practice cross-subsidisation. In general, the nationalised industries' performance has been third rate though with some evidence here and there of first class standards.[16]

Pryke gave some consideration to the question whether ownership was a factor in determining efficiency—i.e. whether public ownership had itself contributed to the performance of those industries which were nationalised. His verdict was that it had. He also made comparisons between similar activities in the public and private enterprise spheres, and concluded that the latter were the more efficient.[17] The above conlusions and comparisons were avidly seized upon by John Moore when Financial Secretary to the Treasury as evidence in support of the privatisation programme.[18] It should also be noted that the reports of the Monopolies and Mergers Commission under the nationalised industry investigation powers conferred by the 1980 Competition Act provided further ammunition.

We turn now to the motives which in the period after 1974 appear to have been influential in disposing the Conservative party towards a policy of privatisation. Undoubtedly a powerful background influence was the revival of interest in the writings of the Austrian school, and notably those of the philosopher and economist Friedrick von Hayek. He saw the growing economic role of the state as carrying with it a threat to liberty and democracy.[19] This view was a key feature of Sir Keith Joseph's analysis of the economic role of the state. In a foreword to a Centre for Policy Studies pamphlet he observed:

> Hence our reiterated conviction that a market economy with freedom to own property and engage in production of goods and services is an essential condition of all other freedoms.[20]

Mention must also be made of the work of Milton Friedman, whose views have already been referred to in discussing the background influences which inspired the deregulatory movement in the US—see Chapter 4. Friedman produced a 'manifesto for *laissez-faire*' in 1962, in the form of a book entitled *Capitalism and Freedom*.

A second factor was the growth of public spending as a proportion of the GDP. In *The Right Approach to the Economy*, the authors pledged the intention of the Conservative party when in office 'to allow State spending and revenue a significantly smaller percentage slice of the nation's annual output and income each year'.[21] It has been argued that in adopting this view the authors had been significantly influenced by the work of Bacon and Eltis, who pointed to the problems faced by an economy when the ratio of non-market expenditure to marketed expenditure is raised significantly. The latter referred to the outputs of industry which are sold in the market as opposed to non-marketed items such as defence, education, the National Health Service, etc. Generally the products of nationalised industries are marketed, but their borrowing is a burden on the exchequer and ultimately on the taxpayer and it was this element to which Bacon and Eltis were pointing. In their view, when the ratio goes up significantly two effects arise. Firstly, workers will resist any reduction of their real incomes stemming from the growing tax burden by pressing bigger wage claims. Consequently wage inflation will accelerate and a tougher macroeconomic response is called for in order to contain inflation. The result is a higher level of unemployment. Secondly, workers had been relatively successful at passing through the bulk of the extra taxation to companies but companies had not been successful in passing it on. Profits therefore declined and investment did likewise.[22]

A key influence in Josephian thinking (and in that of most of those who came to dominate Conservative party policy) was the role of monetary growth in the process of inflation. By 1974 Keith Joseph was obviously a convinced supporter of Milton Friedman's monetarist doctrine. Thus 'if we can in fact gradually start moderating the trend rate of growth of money—which entails also moderating the budget deficit—then the balance of payments deficit, and after a lag, the rate of inflation will ease'.[23] But, as we noted earlier, monetarism was necessary but not sufficient. Factors which led to immobility and lack of adaptability would also have to be rooted out. If they were, then the road to 'spontaneous progress' would open up once more. The monetarist doctrine found its way into *The Right Approach to the Economy*, and its essential ingredients were evident in the 1979 Conservative party manifesto. Control of the money supply, which in the context of the Medium Term Financial Strategy tended to focus initially on Sterling M3, did not automatically imply privatisation. In broad terms the main influences on Sterling M3 are the Public Sector Borrowing Requirement (PSBR), the level of bank advances to the private sector and the state of the external balance. The PSBR could be squeezed if public expenditure could be cut back. The contribution of the nationalised industries to this process had been identified in the Ridley Report. As we have seen it laid great stress on the imposition of absolutely inflexible target rates of return. It should be added that it also called for a progressively decreasing commitment on the part of the government to the financing of nationalised industry investment. If there was any danger of the rates of return not being achieved then the nationalised industries would have to sell off surplus assets, close uneconomic activities or raise prices.

In practice the control over public spending and thus the PSBR and money supply proved much more difficult than expected. As for the nationalised industries, their financial position worsened as the second oil price shock took its toll. They therefore appeared at the Treasury with their begging bowls. In the face of these difficulties the proceeds of asset sales—privatisation of public enterprises plus the sale of

council houses[24]—became an increasingly attractive proposition as a source of relief for a hard-pressed PSBR. Public
expenditure was also seen as crowding out private investment—the prime minister was much taken by this line of
argument. However shifting enterprises to the private sector
does not in itself reduce the pressure of their borrowing on the
capital market and thus on interest rates. It should be added
that whilst the reduction of the PSBR was generally viewed as
a means to an end, there were some who seemed to see it as an
end in itself.

A major plank of the Conservative case against public
enterprise, and notably the nationalised industries, was that
they were inefficient and unresponsive to the needs of the
consumer. This was not by any means a new view, but it was
advanced with greater conviction in the second half of the
1970s and after. Four reasons were advanced by way of explanation of these shortcomings. Firstly, the monopoly status of
at least some of these enterprises meant that, unlike the
private variety, they were not subject to the disciplines of
competition in product markets. Sir Geoffrey Howe pointed
to what he regarded as the ironic fact that some of these public
corporations enjoyed a natural monopoly and might therefore be thought to be protected against competition by their
size and the scale economies which went with it. Nevertheless
they also had statutory monopolies conferred upon them. In
technical terms the natural monopolies were sustainable and
therefore did not require such further legal protection.[25]
There was an important element of truth in the idea that
public enterprises were often insulated from competition but
of course the argument could be over-played. Thus the NCB
(now British Coal) might have a virtual monopoly of coal
production but there were other fuels which had provided a
considerable challenge and of course there was the threat of
imports. Also state owned entities such as British Aerospace
and Rolls Royce were islands of public ownership in a sea of
international competition—much of it private in origin.
Conservative critics were also long on criticism but shorter on
remedies. The above two examples could be sold off and no
regulation would be needed—competition would see to that.
But what about the natural monopolies? How were they to be

dealt with? One possibility was regulation but was that satisfactory? Interestingly Sir Geoffrey Howe felt that British
nationalised industries had been relatively uncontrolled, and
because of this they had become inefficient. He drew a contrast with US natural monopolies, which he argued had been
kept on their toes by virtue of the effective surveillance of the
regulators. In the light of our earlier analysis of US regulation
we must regard that as a considerable misjudgment.

A second critique was that unlike the private variety, public
enterprises were not subjected to the discipline of the market
for corporate control. If private enterprises failed to make
efficient use of their assets, then their share prices were likely
to fall and this increased the possibility of take over by companies who felt that they could make better use of the assets.
The possibility that if such a change of ownership took place
the existing directors and management might well be dis-
placed would tend to keep them on their toes. In other words
the threat of take over has an affect as well as actual take
overs. This is an abstract argument. Whether the market for
corporate control works as effectively as is suggested, particularly in respect of large companies such as British Telecom,
is an empirical matter.

The third critique related to the fact that public corporations could not go bankrupt in the normal sense. Equally,
public limited companies in which the state had a substantial
stake might *de facto* if not *de jure* be said to be in a similar
position. They knew that ultimately they would be bailed out,
and to this extent the will to tackle their problems would be
undermined. This point was neatly summarised by John
Moore when he observed:

> At the end of the day the heart of the matter is that a
> nationalised industry does not have to succeed in order to
> survive. Even if left to their own devices, the industries
> have no real incentive to improve their performance or to
> strive for greater efficiency. If the government stands
> behind the industries and is viewed as possessing a bottom-
> less purse, it is no wonder that inefficiencies flourish and
> market responsiveness does not stand very high on an
> industry's scale of priorities. Nationalisation and the

Morrisonian concept have in effect failed to provide the stimuli that are needed.[26]

With a *mea culpa*, Conservative ministers and former ministers also drew attention to the inevitable temptation to meddle in the affairs of public enterprises in order to use them to achieve objectives which were at variance with their commercial success. Again we can cite John Moore:

Why has these industries' performance been so disappointing . . . They do their best but are faced with an impossible task. The odds are stacked against them. Not only are the industries constantly at risk from political and bureaucratic interference, the managers must at times wonder what it is they are supposed to be managing. Are the industries businesses or social services?[27]

In this connection John Moore also pointed out that nationalised industry borrowing was part of the PSBR, and as a result the individual needs of state industries had to be subordinated to the needs of macroeconomic policy. There was no prospect of treating them differently, and allowing them to borrow in an unconstrained way on the capital market. The market would continue to assume that if the worst came to pass the government would stand behind the nationalised industries. Therefore capital would be supplied on terms which ignored risk whilst the nationalised industries would be free to invest in risky ventures, leaving it to the government to pick up the bill if they failed. If the nationalised industries wished to enjoy financial freedom then they would have to be launched off on a fully independent basis, and they would have to pay a rate return which fully reflected the risks involved.

Two further points are worthy of note in connection with the alleged inefficiency of public enterprise. Firstly, as Samuel Brittan has observed, the original grounds for optimism about the ability of state enterprises to contribute to a rational allocation of resources had been undermined by certain theoretical developments. This optimism, it will be recollected from Chapter 2, was a product of the idea that among other things such enterprises should be required to price on the same basis as the perfectly competitive firm—i.e. at marginal cost. However the subsequent development of theories of bureaucracy and public choice envisaged the possibility that state officials who are deprived of opportunities for financial gain will take them in the form of 'status, security and in-house comforts'.[28] These are also present in the large scale private corporation, but the existence of the market for corporate control together with greater personal involvement via such things as share options would act as a mitigating factor. In other words, even if price was set at marginal cost there was no guarantee that the average cost to which it was related was minimised. Secondly, as John Moore was clearly aware, although the nationalised industries had been called upon to adopt a marginal cost approach to pricing, the 1978 White Paper on nationalised industries indicated that they had largely failed to do so[29]—see Chapter 6.

The concern of the Conservative party about the size of public expenditure and the resulting effect on the PSBR was as we have seen a concern about the consequences for the money supply, and it should be added, the rate of interest. But the heavy burden of public expenditure was held to have other consequences too. It added to the tax burden, and this in turn had an adverse effect on the incentive to work and take risks—i.e. supply side considerations. Whilst the burden of public expenditure might be eased by applying strict financial controls to public enterprises, the problem of keeping it in bounds became such that it is difficult to resist the temptation to view privatisation sales as being motivated if not by a desire to lower taxes at least by a wish to prevent them from rising. The relationship between privatisation and taxation has been subjected to some scrutiny. In the first place, as Alan Peacock has pointed out, the revenue from asset sales has been and is likely to be low compared with the annual public expenditure planning total. As a result the degree of relief which might conceivably have a marked effect on incentives was unlikely.[30] In any case, privatisations do pose problems for future years, in terms of the loss of interest paid by public corporations together with the fact that some have had negative EFLs—i.e. they produced surpluses for the Treasury.[31] The reference to future years also highlights the problem that one–off sales do not provide the recurring finance which is needed to cope with the continuing cut in tax revenue. Of course a stream of sell-offs may provide support for at least a period of years after which the Micawber principle of 'waiting for something to turn up' might be conveniently relied upon.

A major justification for privatisation was the boost which it was felt it would give to the concept of the property-owning democracy. This idea, which was not new to the Conservative party ideology, was emphasised in the 1979 election manifesto, but was only made specific in respect of the sale of council houses. Privatisation was subsequently justified because it would widen share ownership. In pursuit of this goal many of the privatisation issues offered small investors favourable terms or a preference in the allocation of over-subscribed issues.[32] Whilst wider property ownership could have been held to be an end in itself, it was also promoted because it could help in the stimulation of an 'enterprise culture'. It might, for example, contribute to the greater legitimacy of the free enterprise system of private property and the associated profit motive. It will be recollected that Sir Keith Joseph had expressed great concern about the hostility which existed towards the values and principles of the capitalist system. Also sales of shares to employees of privatised firms might create an incentive to greater efficiency in the employing organisation.[33]

It is difficult to resist the conclusion that the electoral events of 1974 were also a contributory factor. The Conservative party was badly bruised by its confrontation with the National Union of Mineworkers—a public sector union. Whilst it would be naive to see the policy of privatisation as a product of political vindictiveness, it seems likely that trade unions, particularly those in the public sector, did not thereafter enjoy great popularity in Conservative party policy-making circles! Students of privatisation have indeed concluded that it was part of a policy for containing trade union power[34]—i.e. privatised firms would (in some cases) be subject to competition and would not be able to turn to the Treasury to finance pay increases. A reading of the leaked version of the Ridley Report leaves the reader in little doubt that the main concern, indeed obsession, was how best to cope with public sector union pressure. Whilst tight financial controls and indeed privatisation could be seen as devices for keeping public expenditure under control, it is also possible to see them as being part of a more fundamental battle about who governed the country. This was really a re-run of 1974 but on a more extended time scale. The winter of industrial discontent, which preceeded the 1979 election, highlighted the issue, and the Conservative election manifesto emphasised the need to guarantee that 'Parliament and no other body stands at the centre of the nation's life and decisions.'[35]

If we look for what may be termed the final straw, then perhaps we need look no further than the prime ministerial frustrations of 1980 and 1981. These remind us of Sir Geoffrey Howe's observation, to which we referred earlier, that the problem of controlling the nationalised industries was greater than had been thought to be the case when the party was out of office. The frustrations which arose from this realisation had been vividly chronicled by Simon Jenkins. They were set against a background of frantic attempts to restrain public expenditure on the nationalised industries. By the spring of 1981 Mrs Thatcher had 'become convinced that the nationalised industries were the most persistent area of failure of her administration.'[36] As indicated earlier, partly because of the recession they had to return repeatedly to the Treasury for assistance. They also argued that their borrowing was treated in an arbitrary way—e.g. some state-owned limited companies, such as BL and BNF, were outside the public borrowing controls largely for historical reasons. More importantly they demanded that they should be free to tap the capital market and employ a variety of borrowing instruments. This, as we also pointed out earlier, was resisted. Financial freedom and the ability to raise *genuine* risk capital would only be possible if nationalised industries were to become part of the private sector.

The nationalised industries seem to have been quite successful in their confrontations with the government—thanks partly to the fact that they acted together in the Nationalised Industries Chairmen's Group, and thanks also to the fact that the chairmen were senior industrial statesmen who seem to have been adept at 'house training' the sponsoring ministers.

Simon Jenkins suggests that from a prime ministerial point of view, a more appropriate description of the sponsoring ministers was that they had 'gone native'.

The government response took the form of a proposal to establish a more stringent and more continuous system for monitoring the activities of the nationalised concerns. (a) Existing sponsoring ministers were re-shuffled out of the way. (b) The Central Policy Review Staff (the 'think tank') under Robin Ibbs were called upon to produce a plan. The Ibbs Report, which was not published, contained some highly controversial proposals. Firstly, a much clearer framework of financial controls and objectives was to be established for each industry and they were to be monitored each quarter by the sponsoring department. Secondly, the boards of nationalised industries were to be restructured in order to have a majority of non-executive directors from outside the industry. The latter would be senior figures from the business world, who would have responsibility for specific areas of the industry's policy. Thirdly, each department would have business groups who would help in setting the financial targets and objectives and would keep an eye on their implementation. They were to consist of seconded businessmen. The emphasis in all this was on the need for a commercial approach in the best Thatcher tradition.

All this provoked a vigorous backlash both within the nationalised industries and among senior civil servants. The main objections focussed on the business group concept and the composition of boards.[37] There was strong opposition to the element of interference and the atmosphere of being spied upon. The result was that the government largely backed down on both these proposals. It seems likely that such experience suggested to the government that wherever possible privatisation was infinitely preferable to government control. John Kay summarised the mood admirably when he refers to the government's 'world-weary anxiety to be rid of the problems of controlling nationalised industries by being rid of the industries themselves'.[38]

One impression which emerges extremely strongly is the contrast between the US experience in connection with deregulation and the UK experience when privatising. The

former does not appear to have been a matter which fundamentally divided the political parties. President Ford, a
Republican, was an enthusiast and President Carter, a Demo-
crat, was responsible for many of the changes. In the UK the
policy of privatisation has exposed fundamental differences of
party ideology with the Labour Party threatening to renationalise.

Two points remain to be made. Firstly, the list of motivations presented above tends to obscure the point that the
nature of the argument changed over time. Whilst a variety of
arguments continued to be deployed in defence of privatisation, the balance changed. In the early years the Conservatives laid stress on PSBR considerations but later the
government tended to make more play of its contribution to
efficiency and wider share ownership. Secondly, opinion poll
evidence suggests that from 1974 until 1980 there was a steady
swing away from more nationalisation and in favour of
denationalisation.[39] How much of this was due to Conservative party publicity is difficult to say, but what is clear is that
for one reason or another they were increasingly pushing at an
open door.

3   ECONOMIC REGULATION

We must begin by noting some contrasts. On the privatisation
front the process of change has been all one way. Public
enterprise has been replaced by private ownership (and
occasionally by private management). But on the regulation
front two conflicting tendencies have been apparent. In a
number of instances regulation has given place to various
degrees of deregulation. But it is also apparent that regulation
has actually advanced in some areas of the economy. Three
processes have been at work. Firstly, some areas have exhibited a simultaneous movement towards deregulation and
towards what may be termed reregulation. Let us take the
case of financial institutions, which from this point on are best
defined broadly so as to include the Stock Exchange. On the
one hand, as we shall see in Chapter 8, regulation has given
place to competition as brokerage and interest rate cartels

have been abandoned, and different kinds of financial institution have invaded each other's markets. But equally in the interests of financial viability, stability and investor protection, a comprehensive system of prudential regulation has been installed. Secondly, industries which were previously in public ownership have been privatised, but because of the problems posed by private market power a system of regulation has been introduced—e.g. telecommunications. We shall say more about that topic in Chapter 8. Thirdly, new industries have emerged which have been subjected to regulation. The obvious example is cable TV, which offers competition against the over-the-air broadcast variety. As we shall see in Chapter 8 the government has given the green light to this form of competition but has nevertheless subjected it to regulation.

Another contrast with privatisation relates to timing. Privatisation has been almost exclusively a product of the period since 1979, but deregulation predates the Thatcher governments. The beginning of a relaxation of the grip exerted by nationalised undertakings over air passenger transport, and a growing role for independent competition can indeed be traced back to the immediately post-war Labour administration—see Chapter 6. Road haulage deregulation was introduced in 1968—by a Labour government (see Chapter 6). Some loosening up of bus licensing occurred in 1978—again under a Labour government. The official opening shots in a process of subjecting banking to more competition were fired in 1971, when the Bank of England produced its famous declaration *Competition and Credit Control.*

Two other contrasts were worthy of note. Firstly, the need to address the phenomenon of regulation does not appear to have been high on the Conservative party's agenda in the period leading up to the 1979 election. As we have seen, privatisation was not greatly emphasised—deregulation was even less of an issue. Only bus deregulation featured in the 1979 election manifesto. Secondly, whereas it was possible to point to a general philosophy behind the policy of privatisation, deregulation has been much more a product of diverse forces and specific arguments. That does not however mean

that the influence of what may be termed Josephian philosophy (see above) was by any means absent from the
deregulation scene.

i Coaches and Buses

A variety of factors can be adduced to explain the deregulatory moves in road passenger transport. Firstly, previous
deregulatory experience had suggested that the relaxation of
controls would not necessarily give rise to the bogy of excessive and destabilising competition. Whilst it is true that fears
of this kind had been expressed primarily in relation to freight
activities, it seems likely that it had exercised some influence
over policy towards all forms of road transport. The Geddes
Committee was not inhibited by it, and post-Geddes experience did not support it as the 1978 report of the Foster
Committee noted. In any case it was still possible to impose
standards in relation to safety, even if quantitative licensing
restrictions, etc., were relaxed or even abolished.

Secondly, UK deregulation of road freight had led to managerial innovation,[40] and there was evidence that there was
scope for service innovation in road passenger transport as
indicated by the limited moves in 1978 which led to community buses and facilitated car sharing.

Thirdly, road passenger transport was the case which most
nearly conformed to Josephian philosophy, since the introduction of competition was a means of bringing pressure to
bear on publicly owned concerns including the National Bus
Company (and its Scottish equivalent), British Rail (notably
its inter-city services), and municipally-owned bus fleets. It
should be added that the system operated by the Traffic
Commissioners had inhibited competition by placing the onus
of proof of the need for new services upon new entrants, and
by affording existing suppliers ample scope to object. We
should also note that the opening up of road passenger transport to competition was a necessary prelude to the privatisation of the nationalised section of the industry. In addition
the Conservatives were only two well aware of the subsidy
burden, and saw that the lack of competition not only robbed
consumers of service innovation but also kept up costs.
Competition would lower costs and therefore reduce the

subsidy bill.

The government indicated that local authorities should seek competitive tenders for the services they wished to subsidise. Particularly in respect of stage services, the government also laid much emphasis on the phenomenon of cross-subsidisation. Whilst some cross-subsidy was commercially desirable in order to preserve an attractive network in the face of competition from car ownership, much of it was regarded as being simultaneously non-commercial as well as uneconomic. It also gave rise to adverse social consequences as when poor passengers subsidised better-off ones.[41] It was confidently predicted that undesirable cross-subsidisation would wither away in the face of competition. To complete the picture, one should add that the decision to phase out licensing on stage services was supported by experience in trial areas where entry controls were greatly eased for experimental purposes and the reported evidence pointed to lower fares, better service and little instability.

ii Airlines

When we come to air passenger transport the situation could be said to be patchy. In certain areas, moves towards liberalisation have been evident but in others powerful resistances to change have been encountered.

On the internal front a major impetus to change seems to have come from bodies such as the Edwards Committee (see Chapter 6) and more recently from the Civil Aviation Authority. The latter has increasingly opted for competition; without doubt it was influenced by US experience. On this side of the Atlantic a great deal of play was made of the relatively high fares (distance for distance) in Europe when compared with the US under a deregulated system. It is also worth pointing out that the fact that the Authority took such a pro-competitive stance undermines the notion that regulatory bodies are inevitably captured. (We drew a similar conclusion when we observed that the Civil Aviation Board in the US started to deregulate before Congress finally acted). The Authority was well aware that, despite the shift in emphasis towards competition which was particularly noticeable from the Edwards Committee onwards, British civil aviation was still unbalanced. British Airways was a monopolist on most domestic routes. If often turned out to be the designated airline in air services agreements[42] although, as we saw in Chapter 6, such agreements named no names. It enjoyed the tremendous advantage that its services were concentrated on the Heathrow hub.[43]

In 1984 the Authority made a number of radical proposals.[44] The size of British Airways should be reduced by route transfers so that other airlines could develop and prosper and therefore be in a position to replace the former on intercontinental routes. This was essential if the Authority was to exercise real control over British Airways. The latter's European routes from provincial airports should also be taken over by other British airlines. Access to Heathrow for domestic services competing with British Airways should be allowed even if the latter's frequencies had to be curtailed. In respect of domestic services, licensing should be dropped for an experimental period and any airline should be able to serve domestic routes (other than those specifically excluded). The Authority should cease to regulate domestic fares, but they would have to be filed in order to permit the policing of exploitative and predatory pricing.

How did the government respond? It was ambivalent on the whole topic of airline competition. On the one hand its natural instinct was to favour free markets as opposed to regulation. Equally it made great play in the European Community context of its desire to see more airline competition. But on the other hand it regarded the Authority's proposals as unduly strong medicine. In particular it opposed any radical attempt to cut British Airways down to size. It did however welcome the internal deregulation proposals.[45] Undoubtedly a major factor behind its refusal to change British Airways' basic position was connected with the airline's impending privatisation, and the fear that the sale price would consequently be depressed. More will be said on this topic in Chapter 8.

On the international front, it has already been explained that the UK government could not act unilaterally in respect of scheduled services. Even if it believed wholeheartedly in absolutely free competition, it could not create such conditions unless another country was agreeable. In some cases such agreement was forthcoming. Following its internal airline deregulation the US adopted a pro-competition stance in its air services agreements with other governments, and as a result a more liberalised situation emerged in UK–US routes. Equally some European countries such as the Netherlands have been in favour of competition, and as a result a significant loosening up has occurred. Competitive forces also began to undermine the IATA price-fixing system, and more will be said on that topic in Chapter 8. However in contrast to all this a relatively tightly regulated system continued to exist on most European routes despite the campaigning efforts of individuals such as Lord Bethell, consumer groups and the European Communities Commission. Whilst the Rome Treaty generally adopts a pro-competition approach, the peculiar position of air transport under the treaty posed problems—we will discuss these in more detail in Chapter 8. It should be noted that, whilst the UK paraded an enthusiasm for more competition in European air travel, when the chips were down and the possibility existed that member states of the European Community might do something, the UK is said to have reneged. It proposed relatively weak reforms. Critics explain this as being due to concern about the selling price of British Airways. The UK Secretary of State for Transport would no doubt dispute that, and argue that it was the result of the fact that when he was president of the Council of Ministers agreement on change was only possible if the lowest common denominator was tabled.

iii Financial Institutions

As we indicated earlier, in the financial sphere, defined broadly to include the Stock Exchange, forces for change have been moving in contrary directions. (a) Some have had a deregulatory impact—i.e. they have led to greater competition between firms in particular sectors of the financial system (e.g. between dealers on the Stock Exchange), and between different sectors of the system (e.g. banks versus building societies.) (b) But equally forces have been at work which have led to a process of prudential reregulation. That is to say, alongside the growing interfirm and intersector competition, there has been a tendency to widen the scope and formalise the controls which regulate the way in which business in the various sectors is conducted. Such regulation gives rise to rules and codes which emphasise the need for prudent management of affairs in the interests of enterprise viability, general financial stability and investor, policy holder and depositor protection. This latter form of regulation is to be distinguished from the monetary policy control variety. We shall consider the forces for change in the above order.

Formally the ending of self-regulatory restraints in connection with activities on the Stock Exchange was a product of UK antitrust policy. In 1956 the UK adopted what turned out to be a basically pro-competitive stance, when it introduced the Restrictive Trade Practices Act. However initially this law did not apply to services. It was only in 1973, under the Fair Trading Act, that agreements relating to services were brought within the ambit of the 1956 legislative approach. It was as a result of that extension of scope that the Stock Exchange rule book was eventually referred to the Restrictive Practices Court for adjudication. The process whereby various agreements were subsequently abandoned will be discussed in Chapter 8. Whilst the antitrust legislation was the formal cause of change, it is generally accepted that the days of the agreements were in fact numbered—indeed they were already crumbling. Basically competitive forces and technological change were undermining the system. Of central importance was the growing threat posed by the New York market which, as we recollect from Chapter 5, had been significantly deregulated from 1975 and indeed earlier. Commissions fell and increasingly transactions in prime UK equities began to shift to New York. The abolition of exchange controls in 1979 (environmental deregulation) facilitated this process. This is an extremely interesting example of the domino effect, whereby financial deregulation in one centre leads to sympathetic deregulation in another. We saw a similar example in Chapter 1 in connection with the impact of US airline deregulation on Canadian airlines.

Another competitive influence derived from the growth of institutional investors, who could use their muscle to undercut the system (see Chapter 4 for the US parallel). As Max Hall points out, they did in effect do so since they were able to benefit from ancillary services which were provided below cost or free. Hall also points out that the single capacity system was inefficient, and if dealers were to compete effectively they needed to be bigger and this rendered restrictions on outsider participation increasingly inappropriate.[46] (The ending of such restrictions of course led to a breaking down of the barriers between security dealing and activities such as banking—i.e. financial conglomeration). Added to all this were the advances in communications technology which increasingly meant that markets such as New York were just as convenient as London. To put it another way the market was being increasingly globalised and differences in the cost of dealing were therefore becoming increasingly untenable.

In other parts of the system competition rather than statutory change has been the major factor in deregulating. As we saw earlier, a shift of emphasis was signalled by the Bank of England as far back as 1971 with the issue of *Competition and Credit Control*. The Bank envisaged a more competitive system and at its request the clearing bank interest rate cartel (a system of self-regulation) was discontinued. But change was not just due to a changing relationship between domestic banks—it was also due to the entry into London of a host of foreign banks. This intensified competition which also had the effect of undermining controls on bank lending. The abolition of controls, together with an erosion of self-imposed restraints on the acceptable range of business, left banks free to offer competition to the building societies in respect of the latter's traditional mortgage business. This external competition, together with the associated growth of rivalry between building societies, helped to undermine the societies' interest rate cartel (itself a system of self-regulation). Thus far we have been emphasising the role of competition on the assets side, but the societies also faced increased competition on the liabilities side from the government (in the form of national savings), from the Trustee Savings Bank and the National Girobank (both had been turned into fully fledged banks) and from clearing banks (in connection with interest bearing cheque accounts). This competitive situation was unfair to the societies, since the banks were relatively unconstrained in their business whereas the societies were constrained by law. In order to create more equal conditions of competition it was therefore necessary to dismantle restrictions laid on the societies (this was, it must be admitted, a case of legal deregulation). It has been this kind of knock-on effect which has been at work in bringing change and deregulation to the system.

But as we noted earlier a parallel process of prudential reregulation has been at work which has affected the whole system. In the case of the banks, the original role of the Bank of England in matters such as capital adequacy, liquidity, etc., was a relatively informal one. This was possible when the banks were mainly British and there were few of them. But when foreign banks, which were less inclined to respond to the force of moral suasion began to crowd in, and particularly after the banking crisis of 1974, the system of regulation had to become more formalised. In the case of other financial institutions a whole series of events has triggered off change. The Wilson Committee Report of 1980, which reviewed the functions of the financial institutions, did not object to the system of non-statutory regulation which characterised the UK system. It did however feel that lay representation was desirable.[47] Subsequent scandals in the City, some of which occurred in areas not covered by the then existing regulatory framework, suggested that a review was called for. That in turn gave rise to an investigation and report by Professor Jim Gower which suggested a comprehensive system of self-regulation, within a statutory framework, which would provide effective investor protection.[48] Such a development was indeed imperative, since increased competition gave rise to the possibility of enterprise failure and might tempt firms to cut corners as far as the investor or depositor was concerned. Moreover deregulation brought in its train structural changes, whereby previously separate lines of businesses were coming together in conglomerate enterprises. Conflicts of interest could therefore arise, and the need for clear cut rules was therefore becoming more urgent. The increased intensity of competition also highlighted the need for reinforcement of the prudential control of building societies. It equally emphasised the need to extend to the system as a whole depositor and investor guarantees in the spirit of the Policy Holders Protection Act 1975. Indeed deposit insurance in the case of banks was foreshadowed in the 1979 Banking Act. These factors ultimately led to the Financial Services Act 1986 and the Building Societies Act 1986, which we will discuss in the next chapter. It should be added that consumer bodies such as the Consumers' Association and the National Consumer Council played a role in calling for change.

iv Broadcasting

Two factors have been at work in explaining the regulatory changes which have occurred in TV broadcasting. Firstly, as in the case of the US, a major force has been technological change which has meant that the traditional over-the-air terrestrial TV has been subjected to the challenges of cable and direct broadcasting by satellite (DBS), whilst subscription TV has offered another new dimension. It would, like the US, have been possible for the authorities to resist these changes but this has not occurred. A major reason, quite apart from the attraction of greater choice for viewers, has been the job and export opportunities which were expected to follow in the train of those new developments—notably in the space and consumer electronics industries. Secondly, the changes were welcomed by the Thatcher governments because they held out the promise of increased competition. The Conservatives appear to have regarded the traditional system as being unduly protected and as a result over-manned and over-renumerated. A two-way squeeze was envisaged. A greater proportion of programme production should be carried out by the leaner outside programme producers, who were also looking for a bigger home base from which to mount an export drive. In addition, new media to carry advertising would put pressure on advertising rates. While the latter pressure was obviously going to be felt by the ITV sector, the shift to more outside programme production was also directed against the public sector BBC.

v The Professions

Regulatory reform has been occurring in the professions. The forces at work have been of two kinds—general and specific.

General criticism has been levelled at the professions. We noted in Chapter 4 and again in Chapter 6 that commentators such as Milton Friedman have questioned the motivations of such self-regulation, particularly when it manifests itself in the form of licensing. The charge has indeed been levelled that income enhancement rather than consumer protection has been the motivating force. Stigler, for example, produced evidence which pointed to the conclusion that incomes in occupations in the US which were subject to licensing were higher than those which were unlicensed.[49] In its 1970 report on the supply of professional services, the Monopolies Commission expressed the general view that restrictions on entry were against the public interest, except where there was a risk of a specially serious kind to users who were unable to assess the likelihood of danger from unqualified practitioners.[50] The other general influence has proceeded from EEC membership. Here we refer to the Rome Treaty provisions concerned with Freedom to Supply Services (across frontiers) and the Right of Establishment (as when a professional person actually sets up in business in another member state). These provisions have meant that professions have been opened up to competition from other member states and this in turn has meant that the member states have had to recognise each other's qualifications and in some cases to harmonise the training leading thereto.

We turn now to the specific factors and will restrict the discussion to opticians and solicitors. In the case of opticians, institutional developments have led to their activities being brought under scrutiny. Secondly, public opinion was unhappy about the prices which they charged. The institutional developments were two in number. During the 1970s the Price Commission, an anti-inflation watchdog, was set up, and it issued two reports which were critical. In 1976 it reported on the price of private spectacles and contact lenses and concluded that they gave rise to a very profitable activity.[51] In its 1979 report a leading firm, Dolland and Aitchison, was under scrutiny, and the evidence also pointed to very high profits.[52] The latter report disposed the Office of Fair Trading (OFT) to refer the activities of opticians to the Monopolies and Mergers Commission (MMC). Here we must note a second institutional development. Initially British anti-trust had focussed on the supply of goods and not services. However thanks to the Monopolies and Mergers Act 1965 that loophole was dealt with. Monopolies in services could be investigated by the MMC, and that position still remains true in the case of professional services.[53] However as we noted in Chapter 6 the opticians were in a special position which rendered a reference to the MMC inappropriate. It should be added that the General Optical Council decided to review its rules on publicity and this prompted the OFT to await events. A second factor also came into play. As we noted above, public opinion was critical of the prices charged for privately dispensed spectacles. Interestingly, attention was drawn to the alleged low prices for reading spectacles which were available 'over the counter' in countries such as the US. Mindful of this criticism, Lord Rugby introduced a bill into the House of Lords to repeal the monopoly enjoyed by opticians in the sale of spectacles. This appears to have provoked the government into action—the Secretary of State for Consumer Affairs asked the OFT to investigate the restrictions operated by the General Optical Council. The bill was withdrawn and the OFT duly reported. The report indicated that the General Optical Council had indeed relaxed its prohibition on the display of prices in windows and that about a third of opticians were displaying them.[54] Whilst no recommendations were made by the OFT, the implications of its conclusion seemed to be that the sale of ready-glazed spectacles over the counter would widen choice and lower prices. There was no evidence that inaccurate spectacles could lead to permanent damage to the eyes. If ministers were concerned about absolutely free dispensing, then it was possible to envisage the possibility of ready-glazed spectacles being sold against a doctor's prescription.[55] The OFT criticised the restrictions on advertising which it believed caused prices to be higher and efficiency to be lower than otherwise would be the case.[56]

In the case of solicitors (in England and Wales) there were three kinds of restriction in operation. Under the Solicitors Act 1974 the Law Society controlled admission and it was an offence for unqualified persons to carry out certain legal functions including conveyancing. Restrictions were also imposed by the Society on advertising. In addition, fee scales were prescribed for certain functions including conveyancing. The maximum fees for conveyancing were however fixed not by the Law Society but by the state—the Lord Chancellor's Committee (upon which the Law Society had representation) performed this function. Again institutional developments were an important factor in causing change since, as we saw above, professional services were ultimately exposed to anti-trust surveillance. The advertising restrictions were investigated by the Monopolies and Mergers Commission, and in its 1976 report were roundly condemned as being disadvantageous to the public interest. The restrictions denied the public and potential new entrants information about services supplied. They were likely to have disadvantageous effects on competitiveness and efficiency, on the introduction of innovatory methods and services, and on the setting up of new practices.[57]

Subsequently the monopoly status itself came in for investigation. Two Royal Commissions on Legal Services, one for Scotland (Hughes Commission)[58] and one for England and Wales (Benson Commission)[59] considered the solicitors' monopoly. The former wanted it brought to an end, the latter wanted it to be maintained! Public opinion, consumer bodies and the press felt that the monopoly was indefensible—particularly in relation to conveyancing. Given the relatively large and growing body of house-owners in the UK, the prospect of competition in conveyancing was bound to be a popular issue. The subsequent course of events was somewhat similar to that in the case of opticians. Austin Mitchell MP lauched a private member's bill in the House of Commons in 1983—the House Buyer's Bill—which sought to end the solicitors' monopoly of conveyancing by opening it up to competition. Mr Mitchell was assisted by the Consumers' Association. The latter had commissioned a survey which indicated that the majority of house-buyers favoured competition. There was also strong support in the press. The government, which initially seems to have been less than enthusiastic, was forced to fall into line. The bill was withdrawn when the government signified its willingness to act. To this end it set up a committee (Farrand Committee) to explore the mechanics.

vi The European Community Dimension

We turn now to two industries which have been dominated by European Community systems of regulation. Pressure for reform of the CAP has been considerable although progress to date has been limited. Three particular forces for change have been at work. Firstly, the UK has constantly called for reform. Whilst as a consequence of membership it agreed to implement the CAP, the CAP has never been popular in the UK. One reason for this is that prior to membership the UK had pursued a much different policy which guaranteed cheap food. The UK approach had been to import food at low world prices and to remunerate farmers by paying deficiency payments on top of market prices. The unpopularity of the CAP in British eyes was further intensified by the financial implications it had for the UK in the context of the Community Budget. The UK, like the rest, made the appropriate payments. However since the UK was not a major producer of agricultural surpluses, and it was upon these that most of the Budget resources were spent, the UK faced the prospect of becoming a major net contributor. This gave rise to a serious dispute, but eventually the UK secured an amelioration of its position. Nevertheless the UK has remained critical of the way in which Community Budget monies are swallowed up by the European Agricultural Guidance and Guarantee Fund, whilst other forms of spending from which it could benefit (e.g. regional development) have been relatively starved of funds. It has therefore used its power to veto additional resources for the Community Budget and has only been willing to make concessions in return for meaningful undertakings to reform the CAP. This type of pressure was exerted by Mrs Thatcher in 1984 and again in 1988.

A second reason for reform has been the obvious failures of the CAP. Space does not enable us to detail all of them. However the outstanding problem has been the existence of surpluses. High prices and technological progress have led to increases in output whilst the low income elasticity of demand for food has meant that demand has grown slowly. Supply outstripped demand and, given the open-ended nature of the guarantee system, the Community had to take all the surpluses off the market. The consumer had to pay high prices for the food he needed and also had to pay for the disposal of food he did not want. Butter for Russians at knock-down prices has not been a popular spectacle.

The third factor for reform has been pressure from food producers outside the EEC. The CAP led to growing self-sufficiency which reduced outlets for food imports, and in addition EEC food surpluses were dumped on world markets. This caused prices to weaken and harmed other food exporting countries. They have been vocal in pressing for CAP reform.

As we indicated in Chapter 6, the UK steel industry falls within the ambit of the European Coal and Steel Community whose regulatory powers are governed by the provisions of the Paris Treaty. During the second half of the seventies and the early eighties, various crisis measures (see Chapter 6) were introduced in order to give the steel industry a breathing space within which to restructure. More recently three factors were at work which were calculated eventually to bring these interventions to an end. The first is that whilst the Paris Treaty is more *dirigiste* than the Rome Treaty, it is still true to say that free competition is the norm. The support systems which were introduced were quite literally crisis measures and as such were bound to be viewed as temporary. This strengthened the hand of the European Communities Commission in seeking to phase them out. Secondly, significant structural change had occurred, in some degree under the threat that subsidies had to be terminated by the end of 1985. Subject to certain exceptions subsidies are now forbidden. One sign of the structural change which had been accomplished is the fact that the nationalised British Steel Corporation is now back in profit and is being identified as a possible candidate for privatisation. The third influence was external in origin. The protective regime in the ECSC led some countries, notably the US, to retaliate. This gave an added impetus to the need to deal with the excess capacity problem and return the industry to conditions of free competition.

NOTES

1. D. A. Heald and D. R. Steel, 'Privatising Public Enterprise: An Analysis of the Government's Case', *Political Quarterly*, 53 (1982), p.337.
2. W. Keegan, *Mrs Thatcher's Economic Experiment*, (Penguin, Harmondsworth, 1984), p.34.
3. Provided it felt that the trade unions were disposed to be co-operative.
4. Keegan *op. cit.*, p.41.
5. *Ibid.*, p.33.
6. Sir Keith Joseph, *Reversing the Trend*, (Barry Rose, Chichester, 1975).
7. Sir Keith's taste in political economy can be judged from the reading list he issued to his senior civil servants during his tenure at the Department of Industry in the first Thatcher government. N. Bosanquet, 'Sir Keith's Reading List', *Political Quarterly*, 52 (1981), pp.324–41. The thinking of the New Right was further explored in N. Bosanquet, *After the New Right*, (Heinemann, London, 1983).
8. Angus Maude (ed.), *The Right Approach to the Economy*, (Conservative Central Office, London, 1977).
9. *The Economist*, 27 May 1978, pp.21–2.
10. S. Brittan, 'The Politics and Economics of Privatisation', *Political Quarterly* 55 (1984), p.109.
11. Sir Geoffrey Howe, *Privatisation: The Way Ahead* (Conservative Political Centre, London, 1981), p.4.
12. S. Brittan, 'Privatisation: A Comment on Kay and Thompson', *The Economic Journal*, 96 (1986), p.35.
13. J. Redwood and J. Hatch, *Controlling Public Industries, op. cit.*, p.18.
14. S. Jenkins, 'Government Policy Towards the Nationalised Industries', in T. J. G. Hunter (ed.) *Decision Making In a Mixed Economy, op. cit.*, p.175.
15. R. Pryke, *Public Enterprise in Practice*, (MacGibbon and Kee, London, 1971).
16. R. Pryke, *The Nationalised Industries, op. cit.*, p.257.
17. R. Pryke, 'The Comparative Performance of Public and Private Enterprise', *Fiscal Studies*, 3 (1982), pp.68–81.
18. J. Moore, *Why Privatise?* (Conservative Political Centre, London, 1983), pp.6, 13.
19. F. von Hayek, *The Road to Serfdom*, (Routledge and Kegan Paul, London, 1944) and *Constitution of Liberty* (Routledge and Kegan Paul, London, 1960). The interactions are also discussed in D. Heald, *Public expenditure: Its Defence and Reform, op. cit.*, pp.58–84.
20. Centre for Policy Studies, *Why Britain Needs a Social Market Economy* (Centre for Policy Studies, London, 1975), p.4.
21. Angus Maude (ed.) *op. cit.*, p.10.
22. R. Bacon and W. Eltis, *Britain's Economic Problem: Too Few Producers* (Macmillan, London, 1976), pp.110–11.

23. Sir Keith Joseph *op. cit.*, p.30.
24. This was a manifesto commitment.
25. Sir Geoffrey Howe, *op. cit.*, p.8.
26. J. Moore *op. cit.*, p.8.
27. *Ibid.*, pp.6–7.
28. S. Brittain 'The Politics and Economics of Privatisation' *op. cit.*, p.115.
29. J. Moore *op. cit.*, pp.8–9.
30. A. Peacock 'Privatisation in Perspective', *op. cit.*, pp.13–14.
31. *Ibid.*, p.14.
32. C. P. Mayer and S. A. Meadowcroft, 'Selling Public Assets: Techniques and Financial Implications', *Fiscal Studies* 6 (1985), pp.50–2.
33. J. D. Tomlinson, 'Ownership, Organisation and Efficiency', *The Royal Bank of Scotland Review* 149 (1986), p.21.
34. See D. Heald, 'Privatisation: Analysing its Appeal and Limitations', *Fiscal Studies* 5 (1984), p.37 and J. R. Shackleton, 'Privatisation: The Case Examined', *National Westminster Bank Quarterly Review*, May 1984, p.64.
35. *The Conservative Manifesto 1979* (Conservative Central Office, London, 1979), p.21.
36. S. Jenkins *op. cit.*, p.174.
37. The idea of spelling out in detail the objectives was not regarded as controversial. Criticism about the lack of clarity on the subject has long been voiced—e.g. by the Select Committee on Nationalised Industries—see R. Rees, *The Control of Nationalised Industries* (Open University, Milton Keynes, 1979).
38. J. Kay, 'The Privatisation of British Telecommunications', in D. Steel and D. Heald (eds) *Privatising Public Enterprises: Options and Dilemmas* (Royal Institute of Public Administration, London, 1984), p.78.
39. K. Newman, *The Selling of British Telecom* (Holt, Rhinehart and Winston, London, 1986), p.4 citing MORI Poll evidence.
40. D. D. Wyckoff, Oral evidence published in Interstate Commerce Commission, *A Cost and Benefit Evaluation of Surface Transport Regulation* (ICC, Washington, 1976).
41. *Buses* (HMSO, London, 1984), Cmnd. 9300. The reverse possibility could also arise.
42. On intercontinental scheduled services BA faced nose to nose competition on only two long distance routes—UK–Los Angeles and UK–Hong Kong via the Gulf—see Civil Aviation Authority, *Airline Competition Policy* (London, 1984) p.8.
43. BA was the only British airline allowed to operate international services from Heathrow and the only British airline having its main base there—*ibid.*, p.4.
44. *Ibid.*
45. *Airline Competition Policy* (HMSO, London, 1984), Cmnd. 9366.
46. M. Hall *op. cit.*, pp.9–12.
47. *Report of the Committee to Review the Functioning of the Financial*

Institutions (HMSO, London, 1980), Cmnd. 7937.

48. *Financial Services in the UK: A New Framework for Investor Protection* (HMSO, London, 1985), Cmnd. 4320.

49. G. J. Stigler, *The Citizen and the State* (University of Chicago Press, Chicago, 1975), pp.128–41.

50. Monopolies Commission, *A Report on the General Effect on the Public Interest of Certain Restrictive Practices so far as they Prevail in Relation to the Supply of Professional Services*, Part 1, Cmnd. 4463 (HMSO, London, 1970), p.75.

51. Price Commission, *Prices of Private Spectacles and Contact Lenses* (HMSO, London, 1976).

52. Price Commission, *Dolland and Aitchison Group—Prices Charges and Margins for Optical Products* (HMSO, London, 1979).

53. Agreements Relating to Commercial Services fall under the UK Restrictive Trade Practices legislation.

54. Office of Fair Trading, *Opticians and Competition* (HMSO, London, 1982), p.3.

55. *Ibid.*, pp.157–61.

56. *Ibid.*, p.161.

57. Monopolies and Mergers Commission, *Services of Solicitors in England and Wales* (HMSO, London, 1977), p.39.

58. Cmnd. 7846.

59. Cmnd. 7648.

8 Privatisation and Regulatory Change

1 PRIVATISATION

It will be abundantly clear from what has gone before that privatisation has been overwhelmingly a feature of the period since 1979 when the Thatcher government came to power. In this chapter we will be concerned with the actual process and in Appendix Table 2 a list of the major privatisations is provided. Critical consideration of the policy is reserved for Chapter 9.

Under the Thatcher governments the role of coordinating privatisation was given to the Treasury. Craig Pickering has pointed out that the Department of Industry as it was in 1979, the Department of Trade and Industry as it became, could well be said to have had a claim. But in fact it was not given the task although it has apparently played an important part in the administration of the policy.[1] The Cabinet Office has necessarily been central to the process, thus giving the Cabinet and Cabinet committees an opportunity to discuss general policy issues and specific cases. The Bank of England had to be brought in since clearly a successful stock market floatation required the identification of a time gap between share issues.

When it has come to specific cases the sponsoring department has taken the lead. Thus in the case of the sale of the British National Oil Company's oil and natural gas interests in order to create Britoil, the Department of Energy was central to the process. When the British Transport Docks Board was sold off as Associated British Ports Holdings, it was the Department of Transport that led the team. The Department of Trade and Industry will also feature when activities under its sponsorship are to be privatised. Given the complexity of the problems involved in producing a track record of past performance of the kind expected by the Stock Exchange, valuing assets, producing an opening balance sheet, devising an appropriate capital structure and selecting a share price, it was imperative that merchant bankers should be called in to advise.

The key initial question was what should be privatised. At the outset the policy was recognised to be novel and, despite the opinion poll evidence cited in Chapter 7, its public acceptability could not be taken for granted. Subsequently, as privatisation flotations proved for the most part to be successful and public opinion was not found to be hostile, the Conservative governments became bolder. At the Conservative Party conference in October 1986 the then Chancellor of the Exchequer Nigel Lawson boasted that by the end of 1987 two-fifths of the state industrial sector would have been privatised and in the subsequent parliament most of what remained would be disposed of.[2] Even British Coal, then a substantial loss maker, was expected to be in profit and ready for privatisation by 1989. This was the forecast of Sir Robert Haslem in 1986.

However not everything was to be privatised in the sense of being sold off. It had long been recognised that the Royal Dockyards needed to be subjected to competition and to adopt a more commercial approach. Consideration was given to the possibility of privatisation as well as to the less radical step of operating the dockyards as a trading fund (as had been the case with the Royal Ordnance Factories). Both these options were firmly rejected. Privatisation was dismissed partly because of the difficulty of separating out the assets which the MOD would need to retain from those that would be transferred to the privatised dockyard companies.[3] The Secretary of State for Defence also pointed out that full privatisation 'would leave the Government with insufficient influence over a major establishment in the defence field at a time of considerable transition'.[4] In the end the government decided to retain the ownership of the yards but to lease out their operation, with some business being guaranteed to the lessees and some being open to competition between the two privately managed yards and outsiders.

In practice therefore, apart from special cases such as the Royal Dockyards, the question became increasingly not one of *what* should be privatised but of *when* particular corporations, companies, trading funds and departmental activities should be sold off. The earlier candidates tended to have some but necessarily all of the following characteristics. Firstly, they were already profitable (or could be fairly easily rendered so by debt write-offs, etc.) and were therefore readily marketable. Secondly, they could be launched off into a competitive setting and therefore the problem of the government having to regulate a monopoly position, etc., did not arise—market forces would do the regulating. Thirdly, there was no need for complicated negotiations about the allocation of responsibilities previously discharged by the public enterprise in the post-privatisation situation. One of the reasons why the privatisation of water supply was delayed was because of complications of this kind. Fourthly, the proposed privatisation was relatively uncontroversial in the sense that the activity in question might normally be expected to be found in the free enterprise sector and was not part of the core of utilities which are conventionally thought to be located in the public sector. An activity which might be typically associated with public ownership might however be privatisable without much controversy if it did not touch too closely upon the consumer interest—thus the mass of the population was not likely to get worked up about what happened to the British Transport Docks Board. Many would not even know it existed. The privatisation of British Petroleum was of course rendered less controversial by virtue of the fact the Labour party had itself sold off part of the government's holding. Fifthly, to the extent that a candidate for privatisation was already a public limited company (in which the Treasury, the National Enterprise Board, etc., had a stake) the time consuming job of turning a public corporation, trading fund or government departmental activity into a public limited company did not arise.

The candidates which came later did so because of some though not necessarily all of the following reasons. Firstly, they were not profitable or sufficiently so. This was a factor which delayed the privatisation of British Airways. Although the power to privatise British Airways was taken in 1980, it was not actually sold off to the public until 1987. In the case of British Coal, even though Nigel Lawson probably anticipated its ultimate privatisation when he made his bold promise in 1986, the losses that it was then still making were such that it was not felt necessary to have the privatisation power in the bag. It should be added that the post-1979 recession generally set back the process of economic recovery among enterprises destined for privatisation.

Secondly, a competitive framework into which to launch the privatised firm was not available. This clearly troubled the Conservative government in its early days in office. Sir Geoffrey Howe, for example, was far from clear as to what ought to be done about natural monopolies even if they were making a profit. It would, he argued, be wrong to entrust private owners with monopoly powers. Whilst he did not reject privatisation, he tended to look to other means of control such as surveillance by the Monopolies and Mergers Commission under the 1980 Competition Act, the ending of statutory monopolies (e.g. by allowing the private generation of electrical power for resale and the connection of 'foreign' attachments to the telecommunications network), and regionalisation of at least some aspects of the monopoly. Whilst the latter might not permit competition between regions, it would facilitate cost comparisons as part of a system of efficiency auditing.[5] In due course however the government came to the conclusion that the absence of competition or substantial competition should not stand in the way of privatisation. The solution was regulation—a system upon which, as we saw earlier, the US has been turning its back. In 1985 the Financial Secretary to the Treasury indicated the degree to which the Conservative government had jettisoned any inhibitions it might have had about the privatising of natural monopolies. He observed 'Where competition is impractical privatisation policies have now been developed to such an extent, that regulated private ownership of natural monopolies is preferable to nationalisation.'[6] John Moore had been critical of competition surrogates such as marginal cost pricing, etc., but was quite happy to embrace another surrogate. The regulatory approach was of course first applied in the case of British Telecommunications, was subsequently applied when the British Gas Corporation and the British Airports Authority were sold off, was envisaged for water supply and was continued in the case of privatised British Airways.

Thirdly, the management of the privatisation candidates needed to be convinced of the desirability of a sell-off. There were two reasons for this. (a) As Sir Geoffrey Howe pointed out, only rarely could the selling off of even a peripheral aspect of a nationalised business be secured by ministerial directive if the management did not agree.[7] The well known resistance of Sir Denis Rooke, Chairman of British Gas, to the sale of its onshore oil property at Wytch Farm gave rise to a substantial delay. (b) Even though the government might not be disposed to give the management a veto over its decision to privatise, it did respect the management's right to be consulted.

Fourthly, privatisation might be delayed by factors outside the total control of the government. The most obvious examples arose in connection with British Airways where legal action for damages in connection with the failure of Laker Airways created financial uncertainty. A further delay occurred as a result of the need to renegotiate an international air agreement with the US (Bermuda Two) which had important implications for British Airways' overseas business.

Fifthly, technicalities could cause delays. In the case of the privatisation of water the plan had to be put back partly because difficulties arose over who would be responsible for land drainage. There were also problems in connection with the financial reconstructions which would be necessary if the less interesting water authorities were to be put in a position to attract the same investor interest as did the Thames Water Authority. Inevitably privatisation tended to get caught up in electoral politics. The privatisation of water was controversial, not least because of its environmental implications, and it affected the mass of the population. The decision to postpone may therefore be partly ascribed to a desire to avoid electoral banana skins in the run up to a general election.

Activities which were to be privatised had to be prepared for disposal. Firstly, as we have already indicated, it was necessary that the management should view it as desirable and indeed inevitable. This might be accomplished by gentle persuasion. However it is apparent that the persuasion was not always gentle—it might indeed be said on occasion to have looked more like bullying. The reader will recollect that in Chapter 7 we noted that Mrs Thatcher and the nationalised industry chairmen were engaged in a vigorous tussle during the 1981–82 period. Moreover we concluded that that experience hardened Mrs Thatcher to the view that the ultimate aim was to get nationalised industries off the government's back. It should be added that it also undoubtedly tended to induce nationalised industry managements to take the view that life would be better if they could get government off their backs. Whilst we noted that the government backed down significantly on the Ibbs proposals, the desire of the Conservative government to bring nationalised industry managements under closer control, at least in the interim, did not then cease. Thus in August 1984 the government produced consultation proposals concerning future nationalised industry legislation. They provoked a strong reaction from the nationalised industry chairmen. Further proposals were produced in the December of that year. These too were strongly opposed. Sir Denis Rooke, Chairman of British Gas, denounced them in these terms:

Not only the price of gas, but the whole gamut of corporate planning, capital expenditure and wage negotiations would become the implicit responsibility of Government. The Corporation's Board would be, to all intents and purposes, reduced to the role of a management committee acting at the ultimate behest of the Treasury. It is difficult to reconcile this with the declared view of the Treasury that state corporations should be allowed a substantial degree of commercial freedom to achieve and maintain commercial viability. Indeed it runs directly counter to that aim, since by effectively weakening the authority of the Board and narrowing its discretion the Board's capacity to provide the stimulus to greater commercial effectiveness is undermined.[8]

There can be little doubt that this sort of experience increasingly disposed nationalised industries which were profitable, or envisaged the prospect of profitability, to embrace privatisation as a welcome deliverance from ministerial criticism and bureaucratic interference. It is also not unreasonable to conclude that the government did not stumble on this reaction accidentally. Whilst government sought to persuade existing managements to go private, it is also true to say that it sought to achieve that objective by putting in new managers who were known to be favourable to privatisation. Such was the case when Sir John King was made chairman of British Airways.

Thus far the emphasis has been laid on securing the compliance of management—but what about the trade unions? Not surprisingly they were opposed, but if we take the case of British Telecommunications their resistance did elicit some assurances from management,[9] and that almost certainly helped to ease the transition.

Getting industries into shape also required that they should be rendered profitable. To that end new managers were injected, who were given the brief of adopting a root and branch approach to nationalised industry over-manning, inefficiency and losses. The most obvious example of that policy was the appointment of Ian McGregor who successively and with ruthless determination restructured the steel and coal industries. The effectiveness of the policy of plant closures and redundancies is revealed in the comparison between the huge losses in the period prior to his appointment and the fact that by 1986 Bob Scholey, his successor at British Steel, and Sir Robert Haslem, his successor at British Coal, could both be contemplating privatisation as a serious (and it seems attractive) prospect.[10] New management was of course necessary, not only to bring to an end the losses which had afflicted industries such as coal and steel, but also to provide prospective privatisees with the more commercial leadership which was necessary when public enterprises became private. Thus in the case of British Telecommunications a new management team was put in place which had considerable outside business experience, not least in marketing. This new team was also intended to cope with the liberalisation of telecommunications which preceded the public sale.[11]

Profitability or increased profitability may of course be achieved in somewhat less painful ways, at least as far as the industry is concerned. One is price increases where competition does not preclude them. Thus in the case of the water authorities the government decided that they should provide more of the funds necessary for their capital investment. This was achieved by requiring them to raise their charges. In the case of the Thames Water Authority this occurred to such an extent that the authority was able to begin repaying its debt to the government, with the prospect that it would be debt-free by 1989.[12] The elimination of such debt charges clearly increased the prospective yield which a given income stream would provide for any given nominal amount of privatised equity. It would therefore improve its marketability. Prospective profitability could also be increased by writing debts off. The government did so in a number of cases including the British Transport Docks Board and the National Freight Corporation. In these two cases it did however replace the debt with equity, but not of equal nominal value.[13] It was also necessary to finance pension funds properly—in the case of the National Freight Corporation four-fifths of the money raised found its way into the new company's pension fund.[14]

There were however other ways in which the government could influence the future profitability of privatised enterprises, and these have attracted considerable criticism. We refer of course to the question of what was to happen to monopoly positions and existing systems of regulation in the post-privatisation period. Clearly the government was faced with two conflicting considerations. Assets would bring the highest price if the enterprises owning them continued to be sheltered from competition. But assets were likely to be most efficiently employed if the force of competition was unleashed. The Conservative party had after all made great play of the point that inefficiency in nationalised industries stemmed at least in part from their protected positions. In practice some liberalisation was introduced, but it fell far short of establishing conditions of free competition. Let us look at a few cases.

British Telecommunications was originally separated off

from the Post Office as an independent public corporation under the British Telecommunications Act 1981. Under that act it enjoyed an exemption from the requirement that all telecommunications suppliers should be licensed. Under the Telecommunications Act 1984 the power was taken to privatise British Telecommunications and in addition the latter was placed on an equal footing with other suppliers in having to obtain a licence to operate. The licensor, who is currently the Secretary of State for Trade and Industry, could have used his power generously in order to create competition. In practice he granted British Telecommunications a master licence for 25 years and the only other competitor (other than the City of Hull) was to be Mercury Communications.[15] Mercury, a small enterprise as compared with British Telecommunications, was allowed to create additional trunk line capacity (in the form of fibre optic cable) linking various cities in England in a figure-of-eight loop system. No new licences were to be issued until November 1990 at the earliest.

The government also commissioned a study by Michael Beesley concerning the possibility that British Telecommunications capacity could be leased with a view to resale. Beesley concluded that unlimited resale should be allowed.[16] However the government did not agree to the proposal, thus preventing the emergence of competition through the use of existing capacity as opposed to through new capacity, as in the case of Mercury. (The leasing of British Telecommunications capacity for private use, as opposed to resale, is allowed). The government defended its refusal on the grounds of the need to let Mercury develop.[17] This restriction stands until at least 1989. The only area where competition has been allowed has been in the provision of terminal equipment—however it was alleged that the setting of standards and the giving of approvals was subject to delays and manipulation.[18]

In the case of British Airways the system of regulation which affected both fares and route allocations has already been described. It guaranteed British Airways the lion's share of domestic business.[19] In 1979,[20] but even more in 1984,[21] the Civil Aviation Authority indicated its preference for more competition and under the Civil Aviation Act 1980, the regulator was for the first time required to have regard to the advantages of competition when allocating routes. Some moves were indeed made in that direction as in the case of granting British Midland the right to fly on the Heathrow–Edinburgh/Glasgow routes. When the proposal to privatise British Airways began to gather pace the smaller competitors, such as British Caledonian, as well as the Civil Aviation Authority, began to press for a reallocation of traffic—see Chapter 7. Not surprisingly this was vigorously opposed by British Airways. It was also substantially rejected by the government. Without its inheritance of routes British Airways would have been a much less attractive asset to privatise. As Mark Ashworth and Peter Forsyth observed—'When BA is sold, it is an airline *plus* regulation which is being sold. The price depends on the regulation expected to be in force.'[22]

A decision to reject the competitive option was also apparent in the case of the privatisation of the British Airports Authority. David Starkie and David Thompson in their study of airport privatisation pointed out that:

> There is considerable scope for increasing competition in the south-east provided that the ownership of BAA's airports is divided. Separate ownership of BAA's London airports would introduce more competition into the large market associated with travel to and from London and the South-east region. Specifically, Stanstead and Gatwick have the potential to complete strongly with each other (and with Luton) in the large and 'foot-loose' inclusive-tour and intercontinental discount fare market. There are indications that the cross-elasticities are high in this market segment. In addition, Gatwick is shaping up as a promising competitor to Heathrow; it now serves more UK regional centres and more cities in the US than does Heathrow. (And if the Docklands STOL–port and its proposed services obtain approval this will add a further, albeit small, competitive element.)[23]

The British Airports Authority was opposed to breaking the London airports up and the government agreed—they have been sold as one entity.

In the case of other nationalised industries some liberalisation has been introduced, but its impact should not be overestimated. In the case of the Post Office, express mail document exchange and other services have been opened to competition.[24] Under the Energy Act 1983, Area Boards and the Central Electricity Generating Board must take their transmission and distribution networks available to private electricity producers on terms which produce a normal return on capital.[25] The Oil and Gas (Enterprise) Act 1982 required British Gas to provide a similar common carrier facility to any other enterprises who wished to enter the gas supply business. The latter is not however thought to be of great significance since any entrant will be using relatively new gas sources which will be costly compared with British Gas, whose prices on average reflect older lower-priced contracts. Finally mention must be made of the changes relating to the private mining and sale of opencast coal. The limit on the size of licensed reserves was raised by a relatively small amount in 1981 but the more substantial increase recommended by the Monopolies and Mergers Commission in 1983 has not been implemented.

As we have already indicated, in several cases privatised enterprises have been subjected to regulation—either that which existed previously or that which was introduced when, with public ownership absent, competition could not be relied upon to police prices, profitability, efficiency and service. Clearly the kind of price control system applied can be a major factor influencing the profitability of a privatised concern, and therefore its attractiveness to investors. We will however reserve our discussion of these issues until later, when we consider the various safeguard mechanisms which have been introduced in certain cases.

Preparation for privatisation also involved the government in making a decision as to whether public enterprises should be sold off as single concerns or should be broken up on sale. The Conservative government has shown a marked preference for the former. In telecommunications the UK has not followed the US down the divestiture path (see Chapter 5)—i.e. separately owned local networks interconnecting with a trunk line monopolist. Equally, as we have seen, it has preferred a private London airport monolith. It also decided to sell British Gas as one concern, rejecting other options such as regionalisation. Thus Beth Hammond, Dieter Helm and David Thompson suggested that the British Gas national transmission system, which takes North Sea supplies from the beach-head to the twelve nationalised regions,[26] is a natural monopoly and should remain as such in the privatised state. But distribution within regions could be carried out by a series of separate private companies. They argued that this would produce more efficient corporate entities, since they would be small enough to feel the threat of takeover (i.e. the market for corporate control) and even bankruptcy. It would also be more likely that the structure of prices would be more closely related to marginal costs since interregional subsidisation would be eliminated.[27] Such a break-up was also possible if electricity was privatised—see Chapter 9.

Prior to disposal it has of course been necessary to make decisions about the appropriate capital structure (the debt/equity ratio, etc.) and also about the price of the privatised equity. The latter of course influences the prospective yield. Where earnings growth is expected to be high, investors may be tempted by a high price and a commensurately low yield since they will be looking to the prospect of capital gains. Where growth prospects are low, as in the case of water which is a mature industry, an attractive yield is required *ab initio*— *The Economist* suggested a rate close to that on gilt-edged government stock.[28]

We now turn to the actual disposal itself. Firstly, an enterprise may be disposed of in whole or only a part may be detached. Thus British Aerospace was sold *in toto*, but in the case of BL car divisions initially it was only Jaguar which was both separable and profitable. Secondly, there is the question of the actual method of sale. The Conservative government adopted a variety of techniques. These included:

(a)   Public Issues of shares on the Stock Exchange (e.g. British Aerospace, Cable and Wireless, British Telecommunications and British Gas);

(b)   Management buy-outs possibly with assistance from financial institutions (e.g. the National Freight

Corporation);
(c) Placement of shares with institutional investors (e.g. the sale of the UK government's minority share-holding in the British Sugar Corporation);
(d) Private sale of assets (e.g. the disposal of the Royal Ordnance Leeds tank plant to Vickers);
(e) Joint Ventures (e.g. Allied Steel and Wire Ltd—an independent subsidiary set up by the British Steel Corporation and GKN Ltd).

In terms of funds raised public issues have been by far the most important and below we concentrate on that approach.

When a public enterprise is already a public limited company, the problem of disposal is that much easier. Where the activity is initially the whole or part of a public corporation, a trading fund or a government department, it is first necessary to turn the activity into public limited company form, with the sponsoring secretary of state holding the shares. The shares can then be sold to the public in whole or part. Such public sales do however assume that the company to be disposed of has an adequate track record of the kind demanded by the Stock Exchange. That would normally require a satisfactory run of results over the previous five years. When the Conservative government first decided to sell the Royal Ordnance Factories it envisaged them being sold as a whole, and they were put into a collective limited company form.[29] Subsequently the government got cold feet about the likely impact of the Royal Ordnance Factories' relatively unattractive performance record. It feared that a sale to the general public would be a flop—just prior to the huge British Gas flotation. It therefore decided to sell the factories off privately.

The reference above to sales in whole or part reminds us that the government has not always decided to sell all of the shares. In a number of cases it has chosen to hold a minority interest. This has given rise to the concept of the hybrid. However in some cases hybridity has only been a transitional state e.g. British Aerospace, British National Oil Corporation's oil and gas exploration business privatised as Britoil and the British Transport Docks Board privatised as Associated

British Ports Holdings. Minority government stakes have however remained in Cable and Wireless and British Tele-communications. The general attitude of the government has been that it would not intervene in the affairs of hybrid companies. But it did indicate in the case of some companies, which as it happened were only temporarily hybrid, that it would use its holding to block foreign ownership or threats to company independence. It seems likely that in the long run minority stakes will be disposed of.

The government adopted two devices in its public issues—offers for sale and tender offers. The former were frequently employed because they were most easily understood by smaller investors. Offers for sale involve the setting of a fixed price in advance of the sale. In the case of tender offers, bids are invited above a certain specified minimum price. Two possibilities then arise. After the bids are in, a common striking price can be set which will clear the market. Alter-natively the shares being tendered for can be allocated on the basis of the highest bidders being given first preference. In this case successful bidders will probably pay different prices rather than one common striking price. This second approach was employed in the British Airports offer—no doubt follow-ing criticisms concerning the degree to which in previous cases share prices had gone to a premium in subsequent trading.

In order to assist smaller investors various devices were adopted. In an offer for sale the issue may be over-subscribed, in which case allocations have to be scaled down, but allo-cations to bigger investors have been scaled down more heavily. In cases where tender offers were employed it was possible to offer to buy at the striking price. This was felt to be attractive to small inexperienced investors. Tender offers have also been accompanied by separate blocks of shares which were available at a fixed price published in advance. This device was employed in the British Airports offer. The smaller investor was also helped by the phasing of payments in two instalments and by offering telephone (etc.) vouchers in lieu of future bonus shares. In order to attract employees special arrangements were made. For example, in the case of British Telecommunications employees were given £70 of shares free. They were also entitled to two shares for every one bought up to a limit of £300. They were also given a preferential allotment in the public offer.

Privatisation has also been accompanied by regulatory systems designed to control the exercise of market power. This has notably been the case in telecommunications and gas, and will presumably apply in the case of water. All these are activities where there are significant economies of scale and elements of natural monopoly. Regulation has also been instituted in the case of airports, where geographical factors confer substantial market power since the privatised British Airports Authority controls the three London airports and the nearest competitors, e.g. Luton, are at a substantial locational disadvantage (as compared with Heathrow) and have limited capacity. Regulation has also been applied to privatised British Airways. However, as we noted earlier in connection with US deregulation, there are no pronounced economies of scale in airline operation, and indeed the market has marked contestable characteristics. Nevertheless the pre-existing regulated state has been carried over into the post-regulation arrangement.

In the case of telecommunications a Director General of Telecommunications has been established who presides over the Office of Telecommunications (Oftel). As we indicated earlier, a licence is required to operate as a supplier of tele-communications services. These are issued by the Secretary of State for Trade and Industry having consulted the Director General. The latter may subsequently modify the terms of a licence with the concurrence of the licensee. He may also make a modification in the absence of such concurrence, but has first of all to seek the approval of the Monopolies and Mergers Commission. If the Commission agrees he then has to see that whatever deficiencies existed are remedied. Licences contain various conditions including a requirement not to show undue preference or undue discrimination.[30]

The Director General is also responsible for operating a system of price control. This is based upon Professor Stephen Littlechild's report which suggested a formula whereby certain prices charged by British Telecom ought not to rise faster than three percentage points less than the Retail Prices

Index.[31] This arrangement will be reviewed in 1989. It should be noted that control is placed on price and not on the rate of return which, as we have seen, is typical of much US utility regulation. As we can see the formula requires that if British Telecommunications is to match the rise in the Resale Prices Index it will have to find savings, through technological improvements etc., of three per cent each year. This provides an inbuilt incentive towards increased efficiency which is largely absent in US regulation. It should also be noted that the Littlechild formula does not apply to all services but only to local and trunk calls and residential and business line rental. These represent fifty-five per cent of revenue. The Director General is not required to prescribe prices but to be reactive—i.e. he could intervene if British Telecommunications sought to exceed the RPI-3 formula. Oftel also ensures that the licensees satisfy reasonable demands for service. (In British Telecommunications's case this included unprofitable services such as public call boxes, emergency services, etc.)

In respect of antitrust phenomena, the Director General of Telecommunications and the Director General of Fair Trading exercise a concurrent jurisdiction in referring cases under the 1973 Fair Trading and 1980 Competition Acts. British Telecommunications has also been allowed to continue to manufacture equipment, but this activity is vested in a separate subsidiary. As a result separate accounts have to be produced which would aid the detection of cross-subsidisation. The British Telecommunications licence also requires interconnection. In the first instance this applied to the separate system run by the City of Hull. Later it applied in the case of the trunk fibre optic loop established by Mercury—this was referred to earlier. Since Mercury has no local circuits and the cost of producing them would be prohibitive, the most economical approach was to use British Telecommunications's existing local connections. British Telecommunications and Mercury were unable to agree terms, and the matter had to be settled in the High Court. Thus Mercury gained interconnection and greatly enhanced the attractiveness of its system.

In the case of the regulation by British Gas, a somewhat

similar system has been devised. A Director General of Gas Supply, presiding over an Office of Gas Supply (Ofgas), has been established. The Secretary of State for Energy, after consulting the Director General can authorise suppliers to supply. The Director General can modify and police agreements on similar lines to the process prescribed for tele-communications. Whereas large industrial and commercial consumers must negotiate prices with British Gas, domestic consumers will be protected by a formula operated by the Director General. The latter allows prices to rise by the same amount as the Retail Prices Index minus an allowance for increased efficiency but plus an allowance for the increase in the average cost of gas. In order to protect standards of service a Gas Consumers' Council was also provided for.

In the case of British Airports the function of regulating airport changes has been vested in the Civil Aviation Authority. The Civil Aviation Authority can also prescribe conditions in respect of accounts in order to police the practice of cross-subsidisation. It appears that this latter provision is mainly designed to prevent the more lucrative airports from subsidising Stansted to the disadvantage of airports such as Luton. The statute indicates that the Civil Aviation Authority must discharge its regulatory role in respect of prices and practices in close collaboration with the Monopolies and Mergers Commission.

Three final points remain to be made. Privatisation statutes have employed the device of the special share—this allowed the government to outvote all other shares on certain issues. This device was not always employed—it was, for example, incorporated in the British Gas statute but was not included in that concerning British Airways. In the British Gas case the provision meant that the consent of the special shareholder would be required for certain matters including in particular the limitation on shareholdings (see below), the creation or issue of shares with voting rights or any variation in the voting rights attached to shares. Statutes have usually set limits to the size of individual shareholdings—a figure of fifteen per cent seems typical. In the case of British Airways a limit was also placed on the proportion of shares which could be held by non-UK nationals. This was justified on the grounds that

BA's operating rights on certain international routes might be at risk if it was substantially owned and controlled by non-UK nationals.

2 REGULATORY CHANGE

i Road Haulage

In Chapter 6 we noted that the regulation of road freight transport was liberalised in the later 1960s and that, following the UK's membership of the European Community in 1973, road freight came under the aegis of the EEC Common Transport Policy (CTP). Broadly speaking the CTP did not reverse that position. It is true that the CTP, as originally conceived, envisaged control over rates via rate brackets, but in the context of the original Six that was in fact a liberalising stance when compared with the fixed rates operated by some states. In practice, rate brackets were not applied to all hire and reward road haulage, but only to the international variety. Moreover within the latter category the width of the brackets, together with the option (favoured by the UK) whereby reference rates may be substituted, mean that rate controls do not currently exercise a significant constraining influence. Earlier we saw that prior to membership the UK had swept quantitative licensing away, and the CTP did not reverse that move. Indeed the original blueprint for the CTP was based on the desirability of easing capacity constraints. The CTP has however required the UK to apply qualitative licensing—hauliers have to satisfy harmonised conditions relating to professional competence, good repute and financial capacity. This involved no great change since similar provisions were already in force. The CTP has also involved the UK in acceding to regulations designed to secure equal conditions of competition as between member states (e.g. rules concerning driving hours and rest periods, and the weights and dimensions of lorries). The objective of fair inter-modal competition through the allocation of track costs to beneficiaries has not been achieved. The CTP has also involved the imposition of licence quotas in respect of international road transport. However in terms of liberalisation that did not represent a step backwards, since member states had previously operated bilateral quotas. Moreover thanks to pressure from the European Parliament, the Community Quota of international licences will be increased and ultimately this quantitative limit will be swept away. It is also anticipated that limited cabotage rights (i.e. domestic hauls carried out in conjunction with international hauls) will be allowed—thus injecting a liberalising influence into domestic markets.

ii Coaches and Buses

A general movement towards deregulation has characterised road passenger transport in the period since 1979. The Transport Act 1980 contained a number of liberalising measures. It further encouraged car sharing. No public service vehicle licence was needed in such circumstances provided the aggregate fares paid did not exceed the running cost of the vehicle for the journey in question and arrangements were made for payment of fares before the journey began. Long distance (express) service was redefined to cover journeys travelled by *every* passenger—the minimum such journey was measured as a straight line 30 miles from the pick-up point to the point of discharge. Licensing restrictions on entry into such *express services* were removed, although safeguards relating to safety and competence were retained. In respect of *stage service* operating, licences continued to be required but the Traffic Commissioners now had to grant an application unless it was against the public interest, whilst objectors to a service faced a new situation. It was now up to them to prove that the new service was not in the public interest. Traffic Commissioners' powers over fares were whittled down to interventions in special circumstances. Finally, the Act also provided for local authorities to be designated as trial areas where operating licence conditions for stage services would be relaxed.

Despite the change of emphasis in licensing, the government was not satisfied with the situation in respect of stage services. For example, it noted that the power to object to the grant of a licence, and to appeal if one was granted, tended to favour existing, and particularly larger, operators—smaller firms seeking a licence might not be able to face the expense of fighting an objection.[32] Under the Transport Act 1985 the need for an operating licence for stage services was therefore abolished—the removal took place in a phased manner with entirely free entry being established in January 1987. Safety standards continued to be enforced. Traffic Commissioners did not disappear—they were required to exercise an oversight which included the prevention of what may be termed competitive disorganisation. A system of competitive tendering was introduced for directly subsidised services and special arrangements were made for London.

iii Airlines

We turn now to air passenger transport. When the Thatcher government came to power it introduced legislation which indicated a preference for a competitive approach in air transport. The 1980 Civil Aviation Act called upon the Civil Aviation Authority to perform its licensing duty in a way which was best calculated to ensure that British airlines competed with other airlines, and in respect of licensing generally (and not just international operations) it was required to have regard to the benefits which might arise from having two or more airlines providing a particular service. Despite this growing emphasis on competition the record is patchy.

In connection with the competitive structure of the UK airline industry we have already noted that the UK government did not accept the Authority's 1984 proposals for building up other airlines as credible alternatives to British Airways. Wholesale transfers of intercontinental and other routes did not occur. British Airways did withdraw from UK–Saudi Arabia routes and these were transferred to British Caledonian. But British Caledonian withdrew from routes to South America, Denver and Morocco, leaving British Airways free to step in. Nor were European services from provincial points transferred. However British Airways indicated its recognition of the fact that other airlines would be encouraged to open up routes in competition with it, and it undertook to provide financial assistance towards such developments.[33]

On the domestic front a gradual process of liberalisation has been apparent. Prior to the Civil Aviation Authority's

1984 statement of policy, independents were allowed to muscle in on British Airways's territory e.g. the entry of British Midland on the London to Belfast and London to Glasgow/Edinburgh routes. In 1984, as we saw earlier, the Authority took a very significant step forward when it decided that domestic routes should be subject to free entry (except for those specifically excluded) and that regulation of fares should be limited to the requirement that they should be filed—this was a device for stopping overcharging and predatory pricing. In practice such interventions have been exceedingly rare.

Turning now to scheduled services on international routes, the tariff fixng activities of IATA were subject to attack from three quarters. The first was charter operations, which IATA failed to regulate and which increasingly made inroads into the scheduled market. The second was the growth of non-IATA carriers, notably in South East Asia, who in various ways undercut the IATA rate levels. The third challenge (a legal one) came from the US and followed in the wake of its own internal deregulation. The effect of all this was manifested in the increased disposition of airlines to operate outside the IATA price-fixing system, and for rates on North Atlantic routes to be cast in terms of zones of reasonableness. The US deregulatory philosophy was also made manifest in its approach to bilateral air services agreements. The Bermuda Two US–UK agreement of 1977 came fairly early in American policy transition, but did nevertheless contain some features which opened up the market. It increased the number of gateways into the US and shifted significantly toward dual designation. Rigas Doganis points out that capacity control posed a particular problem but was ultimately based on traffic forecasts. If the forecasts differed and agreement was not forthcoming, capacity was based on an average of the forecasts. Doganis notes that this limited but important control did not appear in some of the later bilaterals affecting other countries. The 1977 arrangement gave rise to criticism in the US because it was regarded as being protectionist, and in 1980 amendments were negotiated which added more gateways and more dual designation.[34] In 1986 Bermuda Two was renegotiated. It preserved a sixty-forty split in favour of the

US, but the Secretary of State for Transport claimed that the capacity arrangements had been significantly liberalised.

In the European Community a strict regime has until recently continued to exist. Despite the fact that the Rome Treaty, to which twelve European states are signatory, opts for undistorted competition as the centrepiece of the economic integration process, progress on the deregulatory front has been slow. Two problems have been encountered. Firstly, whilst it was evident that air transport was not covered by the Common Transport Policy, it was not clear to what extent other treaty provisions, e.g. those relating to competition, did apply to it. That issue was resolved in 1974 in the case of *EC Commission* v. *French Republic*.[35] It was decided that general treaty provisions including those relating to competition did apply. A second problem then arose. A competition rule such as Article 85, which enables the EC Commission to attack agreements, is only fully applicable if the Council of Ministers *on a unanimous basis* adopts the necessary implementing regulation. This the Council of Ministers did not do. This then left the application of Article 85 very much in the hands of member states, although the Commission could play a limited role. The failure to introduce the necessary implementing regulation was of course a reflection of the lack of enthusiasm of many member states for an open skies policy although the UK took (or claimed to take) a different view. Procedurally it seemed that the Commission's hands were tied.

Three avenues of attack were available. Firstly, deregulation on a piecemeal basis was possible provided that parties to bilateral agreements were of a like mind. This happened notably in the case of the UK–Netherlands bilateral in 1984. Air traffic was substantially deregulated since the agreement provided for the free entry of new carriers, eliminated capacity controls, and allowed the country from where the traffic originated to determine fares. Other agreements, although not as liberal, followed.[36]

Secondly, the member states might be induced to accept at least a limited amount of liberalisation. The EC Commission has been striving to achieve such an end since at least 1972 and memoranda on the subject were addressed to the Council of Ministers in 1979 and 1984. In 1986 a package of measures was under consideration by virtue of which the airlines would be exempted from attack under Article 85 provided agreement could be secured on some degree of liberalisation. These measures involved reducing the share of traffic allocated to the designated national airlines, allowing more than one airline from a given country to fly the same route and permitting certain forms of price cutting. At the November 1986 meeting, when the UK was holding the Council of Ministers presidency, the Community failed to achieve agreement on what was regarded as a fairly weak package of such measures. Thus whereas the EC Commission would have liked to see each national airline's share being reduced from fifty to twenty-five per cent, the UK opted to push a proposal which only required a reduction to forty per cent over three years. Critics tended to see the UK position as reflecting anxiety about the effect which more radical measures would have on the value of British Airways. We gave consideration to an alternative interpretation in Chapter 7. In July 1987 the Council of Ministers once more attempted to reach an agreement. Once more they failed—this time a major issue was a dispute between the UK and Spain over the status of Gibraltar airport.

The third approach was for individuals, companies or governments to seek to invoke Article 85 against airline agreements. Lord Bethell attempted to do this but failed. However in 1986 a breakthrough occurred in the *Nouvelles Frontières* case.[37] This concerned a French budget travel company which had sold air tickets at lower prices than those sanctioned by the French authorities. The case was first heard by a French court which decided to refer the matter to the European Court of Justice for a preliminary ruling. The important feature of the Court's verdict was the additional light it threw on the position which arose when an implementing regulation did not exist. This new light suggested that the EC Commission's hands were not entirely tied—there was a way forward. Thus the Commission could investigate the various agreements entered into in the airline industry, and might then decide to prohibit them. In which case national courts would have to take cognizance of the fact that the agreements in question were null and void. This would then open the door to lawsuits against airlines. Such cases would of course require that those bringing the suits had the required legal standing, and that the Commission had made the correct decision in the first place. Up to June 1986 the Commission held its hand, hoping that the Council of Ministers would agree to a liberalisation package of the kind discussed above. When that failed to materialise the Commission decided to commence proceedings. It obviously hoped that these proceedings might ultimately provoke the member states into an agreement. Happily this seems to have done the trick since, late in 1987, the Council of Ministers reached agreement and this also included the issue which had divided the UK and Spain. A limited amount of competition will now be injected into scheduled intra-EEC airline services.

iv Financial Institutions
Broadly speaking, changes within the financial sector have been a product of competitive forces, together with specific legal developments which have further facilitated competition (sometimes the object has also been to create more equal conditions of competition). In part the competitive forces have proceeded from abroad (the knock-on effect referred to in Chapters 1 and 7) but have also been internal, as firms within sectors began to compete more intensively with each other, and firms in one part of the system began to compete with firms in other parts. The latter tendency has given rise to a more conglomerate structure. All this was discussed in Chapter 7 when we considered the forces for change, and we will not dwell on the matter further. Rather at this point we will concentrate on the specific legally based changes. As we noted earlier, parallel with all this have been moves to tighten up the system of prudential regulation—this could indeed be described as a process of reregulation. We will follow our discussion of legal deregulation with a consideration of these prudential developments.

Formally, deregulation on the Stock Exchange arose out of the reference by the Director General of Fair Trading of the Stock Exchange rule book to the Restrictive Practices Court in 1979. The Office of Fair Trading is said to have identified about 150 restrictions which were thought to be capable of challenge, but without doubt it was the fixed minimum scale of brokerage commissions, the single capacity system and the barriers which helped to sustain the Stock Exchange's near monopoly of security trading, which attracted most attention. In fact the case never came to court. Instead the Secretary of State for Trade and Industry decided to step in. The case was dropped in favour of a negotiated settlement between the government and the Stock Exchange. In effect the government agreed to call off the case provided the Exchange could come up with satisfactory reform proposals.

In practice it proved not to be a government sell-out as was widely predicted at the time. An agreement was reached and a whole series of changes ensued. Lay members were admitted to the Stock Exchange Council in 1983. The single capacity system was dropped. Instead of the old broker/jobber structure a new system of broker-dealers was to be introduced. A firm could decide to act simply as an agent. It would therefore be committed to seeking out the best price for a client from among the firms making a market in the security in question. But there was nothing to stop a firm acting as both agent and principal, although it would have to inform customers as to what capacity it was acting in. This dual capacity system was first introduced in 1984 in respect of international equities, and was extended to domestic equities and gilt edged securities in October 1986. In October 1986 brokerage commissions also became negotiable—the combination of single capacity and brokerage competition was referred to as the 'Big Bang'. In 1986 it was also agreed that the limit on the equity stakes of outsiders should be totally abolished, and new firms were admitted to the Exchange.

In the case of building societies it was, as we noted in Chapter 7, the much more competitive situation on the assets and liabilities side which helped to undermine the interest rate cartel. It was effectively abandoned in 1983. In addition, the need to create more equal conditions of competition between the societies and other institutions (notably the banks) required that the former should be given a measure of relief from the statutory controls which had limited their fields of operation. This was accomplished by the Building Societies Act 1986 which, subject to limits, sanctioned a wide range of new activities which took in the provision of unsecured loans, index-linked mortgages, cheque books, cheque guarantee cards, discount broking facilities, motor insurance, life insurance and pensions business, investment in residential property and land and estate agency. In addition the societies were to be allowed to raise up to twenty per cent of their funds from wholesale money markets rather than from members. Further liberalising measures were announced in 1988.

Parallel with these deregulatory moves has been the creation of a comprehensive system of prudential control. In the case of banks the regulatory function has over the years been discharged by the Bank of England and its nature was briefly described in Chapter 7. The Bank has continued to discharge that role but following the Johnson-Matthey débâcle in 1984, which exposed some loopholes, proposals were made which have led to a tightening up of the system. The other notable development in banking was the introduction of deposit insurance. This, as we noted earlier, was foreshadowed in the 1979 Banking Act which the reader will recollect also made the Bank of England the sole licensor of banks and deposit taking institutions. A deposit protection scheme was introduced in 1982—it is governed by the Deposit Protection Board which is chaired by the Governor of the Bank of England.

On the building society front somewhat similar developments have occurred. The Building Societies Act 1986 has established the Building Societies Commission (successor to the Chief Registrar of Friendly Societies) as the regulator. Increased powers have been conferred on the Commission, which include formal assessment of capital adequacy, liquidity, etc. In addition the act provides for an investment protection scheme similar to that operated in banking. It is operated by the Building Societies Investment Protection Board.

Following the Gower Report (see Chapter 7) a system of prudential regulation under the Financial Services Act 1986 has also been extended to the Stock Exchange and the City (but excluding Lloyds—see below). At the top of the system is the Securities and Investment Board (SIB). It came into existence before the 1986 Act and under the latter the

Secretary of State for Trade and Industry can delegate to it the regulatory powers contained therein. Beneath the SIB are a series of Self-Regulating Organisations (SROs) which will cover different aspects of City activity. The SIB lays down standards concerning regulatory rules. Provided the SROs devise rules which satisfy these standards they will be recognised as the legitimate regulators. In turn those who practise will be regulated by the SROs, and it is illegal to practise unless recognised by the appropriate SRO. Parallel with the devising of acceptable rules will be the establishment of an industry-wide compensation scheme as part of a system which gives high priority to investor protection.

The Financial Services Act provides not only for the recognition of the SROs, but also extends to the recognition of RIEs (Recognised Investment Exchanges), RPBs (Recognised Professional Bodies—these are professions in which investment is incidental to their main business) and RCHs (Recognised Clearing Houses). In total what has emerged is a combination of a statutory system and practitioner-based regulation.

Returning now to the SROs, it appears that five will seek recognition from the SIB. They are as follows. Firstly, The Securities Association (TSA). Following the merger of the Stock Exchange and the International Securities Regulatory Organisation, the regulatory role in connection with dealers in domestic and international equities and bonds was vested in the TSA. Secondly, The Financial Intermediaries, Managers and Brokers Regulatory Association (FIMBRA) will regulate independent investment advisors and managers. Thirdly, The Investment Managers Regulatory Association (IMRO) will supervise those who manage unit trusts, investment trusts and pension funds. Fourthly, The Association of Futures Brokers and Dealers (AFBD) will regulate firms concerned with dealing and broking in futures and options. Finally, The Life Assurance and Unit Trust Regulatory Organisation (LAUTRO) will be responsible for life companies, friendly societies, etc.[38]

Earlier in Chapter 7 we referred to scandals in the City as giving rise to the need to tighten up the system. Some of the scandals were connected with the Lloyds insurance market. A new Lloyds Act was put on the statute book in 1982 but the problems rumbled on. Initially it was decided to exclude Lloyds from the ambit of the Financial Services Act. This gave rise to some controversy since it seemed to be an area of activity particularly in need of reform. A report was therefore commissioned from Sir Patrick Neill QC, which recommended a series of changes similar to those emerging under the SIB. The Secretary of State for Trade and Industry accepted this solution but warned that if firm action was not taken then legislative changes would be imposed.[39]

For completeness we should mention that various sections of the City have created ombudsmen to resolve disputes between investors and firms supplying financial services. To date such systems have been introduced by banks, the insurance companies, the Stock Exchange and two of the SROs. Such a system was also recommended in respect of Lloyds.

v Broadcasting

By the time the Conservatives came to power in 1979 the monopoly originally enjoyed by the BBC had long been broken. Following the creation of the Independent Television Authority in 1954 (by a previous Conservative administration) Independent TV (ITV) made its debut and this was followed by Independent Radio—hence the change of title of the regulatory body to Independent Broadcasting Authority (IBA). Further competition for the BBC TV services flowed from the Broadcasting Act 1981 which allowed the IBA to develop Channel Four. As a departure from previous practice, this was actually managed by a subsidiary of IBA, and was financed by annual subscriptions from the ITV companies who in turn gained revenue from selling Channel Four's advertising time. Incidentally Channel Four was required to supply a form of programming which was different from the fare generally found on ITV and was therefore expected, in cultural terms, to be an important development. Further competition for the BBC followed from breakfast time programming on ITV (TV AM) although the BBC retaliated with its own similarly timed programme.

Subsequent changes (wideband (i.e. multi-channel) cable and DBS) have provided a competitive challenge to both ITV and BBC. The first came from wideband cable. Cable is not new. Cable systems were originally licensed under the Wireless Telegraphy Act 1949. The licensor was the Home Office and in the main licences were confined to the relaying of the outputs of existing broadcast stations. Whilst the main legislative changes in cable occurred under the post-1979 Conservative administrations, it has to be acknowledged that the previous Labour government was itself contemplating change. In a White Paper[40] it proposed two developments. Firstly, it would permit pay–cable systems (as well as pay–TV) which would be freed from the role of merely relaying. Secondly, the function of licensing and supervising pay-cable should be transferred from the Home Office to the IBA. Only the first proposal was adopted. In 1981 the Home Office licensed 13 pilot schemes. These licences were however closely regulated, particularly as to programming. Licensees could only show films which had been registered for public exhibition by the British Board of Film Censors. Films could not be shown until 12 months after registration. No film in category 'X' (unsuitable for persons under 18) could be shown before 10 p.m. A film which had been refused permission for local exhibition could not be shown on cable in the same area. Licensees could not seek exclusive licences for sporting or entertainment events of national importance (This is referred to as an anti-siphoning provision). Advertising was not permitted. Licensees had to submit programmes in advance to the Home Office.

The turning point in cable came in 1982 when the Cabinet Office produced a report on wideband cable systems.[41] It recommended a crash programme, largely because of the perceived need to stimulate British industry in the field of communications technology. For example, if cable was freed from restraints and was allowed to grow rapidly, it would provide an outlet for DBS programming and DBS was an area where the UK had significant potential (e.g. in the field of satellites). The report therefore created a deregulatory stance. The existing restrictions on cable programming should be removed. A new regulatory body should be adopted but the industry should be encouraged to develop an effective system of self-regulation so that official regulations could be reduced to a minimum.

The government responded quickly by setting up the Hunt Committee, to see how the development of the cable industry might be facilitated in a way which was consistent with the wider public interest, and the safeguarding of public service broadcasting. The future role of DBS and the need for an appropriate framework for cable regulation were also included in the remit. The Committee duly reported.[42] It did not see cable as undermining public service broadcasting but as supplementary to it. It did however propose various safeguards including an anti-siphoning rule, a 'must carry' rule whereby all BBC, ITV and future DBS signals should be carried, and a ban on pay-per-view systems. It recognised the need to avoid 'cherry picking'—i.e. the serving of lucrative markets and avoidance of the less dense ones. A new regulatory body should be created, but the emphasis should be on the issuing of general guidelines rather than detailed regulation.

The general thrust of the report was adopted by the governments and the Cable and Broadcasting Act 1984 was the result. The licensing and supervisory body is the Cable Authority. Arrangements for the granting of licences include provisions designed to prevent 'cherry picking'. Licensees can seek remuneration both by advertising and by pay-per-view systems (pay-per-view is also to be available to DBS operators). According to the White Paper preceeding the Act[43] advertising will be restricted to the amount allowed by the IBA. The main protections for public service broadcasting are to be the application of an anti-siphoning rule and a 'must-carry' provision of the kind discussed above. Moreover pay-per-view will not be allowed if as a result one of the existing public service channels is deprived of an event which it has customarily covered. The kind of positive programming standards which are appropriate to public service broadcasting (i.e. to educate and inform as well as entertain) have been deemed inapplicable to cable. Rules have to be laid down in relation to good taste, decency, avoidance of incitement to crime, impartiality and the proper proportion of material of EEC origin. The Authority also has responsibilities in relation to the portrayal of violence, religious and charitable matters and the content of advertisements. Ownership rules have also been laid down whose exclusions cover, amongst others, TV and radio contractors in the area and also local newspaper proprietors. At the time of writing the prospects for a rapid expansion of cable do not seem bright.

The second source of competition for the BBC and ITV has come from DBS. As far back as 1977 the International Telecommunication Union allocated five satellite TV channels to the UK. Thinking in the UK began to quicken in the 1980s as exemplified by the Home Office report of 1981[44] and the provision in the 1984 Cable and Broadcasting Act whereby the IBA could provide DBS services. Originally both the IBA and BBC were envisaged as providing competitive services. Later in the 1984 Act a joint venture mechanism—the Satellite Broadcasting Board—was provided for. In the event this collaboration was not forthcoming. As a result the government decided to ask the IBA to seek contractors for three of the five DBS channels. In December 1986 it awarded the franchise to British Satellite Broadcasting (BSB). BSB (a consortium which includes ITV contractors) plans to use a mixture of subscription and advertising as its means of revenue raising. The UK government has indicated that whilst this DBS venture should remain faithful to the central concept of public service broadcasting, in this case being responsible to the IBA as the trustee of the public interest, it will in order to be profitable have to emphasise entertainment in its programming.

Mention should also be made of low-powered satellite services. These have been inhibited by the size of the receiving dish and its cost. However in May 1985 the government announced that it was prepared to allow individuals to receive TV signals from such satellites provided planning permission was forthcoming. It also allowed the Cable Authority to licence satellite master antennas linked to local cable systems (SMATV). There is however a proviso whereby such arrangements must not be to the detriment of the wideband cable systems which we discussed earlier. It is indeed expected that SMATV should ultimately give way to the wideband system.

A possible future development would be the introduction of pay (i.e. scrambled) TV signals in addition to the existing terrestrial variety. This might be accomplished by inserting a fifth channel into the spectrum space currently occupied by the two BBC and two ITV channels. Alternatively it might be introduced on the old VHF channels. Then again the system might be down-loaded—i.e. scrambled programmes could be broadcast when the existing four channels were not in use and recorded on domestic video recording equipment (with unscrambling capacity) for later use. It should be added that the Peacock Committee on the future of broadcasting were disposed to favour pay TV on the existing BBC and ITV channels.[45]

vi The Professions
Deregulation has been proceeding apace in the professions. The general thrust has been as follows.

(a) The UK government has imposed changes which have broken the monopolies enjoyed by certain professional groups. Allied to EEC membership, the associated concept of mutual recognition of qualifications has meant that some UK professions are already open to entry by professionals from other member states, and others will be opened up in due course.

(b) Arrangements concerning scales of fees to be charged have been abrogated—thanks to pressure from the antitrust authorities.

(c) Restrictions on advertising have been significantly modified. Moreover in 1985 the Minister of Corporate and Consumer Affairs announced a series of studies (to be carried out by the OFT) concerning possible further changes. Subsequent reports suggested that further relaxations of advertising restrictions were needed and that constraints on the formation of multi-disciplinary partnerships should be dropped.[46]

We turn now to the two professions which we singled out for more detailed attention in Chapters 6 and 7. In the case of opticians the government decided on relaxations of the opticians' monopoly and this provision was embodied in the Health and Social Security Act 1984. From December 1984 unqualified individuals could supply spectacles in accordance with a prescription signed by a qualified optician or doctor. Opticians have continued to retain a monopoly of contact lenses and sales to children under sixteen. Then in March 1985 most restrictions on advertising by opticians were lifted. Mutual recognition of qualifications under EEC rules has not however yet occurred.

In the case of solicitors the main changes have been as follows. As a result of the Administration of Justice Act 1985 their monopoly of conveyancing has been broken. The Act provides for this function to be carried out by a new breed of licensed conveyancers. However completely unfettered competition has not been allowed since a Council for Licensed Conveyancing has been established. It is charged with the task of devising and operating tests of competence for those seeking to practise. This is therefore a case of regulated competition. A major cause of controversy was whether solicitors employed by banks and building societies should be allowed to carry out conveyancing. This had been precluded by a Law Society Solicitors' Practice Rule which forbade a solicitor to share his fee with non-solicitors. The Lord Chancellor was opposed to this extension of liberalisation on the grounds of conflicts of interest, but in the event the extension has been allowed. However a financial institution would not be able to carry out both the conveyancing and the financing of a particular transaction.

More generally the legal monopoly of solicitors will in due course be affected by the mutual recognition of lawyer qualifications under EEC rules. Significant relaxations of the restrictions on individual advertising have also been accomplished. As we indicated, the OFT has also called for the removal of restrictions on multidisciplinary practices—this was relevant in the case of solicitors. This change was called for by the National Consumer Council and indeed conglomerate structures (e.g. solicitors and estate agents) are now emerging. Not surprisingly the solicitors have been seeking to invade the territory of barristers. Hitherto the latter have enjoyed a common law monopoly of audience before superior courts in the UK. It has been recommended by the Director General of Fair Trading that this situation should end and it is a matter which is being considered by a committee on the future of the legal profession under the chairmanship of Lady Marre.

vii The European Community Dimension

In connection with the CAP some reform has been achieved but its impact should not be exaggerated. Attempts at reform go back to 1968 when the Mansholt Plan suggested that farms should be made larger and more efficient, and that land should be taken out of production. This provoked a violent reaction from the farmers who had been led to expect salvation not decimation from the Rome Treaty. Mansholt was dubbed a 'peasant killer'. Structural reform was perceived as a political hot potato and was, to continue the food metaphor, put on the back burner.

More recently, under the pressure of inadequate budgetary resources, the emphasis on reform has shifted to the price support system itself. Annual price increases have in some instances been held below inflation. In the case of products in surplus, such as beef, the intervention price has been lowered. The problem of the open-ended nature of CAP guarantees has been addressed by introducing support thresholds. The most dramatic example of this was the agreement in 1984 to introduce quotas for milk—they are now in process of being tightened up. The milk reform was designed to cut the butter mountain. Quality standards have also been raised, thus reducing the quantities which have qualified for intervention purchases. More recently thoughts have been moving towards set-aside measures for land and switching to crops which provide industrial raw materials. More recently the EC Commission has made much play of the so-called budget stabilizers whereby it would be given power to take quick remedial action by price cuts and other devices if agricultural spending got out of hand.

In the case of steel the regulatory system is being wound up. At the end of 1985 subsidies had to be terminated except in certain very special cases and a beginning has been made on the abolition of sales quotas. However the fact that some surplus steel capacity still existed made the total abolition of sales quotas very controversial. The steel producers requested a longer timetable for the abolition of quotas, but were not able to deliver a sufficient quantity of voluntary closures as a *quid pro quo*. The Commission was therefore saddled with the difficult task of solving this problem. Towards the end of 1987 the Commission announced that it had secured a sufficient number of undertakings to close capacity. This paved the way for a decision which will lead to the abolition of quotas by 1990.

NOTES

1. C. Pickering, 'The Mechanics of Disposal' in D. Steel and D. Heald (eds), *Privatising Public Enterprises: Options and Dilemmas op. cit.*, pp.45–6.
2. *Financial Times*, 9 October 1986.
3. House of Commons, *First Report of the Defence Committee. Further Observations on the Future of the Royal Dockyards, Appendices to Minutes of Evidence*, Session 1985/86, HC 18, p.55.
4. *Hansard Parliamentary Debates (House of Commons)*, 23 July 1985, Col.869.
5. Sir Geoffrey Howe *op. cit.*, pp.7–9.
6. J. Moore, 'The Success of Privatisation', Speech when opening Hoare Govett Ltd's new City Dealing Rooms, Treasury Press Release 107/85.
7. Sir Geoffrey Howe *op. cit.*, p.6.
8. House of Commons, *Sixth Report of the Energy Committee, Appendix 1, Nationalised Industries Legislation: Consultation Proposals*, Session 1985/86, HC 302, p.xvii.
9. D. Thomas, 'The Union Response to Denationalisation', in D. Steel and D. Heald (eds), *Privatising Public Enterprises, op. cit.*, p.67.
10. The general recovry from recession also played a part.
11. C. Newman *op. cit.*, p.23.
12. *The Economist*, 21 June 1986, pp.26–30.
13. C. Pickering *op. cit.*, p.53.
14. D. Thomas *op. cit.*, p.67.
15. A subsidiary of Cable and Wireless, itself a privatised company.
16. M. Beesley, *Liberalisation of the use of British Telecommunications Network* (HMSO, London, 1981) and M. Beesley, 'The Liberalisation of British Telecom', *Economic Affairs*, October, 1981, pp.19–27.
17. M. A. Utton, *The Economics of Regulating Industry, op. cit.*, p.210.
18. J. Kay, 'The Privatisation of British Telecommunications', in D. Steel and David Heald (eds) *Privatising Public Enterprises, op. cit.*, p.80.
19. The competitive structure on international routes is of course not a matter for unilateral action on the part of the UK government.

20. Civil Aviation Authority, *Domestic Air Services: A Review of Regulatory Policy* (Civil Aviation Authority, London, 1979).
21. Civil Aviation Authority, *Airline Competition Policy* (Civil Aviation Authority, London, 1984).
22. M. Ashworth and P. Forsyth, *Civil Aviation Policy and the Privatisation of British Airways* (Institute of Fiscal Studies, London, 1985), p.22.
23. D. Starkie and D. Thompson, *Privatising London's Airports* (Institute of Fiscal Studies, London, 1985), p.81.
24. J. R. Shackleton *op. cit.*, p.73.
25. J. Vickers and G. Yarrow, *Privatisation and the Natural Monopolies*, (Public Policy Centre, London, 1985) p.58.
26. British Gas distributes gas which it purchases from oil companies—gas is a joint product of oil extraction. It also extracts gas from its own reserves.
27. E. M. Hammond, D. R. Helm, D. J. Thompson, 'British Gas: Options for Privatisation', *Fiscal Studies*, 6 (1985), pp.1–20.
28. *The Economist*, 21 June 1986, p.30.
29. House of Commons, *Thirty-First Report of the Committee of Public Accounts, Ministry of Defence: Incorporation of the Royal Ordnance Factories*, Session 1984/5, HC. 417.
30. P. Gist and S. A. Meadowcroft, 'Regulating for Competition: The Newly Liberalised Market for Private Branch Exchanges', *Fiscal Studies* 7 (1986), pp.41–66.
31. S. Littlechild, *Regulation of British Telecommunications' Profitability* (Department of Industry, London, 1981).
32. *Buses op. cit.*, p.11.
33. British Airways, *Review of the Year 1984–85* (1985), pp.8–10.
34. Doganis *op. cit.*, p.56.
35. *Commission of EC* v. *French Republic* (1974) 1 ECJR 359.
36. F. McGowan and C. Trengrove, European Aviation: A Common Market? (Institute of Fiscal Studies, London, 1986), pp.138–40.
37. *Ministère Public* v. *Lucas Asjes, Nouvelles Frontières and others* (1986) 3 CMLR 173.
38. D. H. A. Ingram, 'Change in the Stock Exchange and Regulation of the City', *Bank of England Quarterly Bulletin*, 27/1 (1987), p.64.
39. D. F. Lomax, *London Markets after the Financial Services Act* (Butterworths, London, 1987), pp.177–8.
40. *Broadcasting* (HMSO, London, 1978), Cmnd. 7294. See also C. G. Veljanovski and W. D. Bishop, *Choice by Cable* (IEA, London, 1983), Chapter 1 and J. Howkins, *New Technologies, New Policies* (Broadcasting Research Unit, London, 1982), Chapter 5.
41. Cabinet Office, *Cable Systems* (HMSO, London, 1982).
42. *Report of the Inquiry into Cable Expansion and Broadcasting Policy* (HMSO, London, 1982), Cmnd.8679.
43. *The Development of Cable Systems and Services* (HMSO, London, 1983), Cmnd.8866, p.83.
44. Home Office, *Direct Broadcasting by Satellite* (HMSO, London,

1981).
45. Broadcasting, like Financial Institutions, is also undergoing a parallel process of reregulation. In order to protect TV viewers from violence and sex a Broadcasting Standards Council has been created. Whilst it will be able to control domestic broadcasters, its ability to influence material supplied by foreign satellites is less clear. The BBC and IBA are already supposed to regulate standards. This new development in May 1988 therefore adds a further layer of regulation.
46. Office of Fair Trading, *Annual Report of the Director General of Fair Trading* (HMSO, London, 1987), pp.31–2.

Part IV
Conclusion

9 Assessment

1 INTRODUCTION

Having reviewed the various acts of privatisation and regulatory reform, the final issue which falls due for consideration relates to the effects of those actions. Have they led to lower prices, greater efficiency, better service, etc.? How have these effects impacted on various sections of the community? Is it legitimate to assess these policies purely by reference to these criteria? What criticisms can be levelled at the approaches which have been adopted towards regulatory reform and privatisation?

Since privatisation has overwhelmingly been a policy adopted in the UK, our discussion of it will concentrate exclusively on British experience. In the case of regulatory reform, both countries have, as we have seen, been significantly involved and the discussion will be more evenly balanced. We will as far as possible review experience in various industries in parallel.

2 PRIVATISATION

Appraising the UK policy of privatisation runs up against the fundamental problem that it was not purely inspired by narrow economic considerations. It could indeed be argued that the Conservative party would consider privatisation to have been justified even if privatised enterprises had proved to be no more efficient or responsive to consumer needs than publicly owned ones. Josephian philosophy (which no doubt exercised a growing influence as more moderate politicians were dropped from the cabinet) emphasised the threat to political freedom which proceeded from the economic power of the state. Tighter control of public expenditure and ultimately privatisation were also seen as a means of disciplining the trade unions, and there is absolutely no doubt at all that the Conservatives saw this as part of a quite fundamental struggle over who governed the UK. Samuel Brittan seemed to be making a similar point when he observed that economists' appraisals of the UK privatisation programme might lead to a lowish mark, but it was a mark for an examination the Conservatives would not choose to take.[1] The Conservatives had a wider range of considerations in mind than strictly economic matters. Having said that, it cannot be denied that they did look to improved economic performance, and if that has not emerged, or does not emerge in due course, then some of the shine must inevitably be said to have been taken off the policy.

Our focus will be the narrower one of economic performance, and it must be confessed that even when that more limited canvas is adopted the task of assessment is still difficult.

Commentators who have sought to assess the economic impact of privatisation have approached it from three angles. (a) They have pondered the *theoretical* issues, asking whether ownership is *itself* a significant factor. (b) They have reviewed the various empirical studies (and surveys thereof), which have been conducted around the world, concerning the relative efficiency of public and private enterprise. Unfortunately they do not always seem to agree on the implications of these reviews! (c) They have looked at the *actual experience* in UK industries pre- and post-privatisation. Let us approach the question in that order.

The theoretical issues, in an admittedly static framework and British context, are summarised in Table 9.1 where we attempt to suggest what might be the consequences of four combinations of public/private ownership and monopoly/competition[2]. Let us begin with public ownership under conditions of monopoly—which is Scenario A. The lack of the stimulus of product market competition would lead to productive inefficiency (X-inefficiency). Moreover a private enterprise which is neglectful of the need to be productively efficient faces the ultimate sanction of bankruptcy. By contrast public corporations do not go bankrupt and limited companies owned by the government may expect to be bailed out. They are therefore under the strong temptation to buy peace by conceding union claims in respect of wages, labour practices and manning. It should also be added that cost minimisation has been sacrificed for political reasons. The disposition of Conservative as well as Labour governments to do just that was remarked on in Chapter 6. The failure of public enterprise managements to minimise cost has not just been a product of requirements to buy British, even when it was not the cheapest or most effective, or to continue to supply services, even though they were making a loss, etc. It was also caused by the decision making and financial strait-jackets within which such enterprises had to operate. The boards of public enterprises have not been free to act expeditiously and independently in making investment decisions. They have had to wait upon the deliberations of the governmental machine, and to conform to the wider interests of government policy. Thus if for reasons of macroeconomic management government borrowing had to be cut, then theirs had to be cut too—irrespective of the merits of the individual case. On the other hand we will assume that the publicly owned enterprise endeavours to adopt a pricing approach which is associated with the concept of allocative efficiency. Following the prescriptions of Hotelling and Lerner, British public corporations were, however imperfectly, required to price according to marginal cost. Of course, if our analysis is correct, it would be a marginal cost above the minimum attainable under different conditions.

We turn now to Scenario B where public enterprise operates under conditions of competition. In this case pro-ductive inefficiency is reduced because of the stimulus of product market competition but productive inefficiency still exists due to the absence of a bankruptcy incentive and to the inhibiting effect of government interference. However price will be related to cost—an allocative efficiency objective—due to the play of competitive forces.

We turn now to Scenario C. Here we have monopoly under private ownership. Productive inefficiency will exist due to the lack of the stimulus of product market competition. On the other hand the bankruptcy incentive will exercise a moderating influence. In addition the market for corporate control will operate, and it will also exercise some restraining influence on the tendency towards productive inefficiency. Thus if efficiency suffers, shares will be sold and share prices will be depressed. In technical terms the valuation ratio will fall—that is to say the ratio of the stock market value of a company to its book value will decline. This makes the company vulnerable to take over with the likely consequence that the managers will be replaced. The threat of all this will keep managers on their toes. But we cannot rely too much on this corrective influence. Such evidence as is available indicates that whilst the market for corporate control exercises an influence, its disciplinary role is not strong and it tends to decline as firm size increases.[3] Nevertheless productive inefficiency in Scenario C appears at first glance to be lower than in Scenario A, thanks also to the absence of government interference. It might therefore appear that privatisation is beneficial. However we have not yet taken account of the fact that once released into the private sector, a firm which follows the conventional private enterprise path of profit maximisation would be tempted to exploit its market power and price would be raised above cost with allocative inefficiency consequences. This would have to be set against any moderation in productive inefficiency. It is indeed possible that the monopolist would devote resources to the defence of its monopoly position which would be a quite unambiguous loss from monopolisation behaviour. These latter factors, by pulling in a contrary direction, suggest that private ownership under monopoly might not be superior to public ownership under monopoly—although where the balance ultimately lies is an empirical matter which depends on the strength of these conflicting influences.

We come now to Scenario D where private ownership is coupled with competition. We may expect full productive efficiency since product market competition is now reinforced by the market for corporate control. Moreover the firm faces the bankruptcy incentive, and is no longer inhibited by government interference. Competitive conditions will also lead to price being aligned on cost—i.e. allocative efficiency.

How then do we appraise privatisation? There are four possible tracks in Table 9.1 of which three are likely and these are represented by the arrows labelled I, II and III. Track I and track III involve changes in ownership (i.e. privatisation) without any change in product market conditions. Track III is superior to track I since it incorporates factors which improve productive efficiency without any counterbalancing loss. Indeed, as we have seen, it is open to doubt whether track I is beneficial. Of course the best line of action is represented by track II—i.e. privatisation accompanied by the opening of the market to competition.

As we indicated above, various studies have been carried out of particular industries where the opportunity presented itself to compare the performance of firms under public ownership with firms under private ownership—e.g. investor-owned and municipally-owned electricity utilities in the US. It should however be noted that substantial methodological problems arise in making such comparisons. One such study, which attracted a good deal of attention in the UK, was carried out by Richard Pryke. It related to UK airline passenger operations (nationalised British Airways versus privately owned British Caledonian), short distance ship and hovercraft operations (nationalised Sealink UK versus privately owned European Ferries) and gas and electricity appliance sale and contracting (nationalised British Gas Corporation and the Electricity Boards versus privately owned retailers Currys and Comet). Pryke concluded that public ownership led to a performance which was poor by private enterprise standards. He concluded:

> What public ownership does is to eliminate the threat of takeover and ultimately of bankruptcy and the need, which all private undertakings have from time to time, to raise money from the market. Public ownership provides a comfortable life and destroys the commercial ethic.[4]

Table 9.1: Effects of Privatisation and Competition

	Public Ownership	Private Ownership
Monopoly	*Scenario A* 1 Productive inefficiency due to lack of product market competition allied to 2 Absence of bankruptcy incentive and to 3 Inhibiting effect of government interference. 4 Price related to cost (an allocative efficiency objective) but AC > minimum attainable due to 1–3 above.	*Scenario C* 1 Productive inefficiency, due to lack of product market competition, 2 Is reduced (in varying degrees) by market for corporate control and by 3 Presence of bankruptcy incentive and by 4 Absence of government interference. 5 Price may not be related to cost due to monopoly behaviour. AC > minimum attainable due to 1 above and any weakness in 2. Waste may also arise from resources used to defend monopoly position.
Competition	*Scenario B* 1 Productive inefficiency reduced due to presence of product market competition but 2 Productive efficiency not maximised due to lack of bankruptcy incentive allied to 3 Inhibiting effect of government interference. 4 Price related to cost but AC > minimum attainable due to 2 and 3 above.	*Scenario D* 1 Production efficiency due to 2 Presence of product market competition allied to 3 Market for corporate control (variable in effect) and 4 Presence of bankruptcy incentive and 5 Absence of government interference. 6 Price related to cost and AC at minimum—i.e. both allocative and production efficiency.

I

II

III

Interesting as these results are, they only refer to three areas of activity. Firm conclusions require a wide range of results. Two major international surveys of public/private ownership studies have indeed been produced. Robert Millward, surveying North American literature, found overall 'no broad support for private enterprise superiority'.[5] The other major study was carried out by Thomas Borcherding *et al.*—it cites more than fifty studies from five countries.[6] They conclude that the findings of most studies are consistent with the notion that public firms have higher unit cost structures. However they complement this by observing that, given sufficient competition between public and private producers, the differences in unit costs turn out to be insignificant. From this they conclude that it is competition rather than the ownership factor which is the major force influencing performance. There is a lot of support for this view and it has been taken by some to indicate that liberalisation without change of ownership would confer substantial benefits.[7]

George Yarrow has carried out an analysis of the actual performance of UK firms which have been privatised.[8] He selected five firms which were operating in workably competitive circumstances and observed their performance pre- and post-privatisation (during the period 1981–85) in terms of real turnover and profit margins. He also looked at similar data relating to another five firms in workably competitive industries which had remained in the public sector and he also compared their profit margin performance with that of all UK commercial and industrial companies. Finally he looked at the share price behaviour of four firms post-privatisation and compared it with the movement of share prices in their particular section of the market. He appeared to be arguing that any marked rise in the former relative to the latter indicated a favourable view of actual privatisation performance on the part of informed members of the financial community.

There are of course formidable problems in drawing any conclusion from such an exercise. Firstly, the sample size is so small. Secondly, as Yarrow himself points out, ideally we need appropriate counterfactuals—i.e. evidence of how the firms would have performed under continuing public ownership—which could be set against how we know they have performed. This counterfactual evidence is not available. Thirdly, as Yarrow also admits, comparisons of performance pre- and post-privatisation run the risk of financial rearrangements and other essentially one-off changes being made, which render the enterprise more profitable and saleable but also make the comparisons misleading. Fourthly, it is too soon to expect to pick up the full effects of privatisation. Managements steeped in the public enterprise ethos are not likely to change their spots overnight. Indeed it may only be when managements have substantially turned over through retirements, etc., that the full response to the new atmosphere will show through. Fifthly, without going into details about the evidence, it has got to be admitted that some of the biggest jumps in the profits-to-sales ratio occurred in the run-up to privatisation—a point which Yarrow concedes. Sixthly, there was a general improvement in industrial performance over much of the period covered.

What general conclusions do we then draw? The theoretical answer seems to be that changes of ownership in the absence of competition do not inevitably lead to improvements in performance. Changes of ownership which occur under conditions of competition, and particularly those that are accompanied by the creation of competitive conditions, are likely to be beneficial—this point draws support from the empiricial evidence of Borcherding, *et al*.

Against the background of those conclusions, how then do we appraise the UK privatisation programme? Given that government sell-offs have occurred in the case of firms which operated in, and after privatisation continued to operate in, a workably competitive environment, we can conclude that such disposals are likely to have been beneficial. However a problem arises from the fact that some firms which have been privatised (or may be privatised) have had a protected status. Either they have in the past had a statutory monopoly (telecommunications, gas, electricity, water) or have benefited from a privileged position within a regulatory system (British Airways) or have enjoyed an element of geographic protection (British Airports). Moreover in value terms these firms have constituted a large slice of the assets available for privatisation. Given that there is good evidence and fairly general theoretical agreement that privatisation is most effective when accompanied by competition, the crucial issue has been the government's attitude towards the introduction of competition in such cases or, in its absence, to the institution of imaginative regulatory solutions.

In practice the government has been criticised because it has fought shy of a bold competitive approach, and it is for this reason that Kay and Thompson arrived at the critical view to which Samuel Brittan referred. It could be argued that the government should have broken the monoliths up, or in the case of the airlines should have created greater competitive equity in terms of routes and route location. In fact in some cases it refused to adopt that approach although National Bus is an exception. It is argued that in so refusing it was bowing to management pressures. There may be an element of truth in that view, although the government would no doubt defend itself by arguing that considerations of natural monopoly have militated against fragmentation. However whilst it is true that there are elements of natural monopoly within this collection of enterprises, they are by no means all natural monopolies. Natural monopoly considerations did not dictate that the British Airports Authority should be disposed of as one— because of that decision some beneficial inter-airport rivalry was lost.[9] The government also shied away from the more radical proposal of cutting British Airways down to size, and natural monopoly was not a constraining factor although the effect on prospective privatisation receipts may have been. Indeed the government subsequently allowed British Airways to take over British Caledonian. This followed a controversial report by the Monopolies and Mergers Commission which found in favour of the bid. However if the merger was to go ahead the merged enterprise would have to relinquish some route licences (although it could re-apply), would have to drop appeals against the award of licences to competitors and would have to accept competition from other airlines on long distance routes where dual or multiple designation is allowed. On the other hand it has to be admitted that whilst the government has not broken British Telecom up, it has established some limited competition via Mercury and allowed competition into the equipment section.

Natural monopolies are typically found in those industries which involve distribution networks—this means that local telephone services (longer distance activities seem likely to offer increasing opportunities for competition hence Mercury), gas, electricity distribution (but not generation) and water are cases in point.[10] Here the government has already chosen (or is likely to choose) a system of regulation. Regulation is not essential where only one supplier is feasible. As we noted earlier competition for the field can be substituted for competition in the field (i.e. franchising) and it is possible to devise a system which will produce allocative as well as productive efficiency. Commentators have given serious consideration to this possibility but have encountered snags. John Kay, for example, doubts whether a franchise offered to British Telecom would ever be in serious danger of non-renewal, and if it was not then the system would lose credibility. In practice franchise systems may end up very much like the normal form of economic regulation—a point we noted earlier in the book. There are also other technical problems.

Whilst therefore in some cases regulation may be a *fait accompli*, and the system of RPI – x does at least build in an incentive to efficiency which is markedly lacking in US systems, the organisational setting which has been chosen is in some cases open to criticism. Thus in the case of privatised gas a monolithic structure was not essential. It would have been possible to envisage a series of independent regional distribution companies. Whilst they would have been monopolists in their heartlands, some competition would have been available at the edges of their territories, the existence of more than one distributor would have provided useful cost comparisons for the central regulator, and the market for corporate control would have exercised a more effective discipline.[11] Regional possibilities also suggest themselves when electricity is privatised[12]—and indeed the proposals unveiled in February 1988 appear to take account of that possibility.

Some final observations remain to be made. Firstly, the market for corporate control in privatised companies does not operate at all in one case. The shares of the National Freight

Corporation are not available to the general public but are only traded amongst the owning management and employees. In the case of some of the hybrids, the government has indicated its intention to use its votes to block foreign ownership. Whilst there are good reasons for this in the case of British Airways, in other cases it obviously precludes the possibility of foreign take over. Secondly, we have said nothing about the role of the shareholder in monitoring the activities of privatised managements. Whilst the Conservative government may rejoice at the prospect of stock falling into the hands of small shareholders, the latter are not likely to be as effective as the institutions in uncovering managerial weaknesses and forcing change. It is true that the institutions have been criticised for not being more active in this respect. But undoubtedly they do intervene when real difficulties emerge and also exercise influence in ways which are less direct than the annual general meeting. Thirdly, the emergence of large profit maximising companies with substantial market power raises the possibility that various anti-competitive tactics, including predatory pricing, will be employed. Some commentators have quite properly asked whether British antitrust policy is adequate to the task of dealing with such behaviour. Tom Sharpe has observed that British antitrust policy is not strong on penalties. He observes:

> An aggressive competitor need fear only public displeasure, not the consequences of compensating his victim who, by the time an investigation is completed, may well no longer be trading.[13]

Fourthly, some doubts exist as to the powers enjoyed by the regulators in relation to these larger privatised utilities. At the time of writing Ofgas is engaged in a legal tussle with British Gas concerning the alleged inadequacy of data supplied by the latter. Finally, we did earlier raise the issue of the effect of privatisation on the quality of service. The evidence yet available is limited but what there is has given rise to considerable misgivings. We are of course referring to the widespread and vociferous complaints (not denied by the firm) in 1987 about the service supplied by privatised British Telecom notably in respect of installing lines. The Director General of Oftel indicated that British Telecom might be required to accept contractual liability for failing to provide new lines by a specified date, and this approach might also be applied to fault repairs.[14] Some of these problems are obviously an inheritance from public corporation days, and to that extent no final judgement can yet be made. That defence will of course progressively lose credibility.

3   REGULATORY REFORM

Before turning to the particular industries which have been affected, there is one issue which invites some comment. Much play has been made of the idea that regulators are captured by the producers who are regulated. Actually the question is wider than that, since it also takes in the idea that legislators may be in the pockets of those who will be legislated about. Does the evidence support this view?

In the first instance it has to be said that these ideas tend to be expressed in relatively sweeping terms, whereas experience suggests that in the field of human affairs matters are rarely so clear cut. There have undoubtedly been a number of instances which seem predominantly to support the capture thesis. The introduction of the CAB regulatory system in American airline operation seems substantially to be a good example. The application of regulation to the US telephone system also appears to have owed much to the pressure of Bell and Theodore Vail in particular. The extension of regulation to trucking was undoubtedly a response to the clamour of the railways for protection, but other elements were also at work and we shall return to these below.

It is also important to appreciate that capture is a deceptive concept. Regulators may act in a protective way but this does not mean that they do so in response to the campaigning of those who are regulated. When a body of individuals is placed in charge of an industry it inevitably tends to behave protectively towards it, because if the industry should collapse the public spotlight will be on the regulators, and they will be judged to have failed. Some of the response of the railway regulating ICC towards trucking was inspired by that consideration. Furthermore when regulators protect an industry it may not be because they are truckling to the regulated. Rather the protection may be part of a plan whose motivations are those of the regulators. For example, protection of the traditional TV and radio systems in the US by the FCC was almost certainly inspired by the commission's hope that the profits from popular offerings would subsidise minority programming. Posner's internal cross-subsidisation motive has undoubtedly been an important feature of the economic regulatory scene. It was also at work in the CAB system in which revenues on popular routes subsidised airline service on the less densely used ones. Incidentally fare protection also helped to keep down the need for external subsidies.

Earlier in the book we observed that in some cases coalitions have been at work. Electricity is a classic instance in which producers, progressives and consumers all favoured regulation. The thing producers and political progressives disliked, in other words the factor which united them, was public ownership, whilst consumers looked to protection from the exploitation which would arise from uncontrolled monopoly. The introduction of ICC regulation of railways was also a product of a coalition of interests—both the railways and shippers had something to gain, and the public interest motivation of western development was also important. The application of regulation to US trucking was also one in which there was a coalition of interests, since some truckers and indeed some shippers saw possible benefits in the system.

But there are cases where the capture thesis just simply does not hold. It is difficult to see the application of regulation to the US gas industry as being motivated by producer pressures. Their best interests lay in allowing prices to rise to market clearing levels. The industry also opposed the extension of control to wellhead prices. Public interest considerations seem to have been uppermost here although the system of regulation proved to be inept. We also recollect that the CAB and the ICC had initiated deregulation before Congress got around to legislating. These two episodes (and there are others) do not support Bernstein's thesis that at the end of the day the regulators become the helpless tools of the regulated. In the case of US banking a public interest explanation has been afforded although George Benston has viewed the regulatory regime of the 1930s as one which also suited a variety of producer interests.

We turn now to consider the consequences of regulatory reform. The airline industry is an obvious first candidate for consideration. We will focus on US internal services, the North Atlantic routes and the UK-Netherlands bilateral.

Following, and indeed preceeding formal deregulation, the US airline industry became more competitive. T. Gale Moore points out that between 1976 and 1983 the number of carriers (passenger and freight) approximately tripled. Within that total, passenger carriers more than doubled from twenty-eight to sixty-one. The increase in the number of scheduled carriers that the old trunkline operators had to contend with stemmed from three sources—intrastate carriers were the first to enter. They were followed by former charter operators and then by completely new entrants. Not only were there more carriers but more importantly the number on particular routes increased.[15] A notable new feature of the system has been that airlines have tended to centre their activities on one or more hubs, within a hub and spoke route pattern. Thus instead of flying directly from A to B, passengers fly from A to hub X and then from hub X to B. Richard Pryke[16] has pointed out that although some airlines are strongly entrenched on particular hubs, this does not mean that they are totally insulated from competition. Firstly, a passenger may get from A to B via hub Y and secondly, some airlines will offer direct service from A to B.

Not surprisingly, given that between 1976 and 1982 average costs in real terms rose by fifteen per cent (fuel prices rose by seventy-three per cent), nominal fares tended to rise. But in real terms over that period they fell on average by 9.5 per cent on a per mile basis.[17] Another way of measuring the effect of competition is to compare what actually happened to fares with what would have happened under the regulatory price formula. Whilst on long distance routes in large markets fares fell markedly below the CAB predicted level, on short hauls, in small markets they rose above it. Thus comparing the fourth quarter of 1983 with the first quarter of 1975, fares fell to sixty per cent of formula level in markets of 501–1000 passengers a day on routes of 1500 + miles, whilst they rose to 114 per cent of the formula level in markets of ten to fifty passengers per day on routes of up to 400 miles.[18] In short the effect of deregulation was to reduce cross-subsidisation and to relate fares more closely to costs. The more economic use of resources which flowed from the disappearance of cross-subsidisation has indeed been a feature of most deregulated markets.

The pressure on fares in real terms was of course a reflection of what happened to costs in real terms. Some of the cost improvement can be attributed to the emergence of new aircraft, but in the period after deregulation the major part of it was due to internal management strategy.[19] Here the intrastate and new entrant jet carriers played a key role. They had a decided cost advantage, which stemmed from more efficient use of low cost non-union labour, a streamlined no-frills operation and intensive utilisation of relatively fuel-efficient but older twin-engined jets.[20] Incidentally this use of non-union labour points up the fact that one of the main beneficiaries of regulation had been unionised labour, which was able to secure levels of remuneration well above normal market levels.[21] As we shall see, the tendency for union labour to be a loser, and non-union labour to be a gainer, from deregulation has not been confined to airlines. The no-frills point reminds us of the emergence of a price versus services choice for consumers—again this experience has been repeated elsewhere. The no-frills approach represented a reversal of Posner's observed tendency for price agreements and price regulation to force rivalry into cost-escalating non-price channels. Competition also led to higher load factors, although not as high as had been predicted. The new system also allowed airlines to take advantage of unit scale economies.

Greater competition was also seen as posing possible problems. Firstly, there was what may broadly be described as the excessive competition thesis. It is true that firms have gone under, but major instability has not been observed. Mergers have also taken place but they appear to have been predominantly end-to-end rather than between firms on the same route. If the latter occur, the hope must be that the contestability of the market will still exert its influence. However in the latter connection the decision (in the case of major airports) to transfer the ownership of landing slots to the incumbent airlines does not represent an ideal way of dealing with the sunk cost problem. Some also feared that increased competition would lead to an erosion of safety standards, but this is not supported by the accident statistics. Secondly, fear was also expressed about loss of service to small communities. There has been some loss but it has not been as great as some predicted. Moreoever it should be remembered that some loss arose under the CAB system. Also the loss which has occurred is not necessarily due to deregulation. Furthermore commuter airlines have in some cases moved in where traditional carriers have moved out. Finally, most people possess cars and can commute to an airport, and in addition deregulated bus operators have introduced airport express services.

On North Atlantic routes deregulation has been accompanied by increased competition. New carriers entered the market—these included People Express and Virgin Atlantic. A no-frills approach has also emerged, and discounting has grown very considerably. Notably after about 1981, economy fares in real terms tended to fall.[22] Load factors are reported to have increased. There have however been some signs of financial instability in that prestige factors tended to induce airlines, sometimes in league with their governments, to carry on operating even when losses are made. Deregulation has not worked out as well as could have been hoped, although this may be more a criticism of governments than of competitive markets. The new UK-Netherlands bilateral may not yet have had time to reveal its full possibilities. Nevertheless there have been a number of new entrants to the UK-Amsterdam and UK-Rotterdam routes and economy fares in real terms have tended to fall.[23]

The evidence in US trucking also points to beneficial effects. Here again the process of deregulation preceeded the formal act of 1980. From 1979 the number of licensed carriers began to increase and by 1982 was fifty-five per cent up on the

1976 level. The evidence indicates that increased competition caused trucking rates to fall in real terms. Within a sample of between thirty and thirty-five firms, T. Gale Moore found that real truckload rates fell by twenty-five per cent between 1975 and 1982 whilst less than truckload rates fell by eleven per cent. The effect of liberalised entry and rate competition was revealed in the fall in the price of trucking licences. In 1976 they averaged \$579,000 but by 1982 they commanded only \$15,000. Existing operators were of course losing their monopoly rents.

Inefficiencies of the regulatory system, such as those involving the use of circuitous routes, disappeared. Another factor helping to explain the downward movement of rates was that deregulation stimulated the development of non-union trucking firms. Wages and earnings fell, and the bargaining position of the Teamsters Union was weakened. According to J. C. Nelson the new deregulatory climate also encouraged truckers to study their market opportunities more alertly and aggressively, to design new packages of rates and services, to seek out intermodal opportunities which combined low cost road with low cost rail journeys and to cease supplying services which were not profitable or only marginally so.[24] The evidence also indicates that service to small and remote parts of the community was not adversely affected. Service standards were not eroded. The industry did not come to be dominated by large firms.[25]

It is also apparent that within US surface transport, deregulation has enabled the relative advantage of different modes (i.e. rail and road) to assert themselves. Intermodal usage has also increased as we suggested earlier—e.g. trailers on flat cars. Elizabeth Bailey points out that the inefficiencies imposed by artificial regulatory boundaries have been removed, and shippers can now search out the lowest cost mode of carriage.[26] The railways have also benefited financially from more permissive policies towards route abandonments and merger processes have been speeded up.[27]

In the bus and coach sector, the UK was in terms of timing ahead of the US. The first area to be deregulated was express coaching. Whilst the Transport Act 1980 opened up such longer distance activity to competition, the structure of the industry has not changed fundamentally. National Express (the marketing division of the nationalised National Bus Company) retained its dominant position. It was challenged by British Coachways (BC), a consortium of independent operators, but BC met a prompt competitive response from National and subsequently collapsed. Nevertheless the ability of the independents to offer competition has undoubtedly helped to keep National on its toes. Evan Davis reports that fares fell substantially, and in 1984 were lower in nominal terms than they were in 1980. Traffic grew quite healthily. The pattern and quality of service has changed quite significantly. Frequency of service on intercity routes increased. Some smaller towns lost express services. Innovations included airport-linked services and luxury services. This long distance competition also impacted on British Rail (BR). BR travellers obviously gained but BR itself suffered a loss of revenue. One matter of considerable importance has been the benefit which National has continued to enjoy by virtue of its hold on terminal facilities.[28] Local bus services too have exhibited significant response in the wake of deregulation. Entry and price competition have been vigorous. Service innovation has also emerged, notably from independent minibus operators. They have been searching out profitable routes within towns and cities—very much on a door-to-door basis.

In the US bus deregulation flowed from the 1982 Bus Regulatory Reform Act. According to Kenneth Button the immediate impact of the act was a substantial increase in licence applications to supply intercity services. Added to that has been the introduction of new types of product, notably airport express bus services and services to casino facilities. At the same time greater commercial freedom led to significant route abandonments, and the ICC has tended to support the bus operators against state opposition to these discontinuances. The impact of increased competition has taken the form of higher levels of service provision, including better terminal facilities, rather than lower fares. Competitive pressures have also focussed the attention of bus operators on the need, not only to root out unprofitable services, but also to improve their own internal efficiency and to seek wage and other benefit concessions from their employees.[29] We encountered this reaction earlier. Two-tier wage structures, with new employees being paid on a lower scale, have been a feature of surface transportation as well as aviation.

As we saw earlier in the book, security dealing has been deregulated in both the US and the UK. In both cases self-regulating cartels had to be abandoned. In the US this led to marked competition in brokerage commission rates on the New York Stock Exchange (NYSE). Between the first quarter of 1975 and the first quarter of 1981 large institutional investors enjoyed a rate decline of fifty per cent in brokerage commission. Smaller institutional investors over the same period were less fortunate—their commission rate fell by twenty per cent. Commission rates for the smallest trading blocks in the case of individuals actually rose. However in the case of individual trades in large blocks there was a fifty per cent fall in the commission rate.[30] Here again, differential impact was the result of the erosion of regulatory cross-subsidies. The effect of falling commission rates and more open access (the latter arising from nationwide market integration under the Securities Acts Amendments of 1975), was reflected in a precipitous fall in seat prices on the NYSE. Seat prices hit a peak in 1968 and fell continuously until 1977. The early fall was no doubt due to the earlier reductions in the commission on large block trades secured by the institutions. The parallel with the fall in the price of trucking licences (see above) is obvious. Pricing nearer to costs has had an effect on the type of trades. Before deregulation trades were inefficiently small. Since deregulation large block trades have become more prominent. As in the case of the airlines, service variety has increased—discount brokerage houses offering retail services but no advice have prospered in competition with full-service brokers. A large number of brokerage firms left the industry and there were numerous mergers. The share of assets accounted for by the largest twenty-five NYSE members rose from fifty-six per cent in 1971 to seventy-seven per cent in 1980. Concentration was still however quite low.[31]

In the UK, following the Big Bang, the cost of dealing plummeted. Commission rates on equity deals of £100,000 to £1 million fell from about 0.4 per cent to 0.2 per cent. On very large deals in excess of £2–3 million rates of 0.125 per cent are said to be obtainable. Apparently even bigger concessions can be obtained by dealing on a net-of-commission basis directly with market makers, or by approaching broker/dealers who may be willing to operate on this basis from their own book. On the other hand, the ordinary investor with £1000 to spare is likely to find that the commission has remained at 1.65 per cent although a few firms have cut their rates to 1.5 per cent and some firms, on an execution-only basis, charge only 1.0 per cent.[32] The phasing out of cross-subsidies has obviously also been at work in the UK. It should also be mentioned that security dealing has been caught up in the conglomeration process which has been a feature of the reorganisation within the City of London.

Earlier in the book we also noted that over a fairly extended time period competitive forces have been at work in British banking. Given the increased competition both between institutions within a sector (e.g. banks) and between sectors (e.g. banks versus building societies), it would not be surprising if there had been some narrowing of the spread between borrowing and lending rates. This has indeed been apparent in the case of banks, both in respect of their international, and domestic wholesale, lending. In the case of building societies deregulation (in the form of the abolition of the interest rate cartel) lead initially to an increase in profitability as interest rates were adjusted to the market clearing level, but subsequently the spread between the borrowing and lending rate narrowed under the pressure of increased competition. A narrowing of the spread is beneficial to members of the public as lenders, borrowers or both. On the other hand the extensive prudential regulation, which has been introduced in the financial markets, and which is designed to protect investors, will give rise to a significant burden. It has been alleged that the administrative costs alone are greater than any identified losses by investors in public scandals. Critics have also pointed to other losses and detriments arising from the new system of prudential regulation. These include the financing of compensation funds, the diversion of business abroad, the restrictive effect on competition and the stifling of financial innovation.[33] Yet other critics have doubted whether the emphasis on self-regulation is a satisfactory basis upon which to found a system of investor protection.

Deregulation (without statutory assistance) and antitrust restructuring have both occurred in US telecommunications. Elizabeth Bailey points out that competition in telecommunications will lower prices.[34] This is most likely to be the case in long distance services, since competition has been admitted to most of the market and technological change is making a significant cost-reducing contribution. Bell is reported to have just under eighty per cent of the market—the main competitors (in an area where about 400 companies are competing) are MCI (recently acquired in part by IBM) and GTE Sprint—the former has about seven per cent of the market and the latter about four percent. Forecasters originally expected the intense competition to erode Bell's share to sixty per cent—however they now look to a figure of seventy per cent. This is because Bell has made a determined and successful attack on its costs, notably labour, which, as Elizabeth Bailey observes, were inflated much as was the case in other regulated sectors. Because of this successful cost cutting, the low cost advantage which firms like MCI enjoyed has been diminished. Whilst prices are confidently expected to fall in the long distance market, commentators expect them to rise in local service. This expectation arises from the point that there is likely to be a move towards a more cost based pricing system and in the past local rates have been kept down artificially. In other areas, such as terminal equipment, we saw earlier in the book that, thanks to a series of deregulatory decisions, competition was allowed to break through and this has happened on a substantial scale.

In the case of the US and UK TV broadcasting, the main deregulatory events were sketched out in Chapters 5 and 8. In the US the main effect has been to create a multiplicity of offerings, thanks to a series of FCC decisions and court judgements over a long period. Whether multiplicity has contributed to greater choice and improved quality of viewing is a matter for subjective judgement. In the UK the authorities were less resistant to cable and DBS, but the expectation that throughout the land the viewer's lot will as a consequence be revolutionised is open to doubt. This judgement has nothing to do with the impact on choice and quality but is simply a reflection of uncertainty about the future financial viability of these services.

Finally we noted that during the Thatcher years the UK professions have been subjected to significant deregulation and that there is more to come. We focussed on two areas—the solicitors' monopoly of conveyancing and the activities of opticians. In both cases intense competition has ensued. In the case of solicitors, a study published in January 1987 indicated that conveyancing fees had dropped by twenty-five per cent, and that conveyancing costs represented 0.7 per cent of the average house price as compared with 0.9 per cent in 1983. In some cases fees had been cut by fifty per cent. As compared with 1983, solicitors' income from conveyancing was down by up to thirty per cent.[35] Strictly speaking deregulation is not an appropriate term to use in this connection, since the new breed of competing licensed conveyancers are themselves regulated. In the case of spectacles the market, previously dominated by licensed opticians, has been revolutionised by an invasion of firms offering ready-glazed spectacles. The new entrants include the major high street retail chemist Boots. Price competition is reported to be extremely vigorous. This has had a reinvigorating influence on the marketing strategies of the established opticians.[36]

4   ASSESSMENT

The general impression which emerges is that privatisation in the UK has been substantially inspired by considerations of political ideology. That of course is not the whole of the story. By contrast the deregulation movement in the US, whilst not free of ideological content, was largely conceived as a technical exercise in which economic benefits were looked for. In contrast to privatisation, the economic benefits of deregulation (which the UK has also engaged in) have been much more obvious. In some cases prices have fallen across the board with evident direct or indirect benefits for consumers. Better utilisation of resources has come from the termination of unprofitable services, the elimination of perverse regulatory rules and the ending of cross-subsidisation. Where cross-subsidisation has been pronounced, some groups will have, or already have had, to pay more—the main beneficiaries of price falls have been, or will be, business users. But even if some consumers have to pay more, they have nevertheless gained from a wider choice as between price and service. Competition has meant that monopoly rents have been eroded. Productive efficiency has increased and technological change and service innovation have been stimulated. The bogy of excessive competition has proved to be just that—a largely unfounded fear. Market instability has not resulted, although there have been victims in the new competitive environment. In air and surface transport, safety has not been sacrificed. Mergers and conglomeration have occurred but markets remain broadly competitive. The main loser has been organised labour, which proved to be a major beneficiary of regulation. Non-union labour has gained, as have firms which have been able to secure a share of the deregulated action. Against all that it has to be recognised that the consumer protection, which sometimes has to be introduced in the more competitive and newly structured systems (e.g. UK financial markets), will give rise to additional costs. Follow-up action is needed in respect of terminal facilities, etc., if markets are to be rendered more contestable—e.g. UK coach operation. Some loss of service has been sustained by small communities, although the loss is much less than anticipated and not all of it can be blamed on deregulation. Privatisation too has conferred some resource utilisation benefits, although those benefits are likely to be most obvious when markets are substantially liberalised or imaginative regulatory frameworks are introduced. Here the report has to be a more cautious one which might well read as follows—some improvement seems evident, but those concerned could do better and hopefully will do so in future.

NOTES

1. S. Brittan, 'Privatisation: A Comment on Kay and Thompson' *op. cit.*, p.34.
2. For an approach to this type of analysis which also takes in corporate objectives and managerial incentives, see S. Domberger and S. Piggott, 'Privatisation Policies and Public Enterprise: A Survey', *The Economic Record*, 62 (1986), pp.145–62.
3. D. A. Kuenne, *Takeovers and the Theory of the Firm* (Macmillan, London, 1975) and A. Singh, 'Takeovers, Economic Natural Selection and the Theory of the Firm', *Economic Journal*, 85 (1975), pp.497–515.
4. R. Pryke, 'The Comparative Performance of Public and Private Enterprise', *op. cit.*, p.80.
5. R. Millward, 'The Comparative Performance of Public and Private Ownership' in Lord Roll (ed.), *The Mixed Economy* (Macmillan, London, 1982), pp.58–93.
6. T. E. Borcherding, W. W. Pommerehne and F. Schnieder, 'Comparing the Efficiency of Private and Public Production: The Evidence from Five Countries', *Zeitschrift für Nationölokonomie*, Supplement 2, (1982), pp.127–56.
7. J. A. Kay and D. J. Thompson, 'Privatisation: A Policy in Search of a Rationale', *Economic Journal*, 96 (1986), pp.18–32.
8. G. Yarrow, 'Privatization in Theory and Practice', *Economic Policy*, 2 (1986), p.340.
9. See D. Starkie and D. Thompson, *Privatising London's Airports op. cit.*, pp.79–87.
10. On Natural Monopoly and its sustainability see W. Sharkey, *The Theory of Natural Monopoly* (Cambridge University Press, Cambridge, 1982). See also J. Vickers and G. Yarrow, *Privatization and the Natural Monopolies* (Public Policy Centre, London, 1985).
11. See E. M. Hammond, D. R. Helm and D. J. Thompson, 'British Gas: Options for Privatization' *op. cit.*, pp.10-15.
12. Vickers and Yarrow, *Privatization and the Natural Monopolies op. cit.*, pp.51–85.
13. T. Sharpe, 'Privatization, Regulation and Competition', *Fiscal Studies* 5/1 (1984), p.59.
14. *Financial Times*, 15 July, 1987, p.1.
15. T. Gale Moore, 'U.S. Airline Deregulation: Its Effects on Passengers, Capital, and Labour', *Journal of Law and Economics*, 29/1 (1986), pp.5–6. On US airline deregulation generally see also E. E. Bailey, D. R. Graham and D. P. Kaplan, *Deregulating the Airlines* (MIT Press, Cambridge, Massachusetts, 1985).
16. R. Pryke, *Competition among International Airlines* (Trade Policy Research Centre, London, 1987), pp.43–4.
17. T. Gale Moore, 'US Airline Deregulation' *op. cit.*, p.8.
18. E. E. Bailey, 'Price and Productivity Change Following Deregulation:

The US Experience', *Economic Journal*, 96 (1986), p.5 citing evidence by D. P. Kaplan.

19. D. Sawers, *Competition in the Air* (Institute of Economic Affairs, London, 1985), pp.18–19.
20. J. R. Meyer and C. V. Oster, *Deregulation and the New Airline Entrepreneurs* (MIT Press, Cambridge, Massachusetts, 1984), pp.51–86 and 123–37.
21. See D. Sawers *Competition in the Air, op. cit.*, p.19.
22. J. Pelkmans, 'Deregulation of European Air Transport' in H. W. de Jong and W. G. Shepherd (eds), *Mainstreams of Industrial Organisation* (Nijhoff, Dordrecht, 1986), pp.375–6.
23. *Ibid*, pp.378–9.
24. J. C. Nelson, 'The Emerging Effects of Deregulation of Surface Freight Transport in the United States', *International Journal of Transport Economics*, 10 (1983), p.221.
25. This account is based on T. Gale Moore, 'Rail and Truck Reform—the Record So Far', *Regulation*, Nov./Dec. 1983, pp.33–41.
26. E. E. Bailey, 'Price and Productivity Change' *op. cit.*, p.6.
27. J. C. Nelson, 'The Emerging Effects', *op. cit.*, pp.322–3.
28. Based on E. Davis, 'Express Coaching Since 1980: Liberalisation in Practice', *op. cit.*, pp.76–86.
29. Based on K. J. Button, 'The Effects of Regulatory Reform in the US Inter-city Bus Industry', *Transport Reviews*, 7/2 (1987), pp.145–65.
30. E. E. Bailey, 'Price and Productivity Change' *op. cit.*, pp.4–5.
31. G. A. Jarrell, 'Change at the Exchange' *op. cit.*, pp.302–3 and 306–7.
32. D. H. A. Ingram, 'Change in the Stock Exchange' *op. cit.*, p.59.
33. *Financial Times*, 4, June 1987, pp.1 and 48.
34. E. E. Bailey, 'Price and Productivity Change' *op. cit.*, pp.6–7.
35. *The Times* 14 January 1987, p.12 quoting a report by Peat Marwick.
36. David Hall, 'An Eye for an Eye', *Management Today*, Nov. 1986, pp.62–3 and 141.

Appendix Tables

Table 1: UK Public Corporations—Share in UK Economy in 1975

	Percent of UK Totals	
Major Nationalised Industries	Output	Employment
British Airways[1]	0.3	0.2
British Gas	0.8	0.4
British Rail[2]	1.2	1.0
British Steel Corporation	0.8	0.9
Electricity in England and Wales[3]	1.5	0.7
National Bus Company[4]	0.2	0.3
National Coal Board	1.5	1.2
National Freight Corporation[5]	0.2	0.2
Post Office[6]	2.8	1.8
	9.2	6.7

Other Nationalised Industries	Output	Employment
British Airports Authority		
British National Oil Corporation		
British Transport Docks Board[7]		
British Waterways Board[8]	0.4	0.2
Scottish Transport Group[9]		
North of Scotland Hydro Electric Board		
South of Scotland Electricity Board		
	9.6	6.9

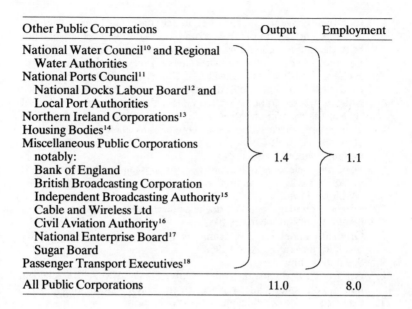

Other Public Corporations	Output	Employment
National Water Council[10] and Regional Water Authorities		
National Ports Council[11]		
National Docks Labour Board[12] and Local Port Authorities		
Northern Ireland Corporations[13]		
Housing Bodies[14]		
Miscellaneous Public Corporations notably:	1.4	1.1
Bank of England		
British Broadcasting Corporation		
Independent Broadcasting Authority[15]		
Cable and Wireless Ltd		
Civil Aviation Authority[16]		
National Enterprise Board[17]		
Sugar Board		
Passenger Transport Executives[18]		
All Public Corporations	11.0	8.0

Notes
1. The result of an amalgamation of BOAC and BEA.
2. The original BTC stripped by virtue of the Transport Act 1962 of its docks, inland waterways, road haulage, road passenger and London transport activities. See also notes 4, 5, 7, 8 and 18.
3. Specifically the Electricity Council, Central Electricity Generating Board and twelve Area Boards.
4. Under the Transport Act 1962 the BTC was replaced by a series of separate boards for railways, docks, inland waterways, London transport and a fifth body—the Transport Holding Company. The latter was responsible for the rest of the inheritance from the BTC. The latter was to include the rump of road haulage which was not denationalised following the act of 1953 (hence British Road Services), buses, hotels, ships and Thomas Cook and Sons. Under the Transport Act 1968 the *bus* element was separated off as (a) the publicly owned National Bus Company and (b) the publicly owned Scottish Transport Group which in turn owned the Scottish Bus Group.
5. Under the Transport Act 1962 the BTC stake in road haulage together with the interests of buses, hotels, ships and Thomas Cook and Sons were vested in the Transport Holding Company (THC). Under the Transport Act 1968 a further rearrangement of *freight* transport occurred. A National Freight Corporation (NFC) was formed and it

took over conventional road freight activities and shipping from the THC. As indicated in note 4, a rump of road freight activity had not been denationalised and was called British Road Services. The NFC also took over from the British Railways Board (BRB) (successor to BTC) freight liner etc. services—i.e. services which originated by road. On the freight side BRB was left to concentrate on activities for which it was felt to be best fitted i.e. freight traffic originating by rail such as full train and wagon loads of coal and steel, and trains booked by companies to carry full loads of oil, cement, chemicals, motor cars, etc.—see R. Kelf-Cohen, *Twenty Years of Nationalisation*, (Macmillan, London, 1969), p.94.

6. Posts and Telecommunications became separate public corporations in 1981—see M. J. Daunton, *Royal Mail The Post Office Since 1844* (Athlone, London, 1985), p.342.
7. Originally under the BTC, docks came under a separate board as a result of the Transport Act 1962.
8. Originally under the BTC, canals came under a separate board as a result of the Transport Act 1962.
9. See note 4 above.
10. A forum for discussing water matters and advising the relevant minister on policy—later replaced by the Water Association.
11. Concerned with the efficiency of port operations.
12. Responsible for operating the national dock labour scheme.
13. Specifically the Northern Ireland Electricity Service, the Northern Ireland Finance Corporation, the Northern Ireland Housing Executive and the Northern Ireland Transport Holding Company.
14. Specifically the Housing Corporation, the Commission for New Towns, the New Town Development Corporations and the Scottish Special Housing Association.
15. Change of title due to inclusion of independent radio in remit.
16. Largely a regulatory body but some airport ownership—see end reference number 14 on p.220 above.
17. Not including subsidiaries such as Rolls Royce (1971). In 1982 the National Enterprise Board was merged with the National Research Development Corporation to form the British Technology Group.
18. The pre-war LPTB became part of the BTC under the post-war nationalisation act. In 1962 the BTC was split and a separate London Transport Board (LTB) was created—see note 4 above. Under the Transport (London) Act 1969 the LTB was transferred to the Greater London Council (GLC) and, as a variation from the normal pattern under the Transport Act 1968, the London Passenger Executive was responsible to the GLC and not to a separate passenger transport authority.

Source: NEDO, *A Study of UK Nationalised Industries, Appendix Volume*, London, 1976, Tables A1, A2 and A3.

Table 2: Major Privatisations. Public Offers for Sale (O) and Private Sales (P)

Privatised Entity	Business	Privatised Form		Value of Public Issue or Gross Proceeds of Private Sale (£m)
National Enterprise Board[1] holdings in various companies including International Computers (P)	Various including computers (ICL)	Various including International Computers Ltd (now owned by STC International Computers Ltd)	1979	38
Suiz Finance Company (UK government holding of 7.67%) (P)	Member of French consortium involved in channel tunnel bid 1978-9	Shares placed mainly with French financial institutions	1979	22
British Petroleum Ltd (combined Treasury and Bank of England holding of 51%) (0)	Oil	Already private company— now The British Petroleum Company PLC	1979 1981 1983 1987	290 293[2] 566 7240 (minimum)
National Enterprise Board[1] holdings in various companies including Ferranti Ltd and Fairey Holdings Ltd (P)	Various including mechanical, electrical and electronic equipment (Ferranti) and specialist engineering (Fairey)	Various including Ferranti PLC and Fairey Holdings Ltd which is owned by Williams Holdings PLC	1980	80

Table 2: continued

Privatised Entity	Business	Privatised Form		Value of Public Issue or Gross Proceeds of Private Sale (£m)
British Sugar Corporation Ltd (24.17% government holding) (P)	Sugar refining	British Sugar PLC owned by S & W Berisford PLC. (The government holding was purchased by a group of institutional investors)	1981	44
Cable and Wireless Ltd (O)	Telecommunications	Already private company—now Cable and Wireless PLC	1981 1983 1985	224 275 933
British Rail (Hotels) (P)	Hotels	Various purchasers	1981 to 1983	45
British Aerospace (O)	Aerospace and guided weapons	British Aerospace PLC	1981 1985	150 550
National Freight Corporation (P)	Road Haulage	National Freight Consortium	1982	7
British Steel Corporation (Redpath Dorman Long) (P)	Constructional steelwork and civil engineering	Redpath Dorman Long Ltd itself owned by Trafalgar House PLC	1982	10

Table 2: continued

Privatised Entity	Business	Privatised Form		Value of Public Issue or Gross Proceeds of Private Sale (£m)
Radiochemical Centre Ltd (100% of shares held by United Kingdom Atomic Energy Authority) (O)	Radiochemicals	Amersham International PLC	1982	71
British National Oil Corporation (oil and gas production interests) (O)	Oil and gas production	Britoil PLC (now owned by BP)	1982 1985	549 449
British Transport Docks Board (O)	Seaports	Associated British Ports Holdings PLC	1983 1984	22 52
International Aeradio Ltd (subsidiary of British Airways) (P)	Aviation Communications	International Aeradio PLC itself owned by STC PLC	1983	60
British Gas Corporation (oil and gas production interests) (P)	Oil and gas production	Enterprise Oil PLC	1984	392
British Gas Corporation (Wytch Farm—a 50% interest in petroleum licence PL 089) (P)	Oil	Sold to Dorset Bidding Group	1984	80[4]

Table 2: continued

Privatised Entity	Business	Privatised Form		Value of Public Issue or Gross Proceeds of Private Sale (£m)
British Telecom Corporation (O)	Telecommunications	British Telecommunications PLC	1984	3916[3]
BL[5] (Jaguar group) (O)	Cars	Jaguar PLC	1984	29
British Rail (Sealink) (P)	Harbours and ferries	Sealink UK Ltd owned by British Ferries Ltd	1984	66
British Shipbuilders (Scott-Lithgow) (P)	Shipbuilding, ship repairing and offshore engineering	Sold to Trafalgar House PLC parent of Scott-Lithgow Ltd	1984	20
National Enterprise Board[1] (76% stake in INMOS) (P)	Semiconductors	INMOS International PLC owned by Thorn EMI PLC	1985	95
British Shipbuilders (Yarrow) (P)	Warship building and general engineering	Sold to General Electric Co PLC parent of Yarrow Shipbuilders Ltd	1985	34
British Shipbuilders (Vosper Thorneycroft) (P)	Shipbuilding and engineering	Sold to management consortium—now Vosper Thorneycroft (UK) Ltd	1985	18.5 minimum
Royal Ordnance Factories (Leeds tank plant) (P)	Battle tanks	Vickers PLC	1986	11

Table 2: continued

Privatised Entity	Business	Privatised Form		Value of Public Issue or Gross Proceeds of Private Sale (£m)
British Gas Corporation (O)	Natural gas supply and production	British Gas PLC	1986	5434
British Shipbuilders (Vickers Shipbuilding and Engineering) (P)	Shipbuilders and warship construction (submarines)	Sold to management consortium (Cammell Laird having previously been merged into Vickers)—now Vickers Shipbuilding and Engineering Ltd	1986	60[6]
B.A. Helicopters (P)	Helicopter services	Sold to Robert Maxwell	1986	13
Royal Ordnance Factories (17 manufacturing and R & D centres) (P)	Weapons, missiles and ammunition	Sold to British Aerospace PLC	1987	190
Rolls Royce PLC[4] (O)	Aero engines	Rolls Royce PLC	1987	1363
British Airports Authority (O)	Seven airports located in south east England and Scotland	British Airports PLC	1987	1225
British Airways (O)	Domestic and international airline transport	British Airways PLC	1987	900

Table 2: continued

Privatised Entity	Business	Privatised Form	Value of Public Issue or Gross Proceeds of Private Sale (£m)
British Rail (Doncaster Wagon Works) (P)	Railway wagons	Management buy-out 1987	6

Other Privatisations include:

British Shipbuilders—sale of Swan Hunter and other yards.
British Steel Corporation—various joint ventures e.g. heavy forging and special steel facilities of Johnson and Firth Brown and BSC River Don Works to form Sheffield Forgemasters Ltd, and sales of other interests e.g. Stanton and Staveley and Coated Electrodes.
British Rail—merger in 1982 of Seaspeed and Hoverlloyd (latter being subsidiary of Brostroms Rederi AB) to form Hoverspeed (UK) Ltd. Transfer in 1984 of Hoverspeed to directors and managers for nominal sum.
National Enterprise Board sale of holdings in several companies.
National Bus Company—sale of subsidiary bus companies estimated to raise £150–170 million.
BL (later re-named Rover Group)—sale of subsidiaries including Unipart, which was taken over by a consortium of former managers and investment institutions, Leyland Bus, which was similarly disposed of, Leyland Trucks, in which a new joint venture company was formed with a 40% holding by DAF, and Istel Ltd (a firm concerned with computer and communications development services) which also involved a management buy-out. Rover Group sold to British Aerospace in 1988.

For greater completeness we can add that considerable sums have been raised by other methods notably:

Crown Agents—sale of property.
Forestry Commission—sale of land, plantations and buildings.
New Town Development Corporations and Commission for the New Towns—sale of land and buildings.

Table 2: continued

Property Services Agency—sale of land and buildings.
Sale of commodity stocks and oil stockpiles.
Lease of motorway service areas and sale of land and buildings.
Water Authorities—sale of land.
Local Authorities—sale of council houses.

Possible future Privatisations include:

The Crown Suppliers.
Electricity Supply Industry.
English and Welsh Water Authorities.
British Steel Corporation.
Scottish Bus Group.
British Coal and Channel Four TV are longer term possibilities.

Notes

1. The National Enterprise Board merged with the National Research and Development Corporation to form the British Technology Group.
2. Sale of government rights entitlement.
3. Net of pension fund liabilities.
4. But with provision for further payments rising to possible 135.
5. BL (later renamed Rover Group) and Rolls Royce were transferred from the National Enterprise Board to the Department of Trade and Industry.
6. Plus possible further 40.

Sources: *The Observer*, 25 October 1987; *The Government Expenditure Plan 1985–86—1987–88*, Cmnd 9428; H.M. Treasury, *Economic Progress Report*, No. 145, May 1982; *Keesings Contemporary Archives*; *The Economist*, 23 February, 1985.

Select Bibliography

Ascher, K. *The Politics of Privatisation* (Macmillan, London, 1987).

Ashworth, M. and Forsyth, P. *Civil Aviation and the Privatisation of British Airways* (Institute of Fiscal Studies, London, 1985).

Bacon, R. and Eltis, W. *Britain's Economic Problem: Too Few Producers* (Macmillan, London, 1976).

Bailey, E. E., Graham, D. R. and Kaplan, D. P. *Deregulating the Airlines* (MIT Press, New York, 1985).

Baumol, W. J. (ed.) *Public and Private Enterprise in a Mixed Economy* (Macmillan, London, 1980).

———, Panzar, J. C. and Willig, R. D. *Contestable Markets and the Theory of Industrial Structure* (Harcourt Brace Jovanovich, San Diego, 1982).

Bernstein, M. H. *Regulating Business by Independent Commission* (Princeton University Press, Princeton, 1955).

Besen, S. M., Krattenmaker, T. E., Metzger, A. R. and Woodbury, J. R. *Misregulating Television* (University of Chicago Press, Chicago, 1984).

Bosanquet, N. *After the New Right* (Heinemann, London, 1983).

Breyer, S. G. *Regulation and Its Reform* (Harvard University Press, Cambridge, Mass., 1982).

——— and MacAvoy, P. W. *Energy Regulation and the Federal Power Commission* (Brookings Institution, Washington, 1974).

Button, K. J. *Road Haulage Licensing and EC Transport Policy* (Gower, Aldershot, 1984).

——— and Swann, D. (eds) *The Age of Regulatory Reform* (Oxford University Press, Oxford, 1988).

Cairncross, A. *Years of Recovery British Economic Policy 1945–51* (Methuen, London, 1985).

Caves, R. *Air Transport and Its Regulators* (Harvard University Press, Cambridge, Mass., 1962).

Collins, R., Garnham, N. and Locksley, G. *The Economics of UK Television* (Sage, London, 1987).

Crew, M. A. (ed.) *Regulatory Reform and Public Utilities* (Lexington, Lexington Press, Mass., 1982).

Doganis, R. *Flying Off Course* (Allen and Unwin, London, 1985).

Douglas, G. W. and Miller, J. *Economic Regulation of Domestic Air Transport: Theory and Policy* (Brookings Institution, Washington, 1974).

Erdmenger, J. *The European Community Transport Policy* (Gower, Aldershot, 1983).

Friedlaender, A. F. *The Dilemma of Freight Transport Regulation* (Brookings Institution, Washington, 1969).

Friedman, M. *Capitalism and Freedom* (University of Chicago Press, Chicago, 1962).

Fromm, G. (ed.) *Studies in Public Regulation* (MIT Press, Cambridge, Mass., 1981).

Gatti, J. F. (ed.) *The Limits of Government Regulation* (Academic Press, New York, 1981).

Gies, T. G. and Sichel, W. (eds) *Deregulation: Appraisal Before the Fact* (University of Michigan, Ann Arbor, 1982).

Glaister, S. and Mulley, C. *Public Control of the British Bus Industry* (Gower, Aldershot, 1983).

Green, M. J. (ed.) *The Monopoly Makers* (Grossman, New York, 1973).

Gujarati, D. *Government and Business* (McGraw-Hill, New York, 1984).

Heald, D. *Public Expenditure: Its Defence and Reform* (Martin Robertson, Oxford, 1983).

Hill, B. E. *The Common Agricultural Policy—Past, Present and Future* (Methuen, London, 1984).

Hunter, T. J. G. (ed.) *Decision Making in a Mixed Economy* (Open University, Milton Keynes, 1983).

Jordan, W. A. *Airline Regulation in America* (Johns Hopkins University Press, Baltimore, 1970).

Joseph, Sir K. *Reversing the Trend* (Barry Rose, Chichester, 1975).

Joskow, P. L. and Schmalensee, R. *Markets for Power* (MIT Press, Cambridge, Mass., 1983).

Kahn, A. E. *Economics of Regulation* (Wiley, New York, 1970).

Kay, J. A., Mayer, C. and Thompson, D. *Privatization and Regulation* (Oxford University Press, Oxford, 1986).

Keegan, W. *Mrs Thatcher's Economic Experiment* (Penguin, Harmondsworth, 1984).

Kelf-Cohen, R. *Twenty Years of Nationalisation* (Macmillan, London, 1969).

Kilvington, R. P. and Cross, A. K. *Deregulation of Express Coach Services in Britain* (Gower, Aldershot, 1986).

Kolko, G. *Railroads and Regulation 1877–1916* (Princeton University Press, Princeton, 1965).

Kuhn, R. (ed.) *The Politics of Broadcasting* (Croom Helm, London, 1985).

Llewellyn, D. T. *The Regulation and Supervision of Financial Institutions* (Institute of Bankers, London, 1986).

MacAvoy, P. W. *The Regulated Industries and the Economy* (Norton, New York, 1979).

———— and Snow, J. W. *Regulation of Passenger Fares and Competition Among the Airlines* (American Enterprise Institute, Washington, 1977).

McCraw, T. *The Prophets of Regulation* (Belknap, New York, 1984).

McGowan, F. and Trengrove, C. *European Aviation A Common Market?* (Institute of Fiscal Studies, London, 1986).

Maude, A. (ed.) *The Right Approach to the Economy* (Conservative Central Office, London, 1977).

Maunder, W. P. J. (ed.) *Government Intervention in the Developed Economy* (Croom Helm, London, 1979).

Meyer, J. R. and Oster, C. V. *Deregulation and the New Airline Entrepreneurs* (MIT Press, Cambridge, Mass., 1984).

Millward, R. *Public Expenditure Economics* (McGraw-Hill, London, 1971).

Mitchell, B. M. and Kleindorfer, P. R. (eds) *Regulated Industries and Public Enterprise* (Lexington, Lexington, Mass., 1980).

Mitnick, B. M. *The Political Economy of Regulation* (Columbia University Press, New York, 1980).

Moore, T. G. *Trucking Regulation Lessons from Europe* (American Enterprise Institute, Washington, 1976).

Morrison, S. and Winston, C. *The Economic Effects of Airline Deregulation* (Brookings Institution, Washington, 1986).

Newman, K. *The Selling of British Telecom* (Holt, Rhinehart and Winston, London, 1986).

Noll, R. G. and Owen, B. M. *The Political Economy of Deregulation* (American Enterprise Institute, Washington, 1983).

———— and Braeutigan, R. *The Regulation Game Strategic Use of the Administrative Process* (Ballinger, Cambridge, Mass., 1978).

Petersen, H. C. *Business and Government* (Harper and Row, New York, 1985).

Phillips, A. (ed.) *Promoting Competition in Regulated Markets* (Brookings Institution, Washington, 1975).

Poole, R. W. (ed.) *Instead of Regulation* (Lexington, Lexington,

Mass., 1982).

Posner, R. A. *Antitrust Law An Economic Perspective* (University of Chicago Press, Chicago, 1976).

Pryke, R. *Public Enterprise in Practice* (MacGibbon and Kee, London, 1971).

―――― *The Nationalised Industries* (Martin Robertson, Oxford, 1981).

―――― *Competition among International Airlines* (Trade Policy Centre, London, 1987).

Redwood, J. *Public Enterprise in Crisis* (Blackwell, Oxford, 1980).

―――― and Hatch, J. *Controlling Public Industries* (Blackwell, Oxford, 1982).

Rees, R. *The Control of Nationalised Industries* (Open University, Milton Keynes, 1979).

Reid, G. L. and Allen, K. E. *Nationalised Industries* (Penguin, Harmondsworth, 1970).

Robinson, C. and Marshall, E. *Can Coal Be Saved?* (Institute of Economic Affairs, London, 1985).

Robson, W. A. *Nationalized Industry and Public Ownership* (Allen and Unwin, London, 1962).

Robinson, C. and Sykes, A. *Privatise Coal* (Centre for Policy Studies, London, 1987).

Roll, Lord (ed.) *The Mixed Economy* (Macmillan, London, 1982).

Savage, I. *The Deregulation of Bus Services* (Gower, Aldershot, 1985).

Sawers, D. *Competition in the Air* (Institute of Economic Affairs, London, 1987).

Schnitzer, M. *Contemporary Government and Business Relations* (Houghton Miflin, Boston, 1983).

Shepherd, W. G. (ed.) *Public Enterprise Economic Analysis of Theory and Practice* (Lexington, Lexington, Mass., 1976).

Starkie, D. and Thompson, D. *Privatising London's Airports* (Institute of Fiscal Studies, London, 1985).

Steel, D. and Heald, D. (eds.) *Privatizing Public Enterprises: Options and Dilemmas* (Royal Institute of Public Administration, London, 1984).

Swann, D. *Competition and Consumer Protection* (Penguin, Harmondsworth, 1979).

―――― *Competition and Industrial Policy in the European Community* (Methuen, London, 1983).

―――― *The Economics of the Common Market* (Penguin, Harmondsworth, 1988).

Thompson, F. and Jones, L. R. *Regulatory Policy and Practices* (Praeger, New York, 1982).

334   *The Retreat of the State*

Tivey, L. J. *Nationalisation in British Industry* (Johnathan Cape, London, 1966).
Trebilcock, M. J. and Prichard, J. R. S. *Crown Corporations in Canada* (Butterworths, Toronto, 1983).
Trebing, H. M. (ed.) *New Dimensions in Public Utility Pricing* (Michigan University Press, Lansing, Michigan, 1976).
Tunstall, J. *Communications Deregulation* (Blackwell, Oxford, 1986).
Utton, M. A. *The Economics of Regulating Industry* (Blackwell, Oxford, 1986).
Veljanovski, C. *Selling the State* (Weidenfeld and Nicholson, London, 1987).
Vickers, J. and Yarrow, G. *Privatisation and the Natural Monopolies* (Public Policy Centre, London, 1985).
Weidenbaum, M. L. and Defina, R. *The Cost of Federal Regulation of Economic Activity* (American Enterprise Institute, Washington, 1978).
Weiss, L. W. and Klass, M. W. (eds) *Case Studies in Regulation* (Little, Brown, Boston, 1981).
———— and Strickland, A. D. *Regulation: A Case Approach* (McGraw-Hill, New York, 1976).
Weyman-Jones, T. G. *Energy in Europe: Issues and Policies* (Methuen, London, 1986).
Wilcox, C. and Shepherd, W. G. *Public Policies Towards Business* (Irwin, Homewood, Illinois, 1975).
Wilson, J. Q. (ed.) *The Politics of Regulation* (Basic Books, New York, 1980).

Index